# INTERNATIONAL JOINT VENTURE
# MANAGEMENT

# INTERNATIONAL JOINT VENTURE MANAGEMENT

## Learning to Cooperate and Cooperating to Learn

Bettina Büchel

Christiane Prange

Gilbert Probst

Charles-Clemens Rüling

**John Wiley & Sons (Asia) Pte Ltd**
**Singapore • New York • Chichester • Brisbane • Toronto • Weinheim**

*Other Wiley Editorial Offices*

John Wiley & Sons, Inc.
605 Third Avenue, New York, NY 10158-0012, USA

John Wiley & Sons Ltd
Baffins Lane, Chichester, West Sussex PO19 IUD, England

John Wiley & Sons (Canada) Ltd
22 Worchester Road, Rexdale, Ontario M9W ILI, Canada

Jacaranda Wiley Ltd
33 Park Road, (PO Box 1226) Milton, Queensland 4064, Australia


**Library of Congress Cataloguing-in-Publication Data**

International joint venture management : learning to cooperate and
    cooperating to learn / Bettina Büchel ... [et al.].
        p.      cm.
    Includes bibliographical reference (p.      ) and index.
    ISBN 0-471-82894-7
    1. Joint ventures--Management.   2. International business
enterprises--Management.      I. Büchel, Bettina S. T.
HD62.47.I583   1998
658'.044--dc21                                            98-8257
                                                         CIP


Printed in Singapore
10 9 8 7 6 5 4 3 2 1

# CONTENTS

# PREFACE

The decision to conduct a longitudinal study of joint ventures sprang from many years of interest in joint ventures as an organizational form which combines autonomy with cooperation. According to the literature, joint ventures run a high risk of failure and we started to wonder what factors might play a major part in determining their success or failure. In an initial project supported by the Swiss National Science Foundation,[1] we were able to study the importance of human resource management and organizational structures. It became clear in the early stages of this study that structures and human resources were not the only important factors, so we broadened the scope of our research. Our aim was then to identify the factors which played a crucial role in the development of joint ventures and to determine how these factors influenced the subsequent success and failure of joint ventures.

The theoretical framework of this book is based on analyses of cooperative strategy, of joint ventures and of interorganizational relationships. Our work follows the systems theory approach to applied business management studies, and its subject matter is company practice. We applied a participative approach to research which seemed best suited to our purposes as it linked research with action.

Our research resulted in this book in which we have tried to portray joint venture management from a number of different angles—strategic management, organizational design, and the cultural and human

---

[1] NF Project 12-36188.92, "Significance and role of HRM and organizational structures in organizing and developing autonomous cooperative forms of organization".

resource perspective. Throughout our research, we were able to observe joint ventures in different parts of the world and have summarized crucial points in cases used throughout the text. Our main emphasis lies on joint ventures in Asia and Europe. We are thankful to the managers and companies who provided us with information that led to the various cases.

We are also extremely grateful to Anne Thomas for her excellent job in translating this book from German into English. Based on her helpful comments, we revised sections, included new cases and clarified ideas.

Bettina Büchel
Christiane Prange
Gilbert Probst
Charles-Clemens Rüling
Geneva, Bangkok and Paris, March 1998

# CHAPTER ONE

# JOINT VENTURES AND JOINT VENTURE MANAGEMENT

The largest Swiss German newspaper reported in December 1995 that "the merger of the transportation sector of ABB and AEG of Daimler-Benz Group led to the largest cooperation between two previously independent divisions of the largest groups in the European movable industry..." (*Neue Zürcher Zeitung*, 11 December 1995). The cooperation brought together 22,000 employees and combined business operations across a total of 40 countries. The concise, matter-of-fact style of the report shows how cooperative arrangements, strategic alliances and joint ventures are now routinely accepted as normal forms of organizational design.

Success in cooperative arrangements has become increasingly important over the past decade. The Volkswagen venture Shanghai Volkswagen Automotive Company Ltd has achieved a yearly production of 120,000 Santanas, a 40% market share and profits of 250 million marks (*Manager Magazin*, **3**, 1994, p. 172). It must therefore be included amongst the success stories, as must as the successful cooperation between the Dresdner Bank and the Banque Nationale de Paris. Failures include the almost legendary collapse in 1989 of the alliance between the communications giant AT&T and the computer manufacturer Olivetti. In the medium term, success in cooperative ventures will become even more important because of increasing globalization, growing international competition, and the opening and merging of new markets. The ability to cooperate, and in particular to "manage" cooperative arrangements (i.e. to organize, guide and develop them) will become one of the core competencies which companies must possess in order to ensure their survival and future success.

Joint ventures are by far the most popular form of cooperation. Indeed, we can no longer imagine the business world without them. Scarcely a week passes without news that a new joint venture has been formed or that an existing one has succeeded or failed, been restructured or dissolved. Joint ventures are so common that it is easy to think of them as part of everyday business life. In practice, however, they present extremely difficult challenges. Cooperating with another company, which may also be a competitor, is a demanding and unfamiliar task. Joint ventures quickly expose conflicting goals and cultural differences. Attempts at cooperation may be hindered by divergent strategies, varying organizational structures and procedures, or different approaches to delegation, autonomy and control. Serious conflicts and crises may ensue. Companies are often eager to embark on joint ventures, and at the outset, their willingness to cooperate is at a high level. However, setting up the joint venture is only the first step. A few years ago, many people believed that the most important thing was simply to find the right partner. Now, there is broad agreement in both theory and practice that the real challenge of a joint venture lies in its management, that is in the organization and long-term development of the whole structure of the arrangement, and in dealing with the various problems which arise in its everyday operations.

In the course of a research project lasting several years, we have been able to observe a number of joint ventures over an extended period. We have reached the conclusion that, in general, too little attention is paid to the management of joint ventures compared to such aspects as setting up the legal structure, finding a partner and carrying out the negotiations. All joint ventures are beset by similar problems relating to the content of the cooperative arrangement, the interactions between the partners and the different phases in the development of the venture. Decisions have to be made on how to organize, guide and develop the venture in these difficult areas. In this text, we shall not, therefore, concern ourselves with topics such as the legal aspects of the contract, or particular forms or uses of joint ventures. Instead, we shall examine management problems which can arise in the life of joint ventures.

One aspect of joint ventures and joint venture management which has often been neglected in the past is the question of learning. As the title of this book suggests, we hope to show that learning is an important feature of joint ventures. Cooperative arrangements are more than a means by which companies can gain access to new markets, or make better use of their existing production capacity. They are also an opportunity for companies to learn from their environment and from other companies. They can also help a company to try out something new and make the organization look beyond its daily routines. The joint venture as a field for experiment is valuable from the point of view of learning, as will be detailed in Chapter 10.

## SPOTLIGHT ON JOINT VENTURES

Since the beginning of the 1980s and perhaps even earlier, joint ventures have received a great deal of attention in the context of organization and management theory. Companies must now survive in an environment characterized by increasing speed, pluralization and, perhaps most importantly, a unique pressure towards globalization—a trend which has become particularly strong in the past decade. These factors have prompted an extensive search for new organizational forms suited to the new conditions of business life. The progressive opening of previously closed markets offers enormous opportunities for enterprise. It also throws up a series of questions, especially in relation to knowledge acquisition and ways of spreading risks. The debate is shaped by two main tendencies. First, there is an emphasis on core competencies, which implies specialization, division of work and outsourcing of company functions. Second, partners in the market are increasingly integrating and networking their activities in order to safeguard resources and to preserve access to contested markets. To some extent, joint ventures reflect both these tendencies, since they typically involve cooperation plus the formation of an independent entity.

Joint ventures have proved to be an ideal form of cooperation in a wide variety of settings. In some countries, there have been long periods when joint ventures were the only form in which enterpreneurship and foreign investment were possible. In other situations, joint ventures have offered a way of sharing risks with other companies, for example in the development of new materials. They have also enabled companies to benefit from advantages of size and economies of scale, for example in purchasing, production and sales, and have provided a way of bringing together specialists from different companies to work on a clearly defined project.

Experience has shown that joint ventures can offer a solution to a wide variety of problems. This versatility constitutes both the attraction of joint ventures and one of the main difficulties which they present. The basic form is the same in all applications; however, different aspects dominate the picture depending on the context and circumstances in which a particular joint venture operates.

Recent figures provide clear confirmation that joint ventures have lost none of their importance in company practice in recent years. The 1980s brought a previously unimaginable boom in joint ventures, owing to the progressive opening of the countries of eastern Europe. A recently published scientific study (Raffee and Eisele, 1994) shows that the number of joint ventures in eastern Europe grew from a mere 43 in 1980 in all the former Comecon countries to over 50,000 in 1983 in Hungary alone. In the countries of the former Soviet Union, the number of cooperative ventures rose from 1,200 in January 1990 to 25,000 by the end of 1993. In China, too, an enormous increase was found in the number of joint ventures, from 188 in 1979 to more than 30,000 at the end of 1993—their number had increased by a factor of 160 (Raffee and Eisele, 1994, p. 17). Joint ventures play a decisive part in structuring international relationships between companies. Today, for example, about one-fifth of international equity relationships with a US partner, excluding banking, take the form of a joint venture (Hermann, 1988, p. 3 ff.).

Joint ventures are clearly becoming more popular as a form of cooperative arrangement, not only between partners from different countries but also between companies operating in the same business area. The costs of research and development continue to rise, reaction times shorten and the costs of a poorly judged development project grow heavier. In an environment of this kind, joint ventures offer a way for companies to pool their experience and specific knowledge and share the risks. Joint ventures are a form of cooperation which stand between the traditional mechanisms of economic coordination, that is market and hierarchy. Unlike market-oriented exchange relationships, they offer a way of uniting the strengths of different companies without incurring the disadvantages of a merger or acquisition. This means that a company can be involved in cooperative arrangements in different market areas and with different partners at the same time, bringing different strengths to each partnership as they are needed. In extreme cases, a company may base its whole strategy on bringing its special strengths, such as knowledge of the market in a particular region, or the capital needed for an important investment, into joint ventures with other companies. The Turkish industrial group Sabanci Holding provides an interesting example of a strategy based primarily on undertaking joint ventures with a large number of important partners.

## SABANCI₀HOLDING: JOINT VENTURES AS A GROWTH STRATEGY

In less than 60 years, the companies founded by Haci Ömer Sabanci have grown into an industrial conglomerate which is the second largest private group in Turkey and one of the 300 largest companies in the world. Today, the Sabanci Group consists of about 50 independent companies which employ a total of 27,000 people. Its turnover of approximately US$6 billion represents more than 4% of Turkey's gross domestic product. The conglomerate is extraordinarily diversified: it has 17 different divisions and covers a wide range of activities, including banking, insurance, textiles, synthetic fibers, car tires, car manufacture, cement, food, tobacco processing, production of synthetic materials and paper, electronics, data processing, agricultural products, research and development, and tourism and hotels. The Sabanci Group no longer aims its activities only at the Turkish market: 40% of all its industrial products are already exported to OECD countries.

The vigorous growth of the Group during the past 20 years is attributable largely to its consistent joint venture strategy. In addition to its traditional fields of activity, where it operates independently, it is also a participant in 17 joint ventures, for example with Bridgestone (Japan), Du Pont (USA), Bekaert (Belgium), Philip Morris (USA), Toyota Mitsui (Japan), IBM (USA), Kraft Jacobs Suchard (USA), Hilton International (Great Britain), CIGNA (USA), Philips (Netherlands), Banque Nationale de Paris (France) and Dresdner

Bank (Germany). In addition to its joint ventures, Sabanci has licensing and distribution agreements with companies such as Mitsubishi, Komatsu and Sharp, and a growing number of locations and subsidiary companies abroad.

The Sabanci Group has thus succeeded in positioning itself *vis-a-vis* potential investors as an optimal partner for investment in Turkey. Its extensive experience of cooperative ventures helps it to make an early and realistic assessment of any proposed cooperative project and, more importantly, to recognize and solve the problems in joint venture management which the project is likely to bring. By having worked with many different partners during the years of its operation, the Sabanci Group has amassed strategically important knowledge in widely different fields of activity.

Joint ventures typically face a number of challenges. These include combining the different technologies of the partners, combining the market knowledge of one with the technical expertise of another, selling the products of one of the partners in an unfamiliar market, joint use of resources, joint research and development, setting shared standards, and guaranteeing supplies to the partners.

The establishment of a joint venture may solve some problems, but it usually creates others. The great joint venture euphoria of the seventies and eighties brought a few spectacular failures in its wake, and it is now widely realized that setting up a joint venture does not in itself guarantee success. Many companies have learned from painful experience about the difficulties which beset cooperative strategies in general and joint ventures in particular. Raffee and Eisele (1994) came to the sobering conclusion that more than 50% of cooperative ventures must be classed as failures. The failure of joint ventures can be viewed from different perspectives. The age of the joint venture is one indicator of performance. The older a joint venture, the higher the likelihood that it will be dissolved (Table 1.1). Raffee and Eisele attribute these failures primarily to neglect of the following factors: the importance of equal participation structures (Figure 1.1); the need for cultural compatibility between the partners; careful choice of partner; and a proper approach to operational and strategic leadership in joint venture management.

| Duration (years) | 1 | 2 | 3 | 4 | 5 | 6 | >6 |
|---|---|---|---|---|---|---|---|
| Domestic joint ventures terminated (%) | 5.6 | 13.5 | 5.1 | 12.7 | 10.4 | 8.3 | 25.9 |
| International joint ventures terminated (%) | 3.9 | 5.4 | 10.8 | 4.2 | 20.0 | 24 | 12.6 |
| International and domestic joint ventures terminated (%) | 4.7 | 9.8 | 8.1 | 8.7 | 14.7 | 14.8 | 20.9 |

**Table 1.1**  Failure of joint ventures over time
Source: Based on Kogut, B. (1988) A Study of the Life Cycle of Joint Ventures, In: *Management International Review*, **28**, pp. 39–52

Success and failure of joint ventures will be discussed extensively in Chapter 9. The difficulties inherent in joint ventures have been the subject of an increasing number of studies in recent years (e.g. Harrigan, 1986; Lyles, 1987). This in itself is an indication of the shift in emphasis away from the technical, legal and strategic aspects, which were much discussed in the eighties, and a shift towards the question of joint venture

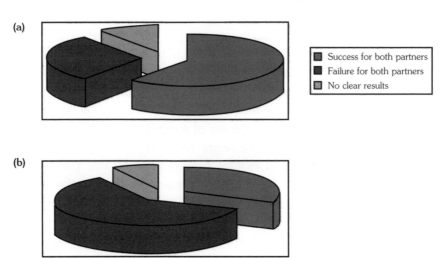

**Figure 1.1**  The relationship between distribution of ownership and success: (a) Equal distribution of ownership; (b) Unequal distribution of ownership
Source: Adapted from Bleeke, J. and Ernst, D. (1993) *Collaborating to Compete: Using Strategic Alliances and Acquisitions in the Global Marketplace*, New York: John Wiley & Sons, p. 28

management. We must now consider what happens once the joint venture is in place. How does it develop? What are the most common pitfalls and sources of conflict? Do the processes of designing the joint venture as a whole and guiding its development involve issues to which we should be especially alert?

## Joint ventures: A double-edged sword?

Most managers have had traditional management training, and they are used to business procedures which do not necessarily include joint venture management. This is just one of the reasons why a multitude of difficulties must be anticipated.

> Interfirm collaborations are plagued by ambiguities in relationships; tensions associated with the need to balance cooperation and competition; managerial mind-sets acquainted with and often suspicious of inter-organizational links; myriad details that need to be managed; and lack of recognition of the complex linkages among the strategies, structures, and systems of both the participating firms and the alliance (Yoshino and Rangan, 1995, p. 106).

Joint ventures are not a cure-all, but if they are approached realistically, they can often provide companies with a meaningful way of extending their scope for action by cooperating with others. Their value lies in the fact that they combine the binding effect of mutual capital involvement with the flexibility and openness of a legally independent entity. In cases where direct foreign investment was difficult or impossible, for example in the countries of eastern Europe until the late 1980s, joint ventures were the only avenue for enterprise. Even today, there is an increasing number of situations in which direct investment, and even straightforward contractual agreements, are possible in theory, but for various reasons they are not desirable in reality. Equity investment is often not desired because the collaboration is intended to last for the limited duration of a particular project, and the partners want to keep their flexibility and autonomy. In situations of this kind, a joint venture offers a certain distance which is preferable to mutual capital involvement. Contractual agreements on the other hand often seem insufficiently binding, especially where long-term, strategically important plans are involved. Considered in the light of organization theory, joint ventures have an advantage over both simple contractual agreements and direct capital investment. This lies in the establishment of an autonomous entity which allows the project to be precisely localized and monitored within the framework of each partner's management systems, yet excluding the core activities of the partners from the cooperative arrangement, and thus from the view of possible competitors. Joint ventures meet all the criteria for a "loose coupling" which offers the advantages of cooperation and increases flexibility, while at the same time sheltering each partner from the full force of any difficulties experienced by the other, and distancing both from any troubles in the joint venture (Weick, 1995a).

Joint ventures are now firmly established amongst business strategies used in almost all branches of industry. Indeed, there are areas in which it is all but impossible to avoid them. This being so, our main aim will be to show how companies can make judicious use of the joint venture form— now a recognized and proven instrument—and manage it to the advantage of all participants. Many of the sources of difficulty in joint ventures can be recognized and analyzed, and if the typical problems are known and understood, it is easier to develop managerial guidelines. Readiness to learn is important in this context. It is only when we are ready to admit our mistakes and those of our organization that we can improve our joint venture practice. We need to be able to ask ourselves what we can learn from a particular situation and how we might improve on it next time.

Up to this point, our discussion of joint ventures has been at a general level. We shall now go on to describe in greater detail what we mean by a joint venture. We shall try to give a more precise definition, describing the essential features and the points where problems often arise. In the following sections, we shall consider joint ventures from three points of view. First, we shall describe several joint venture types. Second, we shall give a brief overview of the reasons for using joint ventures and the forms which they take, both in theory and in practice. Third, we shall outline the argument presented in this book, which is based on the concept of learning in relation to joint ventures.

# THE JOINT VENTURE AS A COOPERATIVE STRATEGY

The following section contains a more precise definition of what we mean by a joint venture. Joint ventures are just one possible form of coopera- tion within a broad range of cooperative strategies. The first step is there- fore to distinguish them from other kinds of cooperative arrangements. We shall then look at the typical structure of joint ventures and the pat- terns of relationships which they involve.

## Joint ventures as an intermediate form between market and hierarchy

Traditionally, economic relationships have been classed under two broad headings, as "market" or "hierarchy". All forms of cooperative arrange- ment represent a middle ground between the two. They are not subject to "anonymous" market forces, nor determined by the rules of a tightly structured hierarchy. A cooperative arrangement is a partnership, a col- laboration based on (contractual) agreement and shaped by a mutual bal- ance of interests.

Market and hierarchy have long been treated as the only theoretical possibilities for organizing economic relations. Nevertheless, in recent years, cooperative arrangements have emerged as a fact of economic life. There is now extensive literature on the subject,[1] largely devoted to discussion of possible legal constraints, or limits on competition. From an economic point of view, however, the existence of cooperative arrange- ments may be attributed to their superior efficiency when compared with the market.

In real life, we often find interesting situations where only some of the relationships between the partners are organized on a cooperative basis. Renault and Volvo, for instance, cooperate in the area of engine development, but still appear as competitors in the market. The wide variety of possible arrangements and combinations within

---

[1] The literature on the theoretical significance of cooperative arrangements has grown sharply in recent years. The interested reader will find more information in Hamel, Doz and Prahalad, 1989; Williamson, 1991; Ring and Van de Ven, 1992; and Williamson, 1992.

the market–hierarchy–cooperation triangle offers a high level of flexibility for structuring mutual relations. At the same time, it conceals an enormous potential for conflict. It is therefore vital to work out the scope of a cooperative arrangement and the obligations of all the partners as early and as fully as possible.

Most discussions of cooperative arrangements as a middle way between market and hierarchy fail to take account of the fact that the term covers a range of different structures. We find many instances in which the same partners cooperate with each other in different areas of their business. Airbus, for example, is the most significant international cooperative venture in civil aircraft construction. The partners have set up Airbus Industrie SA as a joint venture, that is as an independent unit for marketing the jointly produced aircraft; but as far as production is concerned, they cooperate on a purely contractual basis. IBM is another interesting example. IBM entered a number of cooperative arrangements with different partners. With each arrangement, the company pursues a different goal (Table 1.2).

In recent years, many attempts have been made to categorize the various kinds of cooperative arrangement between companies. As shown in Figure 1.2, joint ventures form a relatively small part of the whole spectrum.

The first important distinction to be made among the different kinds of cooperative arrangement is between contractual agreements and coop-

| IBM partners | Goal |
|---|---|
| Ferranti | Market penetration of PS/2 Systems |
| Toshiba | Sharing of development costs |
| DEC, Apollo, HP | Development of a competitive advantage over Sun and AT&T |
| Siemens | Sharing of research and development costs |
| Microsoft | Improvement in competitive position |

**Table 1.2** IBM's cooperative arrangements with different partners
Source: Adapted from Krubasik, E. and Lautenschlager, H. (1993) Forming Successful Strategic Alliances in High-Tech Businesses, In: Bleeke, J. and Ernst, D. (1993) *Collaborating to Compete: Using Strategic Alliances and Acquisitions in the Global Marketplace*, New York: John Wiley & Sons, pp. 55-66

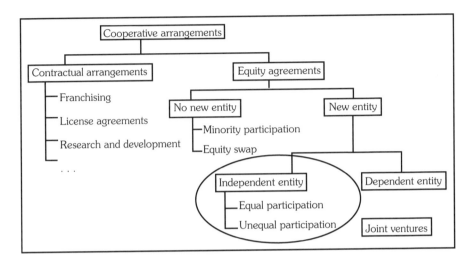

**Figure 1.2**  Range of cooperative relationships between companies.
*Source:* Based on Yoshino, M. and Rangan, U. (1995) *Strategic Alliances: An Entrepreneurial Approach to Globalization.* Boston, Massachusetts: Harvard Business School Press, p. 8

erative arrangements which involve exchange or contribution of capital, that is equity agreements. Amongst the latter, we may distinguish between cooperative arrangements which lead to the creation of a new entity and arrangements which involve equity swaps. The extreme form of equity swap is where the cooperating companies are combined by means of a merger or acquisition.

The following definition of joint ventures is based on the features which are generally considered to distinguish them from other forms of cooperative arrangement: a joint venture is any kind of cooperative arrangement between two or more independent companies which leads to the establishment of a third entity organizationally separate from the "parent" companies (cf. Pfeffer and Nowak, 1976, p. 400; Harrigan, 1986, p. 2 ff.).

Joint ventures thus have two defining attributes which are responsible both for their strengths and for the problems which they can bring. These attributes are cooperation and autonomy. The cooperative aspect derives from the fact that the partners work together to create a new entity, which they usually also run together. However, the unit is autonomous because it is legally and organizationally independent and detached from

the original partners. The apparent paradox of autonomy plus cooperation is solved when we realize that the partner companies which create
the joint venture are often in competition with each other and that they
transfer the cooperative element to an independent unit.

This brings us to another important feature of joint ventures. It is a
mistake to consider the joint venture in isolation; we must always keep
sight of the entire structure of relationships between the venture and the
partner companies. From now on, we shall use the term "joint venture"
to denote the new entity, and the term "joint venture system" when we
mean the whole structure of relationships amongst the partner companies and the new entity. Figure 1.3 shows the pattern of relationships in
a typical joint venture system. Two or more partners enter a cooperative
arrangement and each has its own set of relationships with the newly
created organizational unit. These relationships may exist at different
levels, or between different business areas or functions.

The structure of the joint venture system is therefore less important
from the point of view of joint venture management than the processes
which take place within it, that is between the partner organizations, between the partners and the joint venture, and within the joint venture itself.

The relationships amongst the partners are not necessarily all of a
cooperative nature. It often happens that the partner organizations cooperate in some areas but are competitors in others. The new entity is
generally organizationally and legally independent, but in many cases it is

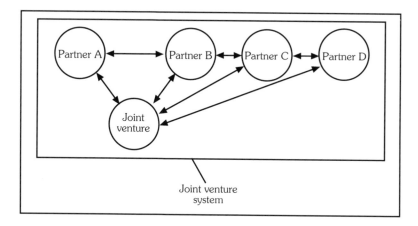

**Figure 1.3** The joint venture and the joint venture system

still subject to strategic and economic control from the parents. It is not difficult to see how this often leads to goal conflicts and continual arguments about control and autonomy. When dealing with these problems, it is vital to distinguish carefully between the different levels of the relationships involved and their complexity.

## COMPETITION AND COOPERATION

Ford Motor Company and Mazda Motor Corporation established a joint venture company in 1995, AutoAlliance (Thailand) Company Limited, which manufactures compact pickup trucks for sale through the companies' respective sales networks in selected markets, excluding North America. Formation of the AutoAlliance was completed after the Thai Ministry of Commerce formally approved the new company's structure. Mazda and Ford each hold a 45% equity in the newly established joint venture and each also has a local partner with 5% equity.

Based on a win–win principle, the two companies jointly conducted market research to decide on which product to develop and produce. Since economies of scale are a critical determinant in the automotive industry, Ford and Mazda felt that a joint production site would enable them to reach the necessary capacity for efficient operations.

Due to the Asian economic crisis in 1997, the joint venture will not reach the expected production capacity, but the nature of the joint venture agreement has not changed.

Both companies will sell the same product in the same market, so competition is unavoidable. For both companies the joint venture is a production base that will design and deliver products for their respective target markets. Within this setup the following issues clearly demonstrate the existence of competition and cooperation.

The marketing companies of Ford and Mazda will order from AutoAlliance directly. The percentage has been set up in the contract with limitation on the extent of change. If, in the future, major changes have to be made, the two parent companies will have to negotiate. There is no direct communication between the marketing companies.

Product development also needs to be agreed upon. If the market demands change, the two companies will jointly conduct market research to determine the best strategy for both companies and the joint venture. As one manager of the joint venture pointed out, "Since both parent companies are present in many markets, the competition is unavoidable." Another manager added, "We do compete to some extent but this is a market issue, not a joint venture issue."

# REASONS FOR THE CREATION OF JOINT VENTURES

Joint venture systems do not happen by chance; they are always the outcome of a company decision. Their structure is always the result of a managerial decision, more so than in the case of purely contractual forms of cooperation between companies. The creation of a legally and organizationally independent entity involves decisions such as points of communication, the transfer of whole departments into the joint venture, and the adjustment of employee development and pay systems. Every joint venture system must be structured according to the needs of the joint venture itself, the relationships between the joint venture and the partner companies, and the relations amongst the partner companies themselves.

Given all these requirements, certain goals and motives must be present to justify creating a joint venture at all. We have already mentioned some of the pressures in the business environment which may prompt companies to embark on cooperative arrangements; these included internationalization, the opening of new economic areas, the decreasing time taken by innovation and development cycles, and the need to diversify and spread risks. In the following sections, we shall examine more closely some of the various needs which may underlie the establishment of a joint venture.

## Motives and goals behind joint ventures

The motives and the company goals which may lead to the establishment of joint ventures cover the full range of business problems. Many authors have paid special attention to the reasons why companies embark on joint ventures. Harrigan (1986, p. 16 ff.) gives a detailed analysis of goals and motives, and draws distinctions between internal, competitive and strategic reasons:

*Internal reasons*
1. Spreading costs and risks
2. Safeguarding resources which cannot be obtained via the market
3. Improving access to financial resources
4. Benefits of economies of scale and advantages of size
5. Access to new technologies and customers
6. Access to innovative managerial practices
7. Encouraging entrepreneurial employees

*Competitive goals*
1. Influencing structural evolution of the industry
2. Pre-empting competitors
3. Defensive response to blurring industry boundaries and globalization
4. Creation of stronger competitive units

*Strategic goals*
1. Creation and exploitation of synergies
2. Transfer of technologies and skills
3. Diversification

This analysis of the various possible reasons for setting up a joint venture should not be taken to imply that they are always prompted by a single aim. A joint venture is much more likely to be the result of a number of different motives, which means that expectations are complex. This is one of the main reasons why it is vital for joint venture management to clarify its goals. All those involved should know from the beginning what goals the partner organizations are pursuing and what expectations they have of the new entity. Those expectations and goals which led to the creation of the joint venture influence the structuring of the organization. They also constitute the only rational measures for evaluating the success or failure of the joint venture at a later stage.

The different participants in a joint venture may be pursuing different ends. Discussion and analysis of goals can therefore help to expose hidden goal conflicts, and make it possible for the parties to find a compromise before the conflicts become manifest and put the whole cooperative venture in jeopardy.

The various internal reasons for embarking on a joint venture are more important than is generally recognized in practice. A joint venture offers valuable opportunities to gather new experience within a cooperative environment, and to move beyond the boundaries of a traditional organization. It is also an opportunity for learning. Joint ventures allow the partner companies to extend their knowledge base in various ways. First, they can learn to cooperate, that is they learn about the characteristics of the cooperation process, the problems involved and how to deal with them. They can also cooperate to learn, that is they may gain specific knowledge which can only be gained through cooperation.

## Basic types of joint venture

Which kinds of joint venture are found most often in company practice? Theoretically, there are countless ways of using and structuring joint ventures, all of them attended by different problems. Figure 1.4 shows some important dimensions which may be used to distinguish between different kinds of joint venture and the areas in which they are used.

Within each dimension, the management and structure of the joint venture face particular challenges which can lead to typical conflicts. When tackling problems in joint venture management, it is important to take into account the different dimensions which characterize the joint venture and not to concentrate on just one aspect.

Only a few basic types of joint venture are commonly found in practice. Based on the existing literature and applications which are common in practice, Hermann (1988, p. 56 ff.) shows six types of joint venture as listed here. The main differences between them lie in the relationships between the partners and in the strategic focus of the joint venture. They make widely differing demands on joint venture management.

- Complementary technology joint ventures: the partners combine their technologies to diversify their existing product/market portfolios.
- Market technology joint ventures: combination of the market knowledge of one partner with the production or product know-how of the other.
- Sales joint venture: the producer and a local partner cooperate in an

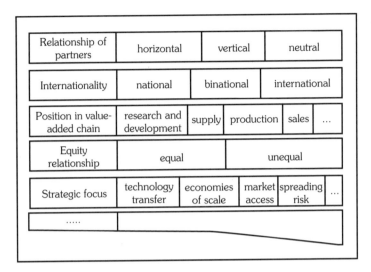

| Relationship of partners | horizontal | | vertical | | neutral | |
|---|---|---|---|---|---|---|
| Internationality | national | | binational | | international | |
| Position in value-added chain | research and development | supply | production | | sales | ... |
| Equity relationship | equal | | | unequal | | |
| Strategic focus | technology transfer | economies of scale | market access | spreading risk | ... | |
| ...... | | | | | | |

**Figure 1.4**  Dimensions for describing joint ventures

arrangement which is a mixture of independent representation and own branch.

- Concentration joint ventures: competing partners cooperate to form larger and more economical units.
- Research and development joint ventures: the aim is to create synergy by making joint use of research facilities, exploiting opportunities to specialize and standardize, combining know-how and sharing risks.
- Supply joint ventures: competitors with similar input needs cooperate to safeguard supplies, reduce procurement costs or prevent the entry of new competitors.

Each of the five dimensions in Figure 1.4, according to which joint ventures can be described, has particular implications for joint venture management and the problems likely to be encountered. However, they are not of equal importance. The most important sources of conflict in the relationship between the two partners seem to be the position of the joint venture in the value-added chain, the ownership relations and the strategic orientation, with the resultant sharing of executive powers and the risks attending the joint venture. The relationship between a partner and the joint venture is determined primarily by the joint venture's position in the value-added chain, the strategic orientation and level of control over the new entity. Table 1.3 shows some of the sensitive areas for joint venture management within each dimension.

Joint venture management includes the design and development of the entire joint venture system. At a later stage in this book, we shall discuss opportunities for joint venture management in particular areas of designing the project. For the moment, we shall content ourselves with a few remarks on the possible implications of problems which typically arise within particular dimensions.

The *relationship between the partners* has far-reaching implications for problems in joint venture management. If the partners are in a horizontal relationship, that is if they are competitors outside the area of

| Joint venture dimension | Potential problems in joint venture management |
|---|---|
| Relationship between partners | Conflicts between partners if they are also competitors; delineation of areas of responsibility; mistrust; fear of loss of know-how; buy-back agreements |
| Internationality | Cultural barriers; different negotiating styles; differing ideas about people; pay systems; business practices; recruitment of personnel for the joint venture |
| Position in value-added chain | Strategic significance for the partners; partners' needs for safety and control; autonomy crises; compatibility of joint venture products with partner organizations |
| Property relations | Profit-sharing; authority to make decisions; dominance of one partner in the new entity; structuring of contracts; control mechanisms; protection of minorities; autonomy of the joint venture; dominance of one partner |
| Strategic orientation of the joint venture | Autonomy of the joint venture versus ties to the partners; measurement of success in achieving goals; need for coordination and continuous renegotiation; adaptability; task sharing between the partners; strategic dominance of individual partners |

**Table 1.3**  Relationship between dimensions for describing joint ventures and some typical problems in joint venture management

cooperation, then a whole series of possible conflicts of interest is pro-
grammed into the situation. Which of the partners will have the greater
influence on joint venture strategy? Who profits more from the joint venture's results? Who feels cheated, that is which partner feels that they are
contributing or sacrificing more than they are gaining from the joint venture? If the partners are in a vertical relationship, that is if their relationship is that of supplier–customer, there are questions about how far the
partners are bound by the joint venture, whether there are supply and
purchasing obligations, which of the partners can exert more power and
influence, and finally, which of them is more dependent on the joint
venture. If the partners are in a neutral relationship, for example if they
come from different business areas, one of the first questions concerns
the strategic orientation of the cooperative venture. Conflicts of interest
can arise, for example, when the markets of the two partners are con-
verging, with the result that partners in a cooperative arrangement sud-
denly become competitors. In joint venture management, the relationship between the partners is expressed most clearly in the way in which
strategy development processes are organized and in the structuring of
interfaces between the parties in the joint venture system.

The *internationality of the joint venture system* has effects which
can be seen in several dimensions. Important factors include the context
in which the venture operates and whether the partners are from different countries. The most obvious effect of internationality is the meeting
of different cultures or cultural groups, which may have different lan-
guages, negotiating styles and business practices, and management phi-
losophies. International equity relationships and joint ventures also face
specific problems arising from different legal systems, different billing
requirements and the extent to which the partner companies can influence the daughter company. The geographical and cultural environment
of the joint venture may affect the ease with which qualified employees
can be recruited and common systems agreed for pay, incentives  and
employee development.

The *position in the value-added chain* influences both the type of
cooperation in the joint venture and the significance of the joint venture from the point of view of the individual partners. Joint ventures in
basic research must clearly differ in their organization and development
from  cooperative arrangements for logistics or sales. Furthermore, the

position of the joint venture in the value-added chain(s) of the partner companies affects the autonomy and control relationships with the partners. The basic pattern seems to be that the nearer the joint venture lies to the core activities of the companies, the less autonomy they will grant it and the more control they will exert. If true, this has far-reaching consequences for the structure of relationships between the joint venture and the partner companies.

The *property relations*, together with the relationships between the partners themselves, play an important part in all decisions affecting strategic orientation, the performance and areas of responsibility of the partners, and the further development of the joint venture itself. The danger inherent in unequal joint ventures is that the partner which owns the greater share of the new entity will dominate it and often exploit its own dominant position by disregarding the interests of the minority partner when decisions are made. The smooth functioning of the joint venture depends on many factors, some of which are especially significant in unequal joint ventures. These include the decision mechanisms shared by the partners, differences in ability to influence the joint venture and the existence of some form of "protection of minorities" at every level in the joint venture system. As we shall see, the balance of power between the partners can lead to conflicts which affect the nature of the work in the joint venture. This is an aspect which companies cannot afford to disregard.

The *strategic orientation of the joint venture* throws up a set of typical problems which are often encountered in the daily operation of joint ventures. The whole joint venture system needs to be structured according to the strategic orientation of the joint venture. First and foremost, the level of autonomy of the newly created entity and the type of control exerted by the partner companies which created it depend on how far the activities of the joint venture affect the core activities of the partners. If the joint venture operates in an area which scarcely touches upon the strategic interests of the partners, then in principle, it can be given greater autonomy than if the joint venture is responsible for selling the products of one of the partners in a particular market area. The strategic orientation of the joint venture is an important basic consideration affecting the construction of the joint venture system, from the development of a concrete business plan for the new entity, through the creation of interfaces and exchange relationships, to matters of human resource policy and cooperative culture.

It is not difficult to demonstrate that the form which a joint venture takes plays a large part in determining the type of problems managers will encounter. Our objective in this book is not to examine the details and practical implications of all the possible forms of joint venture. It is to consider the different problems involved in joint venture management on the basis of a more general model, from which we shall then be able to derive various managerial guidelines.

## JOINT VENTURE MANAGEMENT AS A PROCESS

One of our major themes is apparent in the distinction which we draw between joint ventures and joint venture management. We use the terms to denote two different concepts: on the one hand, the joint venture as a structural form; on the other, the management of the processes which take place within this form.

Joint venture management involves much more than working out structures. Formal structures are relatively easy to create. The real problems begin when the action starts within those structures and processes of change begin. Experience with joint ventures shows that most difficulties are indeed related to structures within the joint venture arrangement, but the essence of the problem can be traced back to difficulties in coping with central management processes. To put this another way, it is important to examine the structure of a joint venture, but even more important to analyze the central processes in joint venture management.

What, in concrete terms, is joint venture management? "Management" in the broad sense embraces all activities involved in leading a goal-directed social system. In essence, these activities can be divided into three groups: organizing, guiding and developing. Management is therefore not isolated or abstract; it always happens in relation to a particular institution, which has its own distinguishing characteristics (Ulrich and Probst, 1988, pp. 240, 270 ff.). Joint venture management embraces all activities involved in organizing, guiding and developing the whole joint venture system at all levels.

*Organizing* means creating the joint venture system in the first place and designing it as a functional whole. This naturally includes tasks such as choosing a suitable partner, considering strategic, economic and legal aspects, and designing suitable structures and processes for working together within the joint venture system. It also includes the actual creation of the joint venture entity, that is personnel recruitment, setting up leadership and incentive systems, and so on. In brief, it means actually designing and creating a joint venture.

In the daily life of the joint venture system, decisions which affect the joint venture are continually made at all levels. The concept of *guiding* is based on the need for continual adaptation of the joint venture system to its environment and to its inner milieu, the need to set new goals, to introduce measures and to monitor their implementation and results. This involves finding solutions to specific problems, creating processes for managing employees and agreeing on goals, finding different ways of working together, and monitoring strategies and outcomes in the joint venture.

*Development* within the joint venture system means increasing learning ability and promoting cooperative activity as a whole. In the short term, the aims are that the partner companies should learn how to improve their functioning steadily in relation to given goals, to rectify shortcomings and not to repeat mistakes. In the long term, it means increasing the company's ability to innovate, to adapt to new demands and to seek and realize new goals and behaviors.

In practice, these three aspects of joint venture management are often interwoven. Because of the large number of protagonists and the complexity of the joint venture system, it is often not even possible to find out who made a particular decision, or who is responsible for a particular solution. This situation differs from "normal" company activity, first in that it is more complicated, and second in that it quickly exposes problems and conflicts, offering difficult challenges to all those with management responsibilities. We shall concentrate on the processes involved in joint venture management, in the hope that this will better equip the reader to meet such challenges.

## "Learning to cooperate" and "Cooperating to learn"

Our process-based approach stems from our view of joint venture systems as non-static entities which are subject to continuous change. The initial relationships change with time, and the cooperative arrangement develops through a series of phases, each of which brings its own particular problems. An essential part of joint venture management consists of watching these stages in development, anticipating possible difficulties and avoiding them by applying appropriate instruments in the areas of strategy, structure, human resources and culture, according to the level and phase of the venture. Joint venture management is a demanding activity, which must be carried out at different points in the joint venture system. There must be a continuous process of organizing, guiding and developing, not only within the joint venture itself, but also in the partner companies.

One of the most serious mistakes that companies often make is to find a joint venture and then leave it to get on by itself, without giving it appropriate supervision and support during the developmental stages. Effective joint venture management is characterized by continuous learning. As time passes, management will refine its use of cooperative instruments and develop a feel for setting up a cooperative venture in a particular market segment, with a particular kind of technology, a specific strategic mission, and so on. This, however, is not the whole story: management must also continue to look for and analyze goals which were previously hidden, and thus learn about the overall aims of the cooperation, as well as the instruments for achieving it.

There is nothing worse than clinging blindly to the status quo, reluctant to question things that have "always been done like that", and unwilling to change them. The concept of learning, of well-considered change and continuous improvement in the ability to cooperate, is a central theme of this book. Learning can take place at two levels. The first level is *learning to cooperate*. This means striving towards a growing understanding of the processes and specific problems involved in joint ventures, and continuing to develop one's own practices and competencies in joint venture management. The second level is *cooperating to learn*. This means using joint ventures as a medium for organizational and interorganizational learning. It is an aspect to which little attention is paid in current joint venture practice.

At the first level, the important thing is to learn how a joint venture works, what are the problems which may arise, and what possibilities exist for organizing, guiding and developing in different areas. At the second level, the aim is to recognize the ways in which joint ventures can be used to enable the partner companies to learn. The focus here is not competence in joint venture management so much as how cooperation in strategically relevant areas can be used to gain knowledge from the business environment and develop competencies (Figure 1.5).

Learning to cooperate and cooperating to learn are interdependent. Learning from cooperative ventures presupposes the ability to deal with such ventures and the problems which they bring; and the desire to learn about the processes involved in cooperation and gaining experience about these processes can be one of the main reasons for embarking on such a venture.

In this book, we shall examine both kinds of learning. First, we shall consider learning to cooperate in some detail. Starting from a general model of joint venture development, we shall discuss action areas in joint venture management. We shall start by considering the classical management areas of strategy, structure, culture and human resources. We shall then examine trust, commitment and the search for common meanings as fundamental issues in any cooperative arrangement. Measurement of success will be discussed in a separate chapter. It seems at first sight easy to tell success from failure; however, closer analysis shows that success and failure can be seen in many different lights and in the joint venture

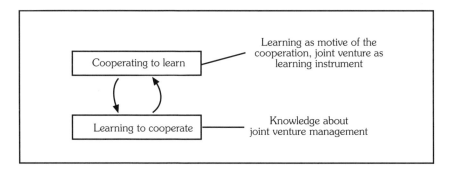

**Figure 1.5**    "Learning to cooperate" and "cooperating to learn"

system they can be determined at different levels. The validity of applying traditional measures of success to joint ventures must therefore at least be questioned, and in some areas, these measures must be broadened.

We shall then move on to the second kind of learning—cooperating to learn. We shall ask how joint ventures can themselves be used as instruments of learning and in what ways cooperative arrangements in general can be used as ways of gaining and applying new knowledge. To illustrate and underpin our theoretical views on constructing joint ventures, we shall make frequent reference to real instances.

## Questions to address

- Is the joint venture the appropriate instrument to implement the company's goals?
- What were the motives for forming the joint venture?
- What goals does the joint venture pursue?
- What goals do the partners pursue?
- What are the central features of the joint venture?
- In what functional area did the partners commit resources?
- What management problems are expected from the joint venture?
- What role does the joint venture play for the partners?
- What relationships exist in the joint venture system?
- Have the partners developed a learning perspective?

# CHAPTER TWO

# JOINT VENTURE MODEL: A DYNAMIC AND MULTI-LEVEL APPROACH

A comprehensive model of joint venture systems should include two major dimensions: the different levels which exist within the joint venture system and the developmental stages in the life-cycle of a joint venture. The literature currently lacks an approach of this kind. It contains many studies of individual variables and their interrelationships, but so far these have not been integrated into a complete model. We shall therefore start by developing a model on which to base our subsequent discussion of joint venture management. Our model will combine the structural aspect, that is the different levels within the joint venture system, with the temporal aspect, that is development of the joint venture system over time. We need to know the interests of the participants at different levels in the joint venture system as well as the developmental dynamics of the whole. Problems differ according to the level at which they arise and the stage of development of the joint venture, and every problem demands its own specific solution.

Our first step in developing the model is to consider the dynamics of the situation over time, highlighting the relationships amongst the participants. A static description resembles a photograph: it creates a picture of relationships as they are at a given moment. A dynamic description, however, is a study of phenomena as they develop. The purpose of our model is to pinpoint opportunities for intervention at different management levels and at different stages during the development of the joint venture.

Historical analysis of joint ventures shows that different levels are more important in different stages. During the formation stage, it is the partners who decide between themselves to set up a joint venture. In the adjustment stage, however, the emphasis is on collaboration between the partners and the joint venture, as well as on the joint venture itself. Finally, in the evaluation stage, the entire joint venture system is under scrutiny. Figure 2.1 shows which levels are important during each stage of development.

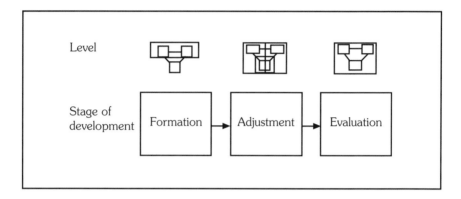

**Figure 2.1**  Relationships between developmental stages of the joint venture and levels in the joint venture system

In the following sections, we shall describe the different levels in the joint venture system, the developmental stages of the joint venture, and the particular problems which arise at different levels during each stage.

## LEVELS IN THE JOINT VENTURE SYSTEM

If we consider the different levels at which the joint venture system operates, we become aware of the different viewpoints of the participants and the ways in which they interact. We can distinguish three main directions of influence within the joint venture system:

- the influence of the partners on the joint venture;
- the influence of the joint venture on the partners; and
- horizontal influences between the partners.

The influence of the partners on the joint venture often takes the form of the exercise of power: they try to control the joint venture by using their power and resources. The joint venture influences the partners, too, but in a different way: it tries to achieve its aims through coalitions or informal exchanges. The initial relationship between the partners is often a horizontal one and they influence each other to a similar degree. However, the relative size of the companies and the changes which take place over time are likely to affect their relative status with regard to the joint venture. The larger the company, or the stronger its competitive position compared with that of its partner, the greater its opportunities to exert influence. Figure 2.2 shows the relationships within the joint venture system.

If we approach the joint venture system from the point of view of relationships, we see a group of entities which interact with each other, but which are in principle autonomous. However, to the extent that they interact, they are interdependent. They are bound together by transactions, each of which has a particular intensity and frequency, and it is the total of these transactions which constitutes the joint venture system. The joint venture itself operates within the framework of its transactions with the partner companies, plus the external environment of the whole joint venture system. It must develop both its relationships with the world outside and its own internal relationships.

When considering the different levels in joint venture systems, it is helpful to concentrate on those relationships which influence the success or failure of joint ventures. We shall describe all three levels in more detail: first, the partners and the relationship between them; second, the

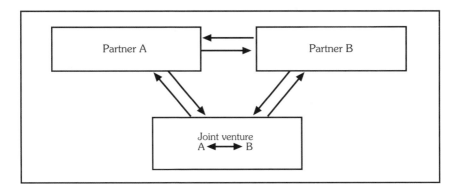

**Figure 2.2** Relationships and directions of influence in the joint venture system

relationship between the partners and the joint venture; and finally the joint venture in its environment.

## The partners and their relationship

The partners are the parties which interact to bring the joint venture into being. Proceeding from their own respective goals, they agree on a set of objectives and activities for the joint venture, and decide upon its structure and staffing. The joint venture is then given the task of realizing the aims upon which the partners have decided, using agreed resources. However, the environment may change, and goal conflicts may arise between the partners, so joint ventures repeatedly find themselves in the position of having to adjust the objectives which have been set for them. It often happens that an adjustment is acceptable to one partner, but that the other is dissatisfied with the way the joint venture is developing. The joint venture must show clear benefits for both partners. For the parent companies, these benefits constitute the collective meaning or sense of the joint venture. If this sense does not exist, then the use of a joint venture as a form of cooperation is also called into question.

The purpose of the relationship between the partners is usually easy to formulate, but its form depends heavily on the partners. Theoretically, the partners often have equal rights, and both (or all) can influence the form of the joint venture. However, if the partners differ in size or importance, this may show in different degrees of influence. Even when the partners have equal formal rights to influence the joint venture, there may still be difficulties if it should become apparent at some stage that the venture is being used to pursue different and conflicting goals.

## The partners and the joint venture

The way in which the aims of the joint venture are implemented is of central importance in the relationship between the partners and the joint venture. The interactions between the partners are to decide on objectives and give the joint venture the task of meeting them. The relationship between the partners and the joint venture is often described in the literature as a "parent–child relationship" (e.g. Harrigan, 1986). This term emphasizes the extent to which the newly created unit is dependent upon the partner companies. However, as time passes, the relationship between the partners and the joint venture may change radically. Lorange and Roos (1992) found that joint ventures gain more autonomy during their lifetime, and become progressively less dependent on their partners. In other words, the joint venture becomes an independent organization which no longer needs the support of the parent companies.

From the point of view of the partners, the joint venture is a means to an end (Harrigan, 1986). All interactions within the joint venture system are therefore complicated by the fact that the joint venture must meet the objectives of the partners as well as its own. The chief coordinating mechanism which helps to ensure this is the linking of the joint venture into the value chains of the partners.

## The joint venture and its environment

In the interactions between the partner companies and the joint venture, discussions center upon how the companies will work together and how the joint venture will be linked to the partner companies. Within the joint venture itself, however, the question is how to survive as an autonomous organization within the parameters set by the business environment. The emphasis is on those aspects of the environment which influence the success of the joint venture.

The joint venture must work within a changing environment to meet the objectives set by the partners. Matters are complicated by the tensions which necessarily exist between the aims of the venture and those of the partners. In order to succeed, the joint venture has to meet the objectives of the parent companies, while at the same time adjusting to the competitive forces in its own business environment. Conflicts may arise in which it cannot do both and a choice has to be made. The original objectives are often threatened at an early stage because of internal differences or an unexpectedly dynamic environment. Joint venture managers are then forced to seek resources which they need to maintain the competitiveness of the joint venture as an independent organization. Although joint ventures are founded by partner companies which set their objectives, they are nevertheless independent companies and must assert their autonomy in their own fields of activity. This means that sometimes, in order to survive, joint venture managers must make decisions which are hostile to the parent companies. Situations of this kind put joint venture managers in the difficult position of having to decide between the goals which the partner companies are pursuing through the joint venture and the goals of the joint venture itself.

## STAGES IN THE DEVELOPMENT OF JOINT VENTURES

A dynamic approach to joint ventures involves describing and explaining changes in the joint venture system over time. In the course of our own research, we have studied a number of joint ventures from their inception. On the basis of our observations, we have developed a model of change which accommodates different developmental stages and feedback cycles.

The literature contains numerous models which show the different developmental stages of joint ventures. Kogut (1988), who was one of the first authors describing the life-cycle of joint ventures, proposes that development is a sequence consisting of creation, institutionalization and termination. Van de Ven and Walker (1984) also offer a stage model, the main purpose of which is to explain the frequent decline of joint ventures. They argue that the reason for the eventual dissolution of a joint venture is already implicit at the formation stage. This is the stage where structures are formalized and control mechanisms agreed. As time passes, however, conflicts which cannot be solved through traditional control mechanisms arise between the organizations. Van de Ven and Walker believe that a second reason why joint ventures are often dissolved lies in the convergence between the activities of the partner companies: cooperation turns into competition and this gives rise to a growing tendency towards ending the joint venture.

Other descriptions of the typical stages in joint venture development are provided by Dwyer, Schurr and Oh (1987) and by Kanter (1994). Dwyer, Schurr and Oh distinguish five stages which they call awareness, exploration, expansion, commitment and dissolution. Kanter uses the terminology of partnerships and describes the different phases in terms of friendship, engagement, housekeeping, learning to cooperate and internal change. All these stage models make valuable practical contributions to understanding the patterns of change which are typical of joint ventures.

A number of authors have gone beyond the traditional linear stage models and have shown how each stage is (pre)determined. Zajac and Olsen (1993) describe stages which they call initializing, processing and reconfiguration, and draw attention to the cyclic relationships amongst them. During the initializing stage the preliminary conditions are set. In the processing stage, learning processes take place and the first behavior patterns develop. In the reconfiguration stage, the joint venture is evaluated and this may lead back to the first two stages. The evaluation can lead to a revision of the original conditions and may call into question the behavior patterns which developed during the processing stage.

Ring and Van de Ven (1994, p. 102) draw attention to the changes in relationships over time. They lay particular emphasis upon the process of socialization, in the course of which the business transaction gives rise to a social relationship. Theirs is a social–psychological approach which stresses the process of institutionalization and emphasizes the change from an initial formal relationship to an informal one.

Based on our observations and the literature, we have extended the quasi-deterministic stage model by recognizing the fact that every assessment of objectives in the evaluation stage, whether at joint venture level or at partner level, affects the two previous stages (see Figure 2.3). Depending on the level of goal attainment and the level of conflict present, decisions are made in the evaluation stage on possible changes to the organizational structure, distribution of resources and strategic orientation. The higher the level of conflict and the lower the level of goal attainment, the more likely it is that fundamental changes will be made to the structure of the joint venture.

## RESULTS OF CONFLICTS

In a Thai–European joint venture, the conflicts had escalated to such a degree that the partners needed to change the relationship in order to sustain the company. The partners could not agree on their roles within the joint venture. The Thai partner no longer saw the benefit of actively contributing to the joint venture and felt dominated by the European partner. The European partner ran the daily operational activities and did not need the Thai partner.

Informal meetings took place to discuss the problems and consider the possibilities. After several rounds of negotiation, there were changes in the management team whereby the Thai partner reduced their involvement in active management and turned their role into a "sleeping partner" with a guaranteed annual dividend.

High levels of conflict have repercussions on the formation stage, because the organizational structure, the resources and the strategic orientation may change the form of the joint venture, and any alterations in these variables lead to a reshaping of the venture. The lower the level of conflict and the higher the level of goal attainment, the more likely it is that any changes will take the form of minor modifications. This in turn affects the adjustment stage.

The feedback cycle linking adjustment and evaluation may be classed as a first-order learning process, since improvements are made without changing the original goals of the joint venture. However, changes to the

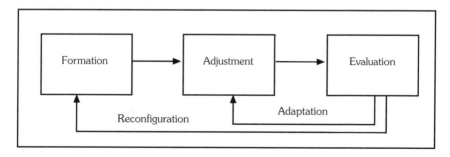

**Figure 2.3**   Feedback cycles linking formation, adjustment and evaluation

goals themselves lead to a higher level in the development process. Analysis of goals initiates a second-order learning process, which leads to a new cycle of formation, adjustment and evaluation.

We shall now examine these three stages—formation, adjustment and evaluation—in some detail and we shall consider the main problems which arise during each phase.

## Formation stage

The main question to be answered at this stage is: What form shall the joint venture take? Other questions to consider include:

- What are the aims of the joint venture?
- How will the resources be allocated?
- What organizational structure will it have?

Companies which set up a joint venture must be willing to cooperate on aims and resources. Typically, the partner companies decide separately what they want from the joint venture. They then negotiate which objectives they wish to pursue together. Reaching an agreement on objectives is important not so much as a way of turning existing agreements into plans, but as a way of emphasizing each company's willingness to set its own activities in a context which is wider than the company itself. The partners have to be committed to doing this and be prepared to sacrifice some of their own interests for the sake of the system as a whole. When they make definite agreements at an intermediate level, they allocate tasks and/or functions, they divide up certain functions and activities amongst themselves, and complete certain tasks together. They must also establish relationships at different levels, initiate contacts between managers and future members of the joint venture, adjust their behavioral styles, examine differences in culture, set up mechanisms for settling conflicts, and coordinate decision making procedures.

For the first stage, Lorange and Roos (1991) have developed a model of joint venture formation which takes account of four critical influences: strategic match, management blessing, internal support and coordination of the roles of the partners and the joint venture. Büchel (1997) suggests that the process of joint venture formation can be broken down into two basic

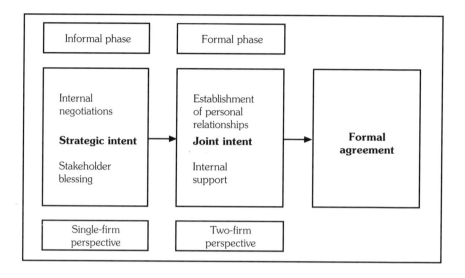

**Figure 2.4** Framework of joint venture formation

phases (Figure 2.4). In the informal phase both partners conduct internal negotiations. These negotiations require the blessing of stakeholders in key management positions. This is consistent with Lorange and Roos (1990) who argue that there are two factors of particular importance: first, the partners to the venture should agree on strategy based on available information; and second, the joint venture should be supported by the partners.

When the partners arrive at a strategic intent on the objectives of the joint venture, both must be able to see the contribution which the joint venture will make towards the achievement of their own particular objectives. It is at this point that the formal phase is entered where the partners aim to establish a congruent understanding that leads to a joint intent. Internal support and good personal relationships between organizational members from both partners help in reaching a joint intent.

Only a win–win situation will produce the level of commitment which is essential in the subsequent phases. If the distribution of benefits is perceived as unequal right from the start, the establishment of a joint venture will be jeopardized. The agreement and support of both direct and indirect stakeholders must be obtained in discussions on how the joint venture will help the companies gain the desired competitive advantage and reach a consensus on cooperative strategy. Lack of management support increases the danger that competing internal projects will emerge and absorb resources which are needed for the joint venture. The main outcomes of the approach phase should be a shared assessment of the expected competitive advantage, a precise evaluation of the contribution the joint venture will make to reaching set objectives, and a judgment of the significance of the joint venture in the total strategic plan of each partner company.

In the second part of the formation stage, that is the formal or negotiation phase, the most important activities have to do with establishing internal support for the cooperative venture and clarifying the roles of the joint venture and the partners within the joint venture system. The main aim in this phase is to develop a business plan specifying the actual tasks of the joint venture, the existing and potential customers, the products, financial means, short-term and long-term plans, and the role of the joint venture in the value chains of the partners. Members of the partner organizations who meet and build up personal relationships during this early formation phase are more likely to be able to successfully mediate in any conflicts which may arise later.

Once the partners have agreed on the objectives of the joint venture, they will discuss its structure and make decisions on the following aspects:

- property rights of the joint venture;
- legal organization of the joint venture;
- staffing policy; and
- financial bonds between the partners.

The two phases of the formation stage differ in importance according to the nature of the joint venture. Product development joint ventures, for example, are set up to diversify and extend the competencies of the parent companies. A company wishing to establish a joint venture of this kind will go through a relatively long phase of looking for and evaluating suitable candidates, because the venture will affect the whole of its value chain. The negotiation phase is usually also relatively long, because the joint venture will have close operational links with the partners and there will be close coordination in various functional areas. Joint ventures in sales or service areas are a different matter. The partners tend to be very similar, so it usually takes only a short time to reach agreement on strategy and to gain the support of relevant stakeholders. The end of the formation stage is usually marked by an official agreement between the two partners to set up a joint venture. This is the demarcation point between the formation stage and the adjustment stage, although there is some overlap between the contents of the two stages: approach and exchange processes between the partners and the joint venture, and within the joint venture itself, are not restricted to the adjustment stage, since the first moves towards mutual socialization are already visible during formation.

## Adjustment stage

The second stage of development may be described as the adjustment stage. The main questions to be answered during this stage are:

- How can the joint venture meet its objectives?
- How is the joint venture to be linked to the partners?
- What socialization processes are taking place between the organizations?
- How does the joint venture adapt to changes in the environment?

The task of the joint venture is to meet the objectives of both partners within the existing guidelines. In the adjustment stage, the emphasis is on the exchange process between the partners and the joint venture. There are two reasons for this: first, it is during this stage that decisions will be made on the coordinating mechanisms between the joint venture and the partners; second, the business plan which was developed during the formation stage is now being implemented in the joint venture. The joint venture now faces the task of fulfilling the chosen objectives with the resources allocated, while at the same time gaining sufficient legitimacy on the market as an independent enterprise.

During the adjustment stage, processes of negotiation and adjustment take place between the partners and the joint venture and within the joint venture as an independent unit. Discussion of the adjustment processes at each of these two levels follows.

## Partner–joint venture relationship

The nature of the joint venture determines the way in which it is linked into the value chains of the partner organizations. The greater the strategic importance of the joint venture in the partners' value chains, the closer the links by which they will bind it to themselves. A product development joint venture, for example, is usually tied more closely to the partners than a basic research joint venture. This is especially true when the output of a product development joint venture forms an integral part of the product range of the partners.

### INTERDEPENDENCE OF PARTNERS AND JOINT VENTURE

Ericsson Hewlett-Packard Telecommunications (EHPT) is a joint venture in which Ericsson holds a 60% and Hewlett-Packard (HP) a 40% interest. EHPT was created in 1993, at the interface of the telecommunications and computer industries. The aim was to develop and produce an integrated product for network management.

EHPT was a product development joint venture, founded to manufacture a product in the border area between telecommunications and the computer industry. The dependency relationships between the partners and the joint venture were approximately as follows. HP provided the hardware, and combined parts of the hardware with the software by arrangement with EHPT. EHPT then added other components used by Ericsson as the basis for their special telecommunications products. The product could be sold by all three organizations, HP, EHPT and Ericsson; in reality, however, Ericsson dominated the market.

Figure 2.5 shows the core technological competencies of the separate organizations in relation to the whole product, which is called TMOS. TMOS is a network management product which is sold to customers as a total integrated system. UNIX, CAP, TAP and XMAS are technological components of TMOS.

As Figure 2.5 shows, the need to link the joint venture to the partners presents a special challenge in the shape of interface management. This will be discussed in more detail in Chapter 3.

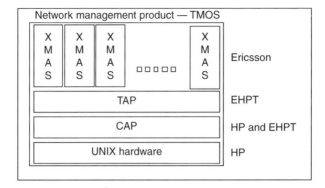

**Figure 2.5** Responsibilities of partners (TMOS = Telecommunication Management Operations Systems; XMAS = Telecommunication Management Applications; EHPT = Ericsson Hewlett-Packard Telecommunications; HP = Hewlett-Packard; TAP = Integrated Hardware Components of TMOS; CAP = Integrated Hardware Components of TMOS; UNIX = Operating System.)

Difficulties can arise in respect of technological compatibility, but these can usually be solved by technical means. Building up relationships between the staff of the joint venture and that of the partners is much more difficult, and maintaining the support of management in the partner companies can also be problematic. It is here that conflicts of culture may emerge between the partners. In the words of Cartwright and Cooper (1993, p. 60): "As culture is as fundamental to an organization as personality is to the individual, the degree of culture fit that exists between the combining organizations is likely to be directly correlated to the success of the combination." The building of relationships amongst staff at the interfaces of the cooperating organizations creates a working culture which enables the joint venture to work towards its objectives even when conflicts arise.

## Joint venture

During the adjustment stage, the joint venture develops its own organizational identity. The members of the partner organizations become acquainted with each other, and as a result the assumptions of the different groups are analyzed and new norms are created. This leads to the development of a new organizational identity for the joint venture. The new identity consists of a culture distinguishable from that of the partners, and a shared meaning or sense for the new organization. The first steps towards joint venture identity are taken when different groups of employees converge and learn to get along together.

## Evaluation stage

The third stage in the development of a joint venture system is the evaluation stage. Questions to be answered in this stage include:
- Have the objectives which the partners set for the joint venture been met?
- Have the partners achieved their objectives by means of the joint venture?
- How is the joint venture changing?

Central to this stage is the evaluation process and its consequences. It is now that the future organizational form of the joint venture is decided. For all types of joint venture, achievement of objectives must be considered at two levels, that is the joint venture and the partners. Decisions are made regarding future cooperation between the partners and the joint venture. The nature of these decisions depends on the degree to which the objectives of the joint venture and the partners have been met, and on whether all participants are perceived to have made a fair contribution. If there is a gap between goals and performance, a possible reconfiguration of the joint venture will be negotiated. The greater the perceived gap, or the higher the level of perceived unfairness, the more likely it is that radical changes will be made to the organizational form.

### RECONFIGURATION PROBLEMS

In Vietnam, there are no legal clauses of liquidation of a joint venture investment which guarantee the investor the right to withdraw the investment in case the joint venture agreement is breached. Due to the lack of laws stipulating the termination of agreements, the

Vietnamese partner is more likely to continue the business after the termination of the joint venture. Therefore, the foreign partner requires a high pay-back or a long-term view of the investment.

## LEVELS, STAGES AND AREAS OF MANAGEMENT INFLUENCE

In the preceding sections, we outlined the different levels at which a joint venture system can be analyzed, and the different stages in its development. We shall now link these levels and stages together, and relate them to the main areas in which the management of the joint venture can influence its development. We shall describe these areas of influence in more detail in Chapters 4–7.

Different objectives and patterns of relationships can exist at different levels in the joint venture system, and the problems which confront management vary according to the stage of development of the joint venture. In the formation stage, the relationship between the partners is of central importance because this is the stage at which they work together to decide the future form of the joint venture. In the adjustment stage, the important factors are the joint venture in relation to its environment, and the relationship between the joint venture and the partners. The joint venture itself needs to develop enough autonomy and identity to be capable of adaptation. In the evaluation stage, the whole joint venture system is assessed.

The areas where management can influence the development of a joint venture are: strategy, structure, human resources and culture (Probst and Büchel, 1997). The relative significance of these areas varies according to the developmental stage of the joint venture and the level in the joint venture system (Figure 2.6). In practice, the emphasis is usually on strategic management during the formation stage, while in the adjustment stage, interface management, that is structural management between the partners and the joint venture, is more important. Management activities in the four areas differ according to the level. At joint venture level, for example, management must decide how to promote a cultural identity for the newly created organization. For the partners, however, the most important aspect is the strategic significance of the joint venture.

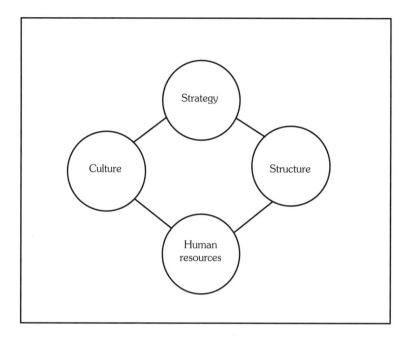

**Figure 2.6**  Areas of joint venture management

In the following chapters, we shall consider the actual problems which arise in the four different areas of development, at different levels and in the different phases.

The main difficulty in managing joint ventures arises from the fact that the four areas of management overlap and interact: "...Alliance management involves consideration of complex systemic issues associated with interrelationships among strategy, structure, systems, and staff in the participating organizations." (Yoshino and Rangan, 1995, p. 113)

## Questions to address

- Which stage of development has the joint venture reached?
- At what level in the joint venture system are you located?
- In what ways can the partners influence the joint venture?
- How much autonomy does the joint venture have?
- Were the objectives of the joint venture established during the formation stage?

- Was the organizational structure established during the formation stage?
- What purpose does the joint venture serve for the partners?
- How does the joint venture adapt to changes in the environment?
- Are mechanisms in place for resolving conflicts between the joint venture and the partners?
- Has the joint venture achieved the objectives set by the partners?
- Were these objectives analyzed during the evaluation stage?

# CHAPTER THREE

# CONCEIVING AND NEGOTIATING A JOINT VENTURE

*Dr. Lalit M. Johri*
*Associate Professor of School of Management*
*Asian Institute of Technology, Bangkok, Thailand*

The elements leading to operational success of a joint venture have to be brought into play at the time of conceiving and negotiating the joint venture. A weak concept of joint venture partnership, negotiations addressing only general principles, and a poorly orchestrated launch can lead to a situation where even the best management practices cannot make a success of the joint venture. In this chapter, experience of several joint ventures, both successful and failed, will be used to describe prescriptions or recipes for achieving success at the conceiving and negotiating phases of joint venture management. These phases can generally be subsumed under the formation stage.

## CONCEIVING A SUCCESSFUL JOINT VENTURE

Usually it is one of the partners who proposes the formation of a joint venture to another partner with the idea of exploiting business opportunities jointly. The choice of a joint venture as an entry strategy may be influenced by external or internal reasons. Among the external reasons may be the government policy requiring foreign companies to join hands with local companies to do business in their country. The internal reasons may include sharing risks, lack of experience in foreign markets or high entry barriers in the form of investments or market complexities. The viability of a joint venture is highly dependent on the interests and perceptions of the outcomes of the joint venture by the partners. The extent to which the interests of the partners are served and their perceptions about the risks and benefits shape their attitudes and commitments towards the joint venture and are thus prime contributors to the success of the joint venture.

## Shared interests of the partners

A joint venture emerges as a strong business concept when there is convergence or a high degree of overlap in the interests of the partners. Looking for corporate growth, business expansion into new product lines and entry into new markets are among the most common interests of the companies that bring them together as joint venture partners. Needless to say, these examples of interests ultimately guide the partners towards higher levels of profitability.

### TOYOTA KIRLOSKAR MOTOR

The Toyota Motor Corporation's (TMC) newly formed joint venture with Kirloskar Group is a US$170 million joint venture which will produce 20,000 family type multipurpose vehicles on the basic platform used in Kijang, India. The production is expected to rise to 50,000 vehicles at the end of the fifth year of operation. Both of the partners are benefiting in terms of their long-term interests. TMC's interest is to enter the fast growing automobile market in India with the ultimate aim of developing an Indian plant and operations to become a major part of Toyota's global strategy for the twenty-first century. The interest of Kirloskar Group, well known for its high quality engines and generators produced in collaboration with Cummins, is to diversify its business portfolio and enter into the automotive sector as part of their future strategy. There seems to be a very good match between the global ambitions of one company and local ambitions of another. Toyota holds a 74% share in the joint venture which facilitates the transfer of technology from TMC Japan to the joint venture.

Besides shared interests, compatibility between partners also helps in crafting a joint venture strategy. Tetsu Araki, chief representative of Toyota in India, considers the joint venture with Kirloskar as a "marriage of minds". He finds three common aspects between the two: similarities in corporate culture, commitment to quality, and manufacturing experience in generators and engines. He feels very optimistic about the success of the joint venture. There is compatibility and a move towards accepting each other's ways and styles in critical areas of activities.

## Competitive advantages and complementarity

Many strategic alliances including joint ventures point towards the fact that partnerships based on respective competitive advantages with strong complementarity lead to success. The Philips–Sony alliance for the development of compact disks was not only successful in enforcing global standards but was also a commercial success. Philips contributed its competence in the area of digital music and Sony contributed its competence in the development of playing systems. Conceptually speaking, the pooling of strengths and their complementarity resulted into potential synergies all through the value chain (Figure 3.1). However, combining strengths and weaknesses produces sub-optimal results because of poor coupling between skills and resources of the partners. In addition, differences in learning curves of partners cause misunderstandings and conflicts resulting in delays and inefficient deployment of resources.

|  |  | Partner A | |
|---|---|---|---|
|  |  | Strengths | Weaknesses |
| **Partner B** | Strengths | 2+2=5 (synergistic) | 2+2=3 or 4 (counterproductive) |
|  | Weaknesses | 2+2=3 or 4 (counterproductive) | 2+2=0 (destructive) |

**Figure 3.1** Pooling together of respective strengths and weaknesses

Table 3.1 presents the contributions of Partners A and B so as to complete the value chain of a joint venture. Each Partner contributes in the areas where it has the most advantage. For example because of superior capabilities Partner A plays a dominant role in three functions, namely, research and development, manufacturing and marketing. Similarly Partner B, having superior capabilities in four areas, plays a dominant role in these areas: purchase, selling, distribution and after sales services. This demonstrates the complementarity between two partners. By focusing on their respective areas of competencies the joint venture partners can keep the functional costs low and maintain high levels of productivity and quality standards.

| R&D | Purchase | Manufacturing | Marketing | Selling | Distribution | After sales services |
|-----|----------|---------------|-----------|---------|--------------|----------------------|
| A   | B        | A             | A         | B       | B            | B                    |

**Table 3.1**  Complementarity between two partners in various areas of the value chain

In some less technologically developed Asian countries the local partners lacking resource competencies often provide the all important relational advantage, thus making the market access easy for the foreign partner. Their relationship networks also help in dealing with the government or suppliers. In China, many foreign companies cultivate *guanxi*, a holistic concept of relationships, at different levels of the society with the help of their local partners.

## Perception of risk–benefit

Another very important aspect influencing the successful creation of a joint venture is the perceptions of the partners regarding the potential risks and benefits of the proposed venture. Empirical evidence points out that when perceived advantages are high and are seen as win–win by the partners the joint venture ultimately proves to be a success (Newman, 1992). In the case of successful joint ventures, not only are the perceived benefits high for both, but also the risks are seen to be equally shared. In the TMC–Kirloskar joint venture described earlier, the perceived advantages by both partners are said to be very high and at the same time there is strong enthusiasm among them to implement the joint venture. Sharing of benefits and risks gives a feeling of equality and acts as a strong motivator for the potential partners.

## Commitment and trust

A strong conception of a joint venture is also characterized by the presence of committed individuals amongst the potential partners who support the creation of the joint venture. Often this commitment is based on mutual confidence exhibited by key individuals. Many successful joint ventures in Asia are based on partnerships with erstwhile agents or distributors. Since many foreign partners do not trust new parties they prefer to go with traditional partners they have had long standing business relationships with and can trust more easily.

Notwithstanding historical business relationships, the starting point for further negotiations is a comprehensive and transparent proposal that establishes the strategic and operational feasibility of a joint venture.

## WESTERN ENERGY: WHY IT FAILED

Western Energy Inc. (WEI), primarily an oil company, entered into a 50-50 joint venture agreement with three Chinese companies to develop and exploit Taibo coal mines in Shanxi province. Incorporated as Taibo Mine Group in 1982, the joint venture involved a total investment of US$700 million. WEI entered China because it was fashionable to do business in China and the Chinese Government's open door policy encouraged US companies to enter China. Prompted by energy shortages in China, WEI wanted to gain from first mover advantages. WEI adopted a high profile approach and made use of relationships with senior power brokers in the Chinese Government. The political processes influenced the negotiations which were more about general principles rather than specific tasks and responsibilities. WEI had some prior experience in joint ventures but not in China. WEI was overly enthusiastic, moved unusually fast and made several irrational or extravagant commitments to the Chinese Government including large-scale exports of coal from China. Declining coal prices in the world market coupled with poor quality coal made it impossible for the joint venture to export large quantities of coal. The use of defective machinery, inability to cultivate *guanxi* with local partners and market-based institutions, and conflicts and disputes further contributed to the failure of the joint venture.

Source: Mike W. Peng, *The China Strategy: A Tale of Two Firms,* University of Washington, 1992

## AMERICAN COPIER COMPANY IN CHINA: WHY IT SUCCEEDED

American Copier Company (ACC) (51%) formed this US$30 million joint venture with Shanghai Photo Industry Company (49%) in 1987. ACC had prior experience in joint ventures and first gained experience in China through the export route. It avoided getting involved with Chinese politics and took four years to finalize the joint venture. It did not make any vague promises to the local partners or the Chinese Government.

The joint venture focused on the domestic market and produced only low end and mid-range copiers with due emphasis on quality. In line with the Chinese Government's policy, ACC adopted a phased localization of components and made investments in training for the development of local vendors. It gave them continuous support and monitored their progress. ACC established a nation-wide distribution network and adopted the strategy of local branding and aggressive advertising. Although the company depended on *guanxi* with politicians and local suppliers, it mainly relied on product appeal as a key success factor.

Source: Mike W. Peng, *The China Strategy: A Tale of Two Firms,* University of Washington, 1992

# NEGOTIATING AND WRITING A JOINT VENTURE AGREEMENT

The process of negotiating and arriving at a joint venture agreement does not follow any rigid structure. Each time a company enters into a joint venture, it faces a new situation because the external environment, the profile of potential partners and the scope of the joint venture will change according to host country requirements and the strategy for the joint venture chosen by the partners. One major issue facing foreign companies entering Asia through the joint venture route is to find an ideal process to accomplish rational and working agreements. Experience shows that as such there is neither an ideal process nor a perfect joint venture agreement. A company with an intent to manoeuvre its partner will always be able to find loopholes even in a well written, detailed agreement. Companies can, however, safeguard their interests by following guidelines as presented in this chapter. Much of what is described here is based on valuable experience accumulated by foreign companies that have entered into successful joint venture agreements in the past.

  The art of negotiating and writing a balanced agreement from the point of view of potential partners starts with signing a memorandum of understanding (MOU), followed by in-depth negotiations based on the development of pre-negotiation strategies and finally ends with writing and evaluating the agreement. This process reduces the probability of misunderstanding or divergent interpretations of the agreement.

## Memorandum of understanding

This is an important step because it is an expression of intentions of the partners to create a joint venture. Without implying any form of legal bondage, an MOU provides a psychological bond for the potential partners to carry on further negotiations towards cementing a relationship. The MOU describes the terms of reference of the joint venture which essentially include the strategic boundaries within which the joint venture will be established. The strategic boundaries of the joint venture indicate such things as product/model choice; scale of production; size of investment;

share of each partner; location. The MOU has no legal standing, but is an important platform for launching detailed negotiations.

## Pre-negotiation strategy

Often the negotiations between potential partners for forming a joint venture fail because the partners have not sufficiently prepared before going into the negotiations. Experience shows that negotiations are smoother and less time consuming if the potential partners come to the negotiation table with their respective pre-negotiation strategies. The process of developing the pre-negotiation strategy helps the negotiators to forecast the issues and expectations from their own and their partners' point of views before they engage in actual negotiations. Thus, the negotiators are better prepared to make offers and counter offers and resolve issues without having to face surprises. A framework for designing the pre-negotiation strategy is shown in Figure 3.2.

To design the pre-negotiation strategy, each partner should answer the following questions grouped under the twelve points outlined in Figure 3.2. Usually the pre-negotiation strategy can be designed in a workshop involving some of the key managers of the company. The time spent in designing the pre-negotiation strategy is important because it saves the potential partners from major surprises and time wasting dialogues. The following questions ought to be addressed for the pre-negotiation strategy.

---

1.  Establishing a rationale for the joint venture.
2.  Identifying sources of synergies between the partners' contributions.
3.  Assessing degree of compatibility between two partners.
4.  Analysing motivations for launching the joint venture.
5.  Identifying the main issues for negotiations.
6.  Assessing expectations on specific issues.
7.  Assessing range of offers.
8.  Assessing concessions during negotiations.
9.  Assessing positions on various issues.
10. Predicting notions and fixations that may influence negotiations.
11. Deciding the flow of negotiations.
12. Final checking of the pre-negotiation strategy.

---

**Figure 3.2** Framework in designing the pre-negotiation strategy

## Rationale for the joint venture

- What is the rationale from your company's point of view?
- What is the rationale from your "would-be" partner company's point of view?
- Is there a strong rationale for the proposed joint venture? If not, how do you justify the creation of the joint venture?

## Synergy between the partners' contributions

- What competitive advantages will your company contribute to the joint venture?
- What are the competitive advantages that your "would-be" partner company will contribute to the joint venture?
- Is there a strong complementarity between your company and your "would-be" partner company's contributions? If not, what are the sources of competitive advantage for the proposed joint venture?

## Degree of compatibility between two partners

- What is the size, company culture, management style, corporate philosophy and profit orientation of your company?
- What is the size, company culture, management style, corporate philosophy and profit orientation of your "would-be" partner company?
- Are these compatible or not? If not, how do you propose to adjust with your "would-be" partner company?

## Motivations for launching the joint venture

- What are the interests of your company?
- What are the interests of your "would-be" partner company?
- Is there a strong convergence between the interests of your company and your "would-be" partner company? If not, how do you propose to bring about a convergence?

## Identification of issues

- What are the issues to be negotiated from your company's point of view?
- What are the issues to be negotiated from your "would-be" partner company's point of view?
- Is there a common set of issues to be negotiated? If not, how do you propose to arrive at an agreement on common issues to be negotiated?

## Expectations on specific issues

- What are your company's expectations with respect to various issues?
- What are your "would-be" partner company's expectation levels with respect to various issues?
- Are there major differences in the expectations of the two companies? If yes, how do you propose to bridge this gap?

### ASAHI–VICHAK JOINT VENTURE

The parties wanted to enter into a 50-50 joint venture partnership in order to establish a boiler manufacturing and marketing joint venture to be based in Thailand. Vichak (VBC) wished to undertake, through its manufacturing division, the assembly, manufacture and distribution of the range of boilers designed and manufactured by Asahi (ASC).

When preparing the pre-negotiation strategy, the parties identified a range of issues for which each party had slightly differing objectives:

| Common issues | VBC | ASC |
|---|---|---|
| Management control | 50–50 | ASC |
| Quality control | ASC | ASC |
| Marketing control | VBC | ASC |
| Royalty fee | None | Yes |

| Profit sharing/margin | 50-50 | 50-50 |
|---|---|---|
| Unilateral right to pullout | written default | Yes |
| Product development | ASC | ASC |
| Research and development | ASC | ASC |
| Head of training | ASC | ASC |

**Table 3.2** Objective of VBC and ASC

The gap between the two parties was overcome by trying to arrive at a win–win situation. The negotiation position was to be flexible but within certain limitations where partners should be fair and should not take advantage of the situation. The outcome relied on the cooperation of Asahi and their motivation for this joint venture to work.

## Range of offers

- With respect to each issue what will be your initial offer and goal offer?
- With respect to each issue what will be the initial offer and goal offer of your "would-be" partner company?
- What tactics will you use to negotiate each issue within the range of initial and goal offers that you would make?
- What tactics will your "would-be" partner company use to negotiate each issue within the range of initial and goal offers that they would make?

## Concessions

- With respect to each issue what concessions are you willing to give or seek?
- With respect to each issue what will be the concessions that your "would-be" partner company will give or seek?
- What tactics will you use to gain concessions from your "would-be" partner company?

- What tactics will your "would-be" partner company use to gain concessions from you?

## Position taking

- What are the issues on which your company may take a certain position?
- What are the issues on which your "would-be" partner company may take a certain position?
- In such a situation how do you plan to resolve the deadlock?

## Notions and fixations

- Are you likely to suffer from any fixations or rigidities during the negotiations?
- Do you think your "would-be" partner company is likely to suffer from any fixations or rigidities during the negotiations?
- What tactics will you adopt to soften these rigid attitudes on your part and on the part of your "would-be" partner company?

## Flow of negotiations

- How will you approach the negotiations?
- How will your "would-be" partner company approach the negotiations?

## Final check of your pre-negotiation strategy

- Is your company's pre-negotiation strategy based on comprehensive analysis of facts and figures and specific considerations?
- Is your company's pre-negotiation strategy drawn from a "big picture" about the joint venture?
- Is your company's pre-negotiation strategy specific?
- Does it cover all the issues for negotiations?

- In overall terms is your company's pre-negotiation strategy constructive?
- In overall terms is your company's pre-negotiation strategy realistic?
- In overall terms is your company's pre-negotiation strategy flexible?
- In overall terms does your company's pre-negotiation strategy create a win–win perception?
- In overall terms is your company's pre-negotiation strategy easy to implement?

---

## NEGOTIATING A JOINT VENTURE: SOME LESSONS OF SUCCESS

The process of forming Nantong Cellulose Fibers Company (NCFC), a very successful joint venture in China, was launched in 1982 when a Chinese delegation sought technology for producing "tow", fluffy synthetic fiber, used for making cigarette filters. After a series of negotiations NCFC was launched as a joint venture between China National Tobacco Company and Hoechst/Celanese Corporation. The experience of NCFC shows that the negotiation phase of a joint venture can be very productive and beneficial to both partners if:

- the negotiations move at a regulated pace and are carried out to develop mutual understanding and trust;
- the negotiations focus on interests of the parties;
- the negotiations lead to strong convergence in the interests of both parties;
- the two parties have a win–win feeling and gain equally and at the same time;
- the negotiations are detailed and with active participation from technical staff;
- the negotiations take into account cultural differences and adjust the tone of agreement accordingly. Through a two phase translation process all the documents are conformed; and
- the negotiations are supported by feasibility analysis and without any sense of "over" optimism.

Source: W. H. Newman, "Launching a Viable Joint Venture", *California Management Review*, **35**, Fall 1992

# Negotiating and writing the agreement

The task of negotiating the final joint venture agreement is somewhat simplified if the pre-negotiation strategy preparations have been done. At the time of launching the negotiations, it is advisable to agree on the scope of the agreement. Generally the main aspects of the joint venture agreements include:

- Definitions (e.g. technical terms specific to the industry)
- Identity of partners
- Purpose and scope of the joint venture
- Activities of the joint venture
- Validity period of the agreement including time span of joint venture
- Contributions of each partner
- Responsibilities and obligations of each partner
- Equity share of the partners
- Capital structure of the joint venture
- Quality commitment from both partners
- Scope of technology transfer
- Terms of technology transfer
- Training of employees
- Management: structure, systems, process and procedures
- Ancillary and supplementary agreements covering suppliers and distributors
- Accounting principles and practices
- Accounting and financial statements
- Business policies and profit sharing
- Implementation schedule
- Settlement of disputes and resolution of conflicts
- Legal details (e.g. compliance with any specific laws of the country)
- Any special clauses.

The experience of many successful joint ventures shows that the negotiations follow a calculated pattern of agreeing on issues. Many specific issues in several broad areas such as technology transfer, management structure, equity structure, purchase of equipment, etc. are identified and a series of detailed negotiations are carried out. During each negotiation session, the minutes are recorded and agreed upon by both parties. The composition of the teams may vary according to the issues and areas of decisions. Overall guidance is provided by the top management of the potential partners.

The pattern or flow of negotiations may vary from one joint venture to another. One very significant aspect of negotiating a joint venture is the attention to details. Sticking to discussions on general principles for the creation of the joint venture may leave many issues unresolved and create problems at the time of implementation. In the case of successful joint ventures, negotiators focus on all the specific issues of critical importance. This also paves the way for mutual understanding and building of trust. A leading European airline entered into an agreement with a local company to operate a domestic airline service in India. The Indian partner had no prior experience in the field of civil aviation. The two companies entered into an agreement at a time when India's air space was being opened to private airline companies. The two companies forged an alliance without much homework and soon the partnership ran into difficulties. Many outstanding issues from the point of view of the two partners were not covered fully in the agreement. An outstanding issue ignored at the time of negotiation was the maintenance contract for the leased aircrafts. Because of ambiguity on the issue of maintenance, the two partners ultimately had to go to court to resolve the dispute. The European airline in the process lost goodwill with the civil aviation authorities in India and the Indian partner lost credibility with the foreign investment community in India.

In another case of a 50-50 marketing joint venture between Proctor & Gamble and Godrej Soaps in India, it was revealed that in the agreement there was no cap on the supply price for the soaps that were manufactured by Godrej and supplied to the joint venture. That was one of the undiscussed issues which emerged at the time of the break up of the joint venture.

In the case of large-scale complex joint ventures such as power generation projects, ancillary negotiations are required with suppliers, government agencies and the unions. For example, a joint venture initially involving three partners, namely, Enron, Bechtel and GE created for power generation in India, had to sign more than 370 contracts with different agencies, suppliers and buyers in the country of operation and abroad. This was in addition to the joint venture formation agreements.

Frequently, the process of drafting an agreement is initiated at the time of developing the pre-negotiation strategy. This draft document should, however, not become an anchor, or frame discussions thus limiting options during negotiations. It should only be used as the basis for discussions and at the same time flexibility should be exercised. As soon as the agreement is reached, after a series of negotiations and re-negotiations, the draft can be changed to reflect negotiated settlement. If all the partners bring their own draft agreements, it is advisable to use these drafts as the basis for preparing the agreement. Companies often use source material and standard clauses from the International Chamber of Commerce for drafting agreements (refer to the Appendix).

In the case of some joint ventures involving large-scale compliance of legal frameworks in the country of operation, the agreement reflecting the final settlement is referred to lawyers for identifying any major lapses or legal implications of the agreement in terms of rights and responsibilities. Any serious doubts raised by legal experts can lead to reopening of the negotiations and the process may go on until resolved to the satisfaction of the partners. Experience shows that in the early stages, the negotiations should be among top management, specialists, facilitators, etc. Lawyers should get involved towards the end.

There are a few special precautions needed for negotiations among managers and companies belonging to different language cultures. At the negotiation stage, a partner may need people who can speak the language of the other partner. In such cases, companies depend on services of interpreters and translators. In terms of writing bilingual agreements, there is a well known practice called conforming. It means that the mother agreement, say English, is first translated into the language of one of the partners, say Chinese, and then the Chinese version is retranslated into English. The retranslated version in English should conform both in letter and spirit with the mother agreement.

An illustration of a joint venture agreement is given in the Appendix.

## Evaluation of the agreement

Just before implementing the agreement, it is necessary to evaluate the agreement. The specific questions asked at this stage are:

- Is the scope of the agreement complete or not?
- Are the business and legal interpretations of the agreement explicit and reflect the negotiated settlements or not?
- Is there scope for manoeuvrability for either partners?
- Do the various language translations conform to the mother agreement?
- Does the agreement raise the spirits and excite the partners in terms of potential benefits? If yes, go ahead!

## Questions to address

- When conceiving a joint venture, do the partners have shared interests?
- Do the partners complement each other?
- Are risks and benefits equally shared between the partners?
- Have the partners been able to develop commitment and trust?
- Before negotiating, have the partners established an MOU?
- Have the partners developed a pre-negotiation strategy?
- Have the agreed issues been formally written into the joint venture agreement?
- After agreeing on issues and writing the joint venture agreement, has the agreement been evaluated in terms of scope and flexibility?

# CHAPTER FOUR

# STRATEGY DEVELOPMENT AS AN AREA OF JOINT VENTURE MANAGEMENT

The term "strategy development" as used here embraces all the processes involved in formulating strategies of varying scope and precision, translating them into practical terms and implementing them at every level in the joint venture system. Strategy development gives rise to a series of questions, such as:

- Who develops strategy in the joint venture system?
- How can the strategic objectives of the partners be harmonized?
- What factors must be taken into account in developing strategy for the joint venture?
- How can the multiplicity of demands within the joint venture system be managed?
- How can provision be made for continuous adjustment of strategy?

The terms "strategy" and "strategic leadership" can be used in a general sense to denote all the objectives and actions of a company which are directed towards making it more competitive. In other words, the function of strategy is to direct the company's activities. The development of strategy for a joint venture has two main purposes: first, to establish a strategic basis shared by the partners; second, and more importantly, to provide the joint venture itself with a set of guidelines on which to base its actions. The process of developing strategy in the joint venture system therefore springs from two basic questions: (i) Why do the partners believe that a joint venture is a good strategic option?; and (ii) What strategy should the joint venture pursue?

The partners need to be able to say why a joint venture makes sense as a cooperative strategy. We have already discussed some of the motives which prompt companies to embark on joint ventures, but there are other reasons:

- exploiting synergy;
- ensuring access to important resources;
- gaining entry to markets; and
- gaining know-how.

If a cooperative venture is to succeed as a way of attaining these objectives, common strategies must be developed and established. The basic strategy negotiated by the partners provides the joint venture with its direction and goal.

The question facing the joint venture is how to behave within its own specific environment, which consists of the markets in which the venture operates, the specific legal conditions and the expectations of various external interest groups. The strategic guidelines must be translated into practical terms. Like any independent company, the joint venture must work out a concrete strategy which fits its circumstances and will enable it to achieve its objectives. The practical problems which it encounters are closely linked with the interplay of autonomy and control in the joint venture. The basic strategy on which the partners have agreed is seldom sufficient to answer all the strategic questions which arise in the daily operations of the joint venture. In reality, repeated adjustments and renegotiations are unavoidable. In the course of these activities, the partners try to redefine their influence and to exert it in various ways. In extreme cases, one partner may try to dominate the strategy of the entire joint venture system.

The position of the joint venture in the renegotiation process is characterized by constant tension between the objectives as originally stated, and the need to act in a way which serves both the specific interests of the joint venture itself and the strategic interests of the partners. The joint venture is obliged to implement the strategic plans of the partners; ideally, it should do this by acting independently, as an autonomous company. However, this rarely happens in real life.

In any joint venture system, strategies and strategic objectives are not the only issues which must be settled in advance. Even more important are the mechanisms and processes for developing and adjusting strategies, methods and institutions for resolving conflicts. These are issues of vital importance, yet they are repeatedly ignored. Even in cases where the partners have little difficulty in agreeing on an initial strategy, joint ventures almost inevitably reach a point where previously agreed fundamental strategic decisions are called into question, and radical renegotiations are needed. This point was made in relation to our stage model of joint ventures. In the adjustment stage, the joint venture strategy is influenced by the interests of the partners. In the evaluation stage, it is subjected to thorough scrutiny. In our model, the outcome of the evaluation stage is either a new adjustment cycle or, if the reality of the joint venture is too far removed from the expectations of the partners, the dissolution of the joint venture.

Strategies are important for assessing success and failure in the joint venture system. Success and failure can only be judged in reference to given objectives or success criteria. If the strategic objectives are clearly formulated at the different levels in the joint venture system, subsequent evaluation of the cooperative venture will be much easier.

We shall now examine more closely the processes of strategy development at the different levels in the joint venture system. This will put us in a better position to offer some suggestions on how strategy development processes in the system might be structured. We are concerned not with the content of the many strategic orientations which are possible within a joint venture system, but with the actual processes of strategy development and implementation. Answers must be found to a number of important questions, for example: What are the requirements which a strategy for a joint venture system must satisfy, if it is to have a good chance of success? How can it be implemented? What are the problems and conflicts which are likely to affect implementation? Experience shows that even the best strategies are of little use if they are not implemented, or if they are not constantly scrutinized and adapted to suit new situations.

The best strategy is always the strategy which one has personally helped to develop and implement. Strategies are not just a matter for the strategic planners; they must always be developed in collaboration with the people who will be directly affected, that is those who will have to use and implement them.

This has implications for the style of leadership in the joint venture system, the hierarchical structures and the decision making procedures.

Strategy development is therefore always a political matter, no matter how hard people try to support their chosen strategies on rational grounds.

When discussing strategy in the joint venture system, it seems reasonable to distinguish between the cooperative strategies which the partners pursue through the joint venture, and the strategies which are developed within the joint venture itself. Problems and conflicts which arise between the partners can have very different causes and effects from those of strategy-related problems within the joint venture. From a theoretical point of view, this distinction seems convincing. However, if we examine the kinds of conflict which actually arise in the everyday operations of joint venture systems, we often find that the problems which lie at their root cannot be clearly localized. This can lead to a situation in which the participants exhaust their energies in mutual accusations instead of getting to the bottom of the problems.

Our joint venture model throws further light on the important distinction between strategic issues at partner level and at the level of the new company (Figure 4.1). In our model, strategy development starts with the strategic fit between the partners. From this the partners derive the strategic objectives which they formulate together for the joint venture. In addition to their explicit objectives for the joint venture, the partners also have various additional expectations and implicit objectives which are not to be found in their formal agreement. As a result, conflicts often arise in the daily life of the joint venture between its "official" mission and the unofficial expectations and individual interests of the partners. Furthermore, the joint venture is usually trying to implement the strategic objectives within its own constantly changing environment, which must also be taken into account in the development of a joint venture strategy. This does not mean, of course, that the environment of the joint venture is completely divorced from that of the partners; but the new unit and the partners are rarely subject to the same environmental demands, if only because of the difference in size.

We turn now to some of the main problems affecting the development of strategy in the joint venture system. We shall then consider the different levels at which strategy is developed. This is followed by a discussion of "strategic fit", that is the degree of alignment which must exist between the basic cooperative strategies of the partner companies,

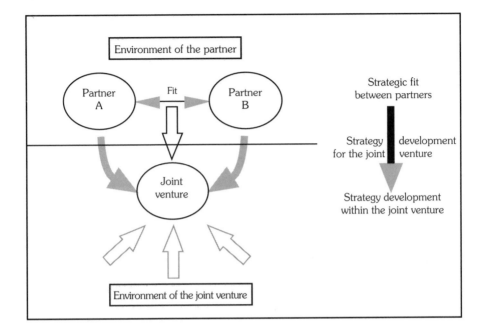

**Figure 4.1**  Strategy development at different levels

and the issue of development and adjustment of strategy in the joint venture itself.

## PROBLEMS AFFECTING STRATEGY DEVELOPMENT IN THE JOINT VENTURE SYSTEM

Our description of the strategic relationships within the joint venture system helps us to categorize and analyze the problems which typically affect strategy development in the system (Figure 4.2).

Different problems commonly affect strategy development at different levels in the joint venture system. We have already mentioned the issue of harmony between the partner companies. There may also be problems of strategy translation between the partners and the new unit, and problems of coherence arising from the differing demands which the partners place on the joint venture. Translation problems arise when the time comes to put the strategy set for the joint venture into practical

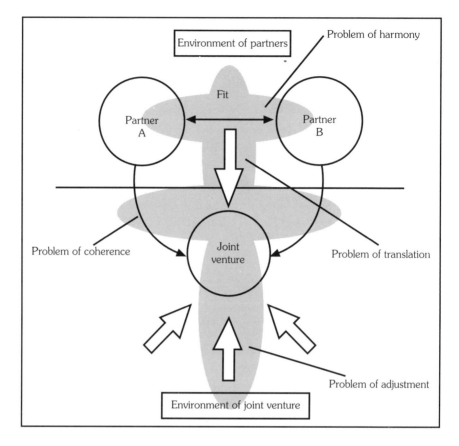

**Figure 4.2** Problems affecting strategy development in the joint venture system

terms and implement it. Coherence problems arise because the partners, although they agree in many areas, are bound to have some conflicting aims and these become apparent when each partner evaluates the joint venture's actions from their own point of view. Other issues relating to strategy development in the joint venture concern adjustment and updating of strategy.

We shall now examine these problems more closely, and consider their consequences for strategy development. Later in this chapter, we discuss in some detail the various processes of strategy development and possible ways of influencing them.

## Problems of harmony: Insufficient agreement between the partners

The partners may have problems of harmony over the strategic aims which they wish to pursue through the cooperative venture. Such problems usually have their foundations in incompatible basic strategies and differing expectations regarding the outcomes of the joint venture. They may also arise if the partners make unequal contributions to the joint venture, or as a result of differences in structure, culture or staffing policy.

In practice, problems of harmony may prove particularly awkward, because they are often recognized late and may therefore be ignored in the initial negotiations between the partners. At some stage, the joint venture is likely to be confronted by a problem not covered by the initial agreement, and it is then that the previously ignored differences come to light. The level of harmony between the partners has far-reaching consequences and affects the degree to which the partners are able to work together in an atmosphere of trust and mutual commitment.

## Problems of translation: From strategic principles to a joint venture action plan

Problems of translation generally arise when the time comes to derive strategic action plans for the joint venture from the basic strategy set by the partners. The partners may have agreed on a joint cooperative strategy, but the issue of how to put it into practice remains to be tackled. Essentially, this is the classic problem which any strategic business unit faces when responsible for implementing a strategic assignment. In the case of a joint venture, the task of translating principles into actual plans is complicated by additional difficulties of several kinds.

Joint ventures often operate in an area with which the partners are unfamiliar, and where they have insufficient experience to develop strategic principles which can be easily implemented. Furthermore, the managing body of the joint venture is made up of individuals from varying backgrounds: they often come from different companies, where they have learned different "strategy cultures". This is one of the great strengths of joint ventures, because it sets the stage for innovation, creativity and mutual learning. On the other hand, if the diversity is too great, it can hinder the attempt to translate basic strategic principles into specific actions. The difficulty is compounded by the fact that there is never one correct way of doing this. There is always room to maneuver, but the management of the joint venture must choose one specific course. Diversity of experience amongst the staff of the joint venture is in itself desirable, but it should not be allowed to lead to a situation in which all questions of strategy are settled by choosing the smallest common denominator.

Another aspect of the translation problem derives from the fact that the objectives and basic strategies which the partners develop for the joint venture are often kept vague and open. In negotiations between potential partners to a joint venture, it often happens that issues which are unclear, unpleasant or threaten to cause conflict are put aside and left for the new unit to sort out. The less the joint venture's freedom of interpretation with regard to its objectives, the less difficulty it will have in translating strategic principles into practice. The joint venture system harbors a certain paradox, in that those systems in which the joint venture has vague objectives and a great deal of freedom are also the ones in which there is the greatest chance of fully exploiting the innovative potential of the cooperative venture; however, conflict is also most likely when the objectives are so vague that they require far-reaching creative interpretation by joint venture managers. When the partners are dissatisfied with the way the joint venture uses the freedom of interpretation they start to interfere more and more in the operational activities of the joint venture.

## DYNAMIC EQUILIBRIUM

Thai Maxwell Electric Co. Ltd is a joint venture established by a group of leading Thai industrials and entrepreneurs from Japan, Taiwan, Singapore and Indonesia to manufacture and distribute transformers. In the case of Thai Maxwell Electric, the joint venture agreement was built on trust between the partners. Since the joint

venture had not been developed in detail, the partners had to rene-
gotiate many issues. To match expectations, top management and
owners of all the partner companies were involved. At this stage,
responsibilities were clearly defined, yet the nature of joint ventures
demands the agreement to be flexible for renegotiation. As a manager of Thai Maxwell Electric pointed out: "We all know the equilibrium is dynamic, so we keep the deal open for renegotiation.
Each year after the operation started, partners meet once to discuss
issues related to the joint venture."

## Problems of coherence: Differing demands on the joint venture

As a business form, the joint venture system is particularly vulnerable to
problems of coherence. Even where the partners have formally agreed
on a basic strategy and a set of strategic principles for the joint venture,
there often remain additional expectations which are unexpressed, or of
which the partners were unaware at the time of the agreement, or which
they regarded as unimportant. In the course of time, these expectations
may become more significant and lead to serious goal conflicts within the
joint venture system. In this situation, the management of the joint venture has a double task: first, to translate into practical terms the explicit
strategic principles set by the partners and second, to harmonize these
with the partners' implicit expectations. The problems which arise in this
context can be particularly serious if one of the partners gains more influence and the joint venture, in addition to pursuing the objectives initially
negotiated, begins to act more and more in the interests of that partner.
There are already some classic cases on record in which one partner
"used" the joint venture to acquire specific know-how and once this
was achieved, the partner either abandoned the joint venture or behaved
in such a way as to push it into a deep crisis of mistrust (Reich and
Mankin, 1986).

The partners have various expectations and demands, partly
unexpressed, which complicate all negotiations and communication
processes within the joint venture system. Sooner or later, this may lead

to open conflicts, and sometimes even to the dissolution of the joint venture. In situations of this kind, the commitment of the partners and the mutual trust of all participants are called into question. The continuing shift, initially unnoticed, in favor of the dominant partner leads to a potentially unstable situation in which the partner who is losing influence will try to regain it, reduces its commitment in proportion to loss of influence, or leaves the cooperative venture. Situations of this kind often lead to "affairs", in which a partner tries to build up alternatives to the cooperative arrangement. This causes further destabilization of the already weakened joint venture.

## Problems of adjustment: Changes in the environmental circumstances of the joint venture over time

Adjustment problems often arise when there is a clash between the strategic principles set by the partners and new developments in the business environment of the joint venture, that is new configurations of markets, interest groups or resources. The new developments may offer the joint venture new opportunities, but they may not have been foreseen at the time when the original joint venture strategy was developed and may conflict with it. In a situation of this kind, the strategic principles must be adjusted. This can involve a wide-ranging process of evaluation, renegotiation and sometimes redefining the joint venture system.

Adjustment difficulties are not unusual and in themselves they are not a problem. On the contrary, periodic reflection of the objectives and outcomes of the cooperative venture provides an opportunity for a company to learn from its experiences and mistakes, and to make progressive improvements in its cooperative skills. However, this becomes difficult if the partners allow the joint venture so little room for strategic maneuver that the management of the joint venture must use up a large part of its resources in renegotiating its given objectives or in testing the limits of its freedom. The extent to which strategy adjustment becomes a problem depends ultimately on the levels of autonomy and control within the joint venture system. It is often suggested that the partners should initially keep the joint venture under close control, and allow it more independence as everyone gains more experience (Chakravarthy and Lorange, 1991). However, it is difficult to make general rules, and it is important not to restrict one's view to the strategic aspects of autonomy and control. It is just as important, for example, that the joint venture develops its own identity at an early stage and that sufficient attention is paid to structure and staffing. Adjustment problems are particularly difficult and imponderable. They may conceal unpleasant surprises, partly because they are difficult to foresee, and partly because they affect many different centers of authority within the joint venture system.

## STRATEGY PROCESSES AT DIFFERENT LEVELS IN THE JOINT VENTURE SYSTEM

We now turn to strategy development processes at the different levels in the joint venture system. In this section we show how these processes can be structured at different levels. The section is arranged according to the three levels at which strategy is developed: (i) strategic fit between the partners; (ii) development of strategy for the joint venture; and (iii) development of strategy in the joint venture.

### Strategic fit between the partners

There is much discussion in the literature of the need for a strategic fit between companies which set up a joint venture (e.g. Chakravarthy and Lorange, 1991). "Fit" and "misfit" are not static concepts, although they are often treated as though they were. We prefer to regard them as processes. It is of course conceivable that two partners might have an optimal strategic fit from the beginning, but this is exceedingly rare in practice. An adequate strategic fit is not something which two companies either have or do not have; it is the outcome of a continuing process of negotiation between them—a process which does not end with the establishment of the joint venture. The partners must be prepared to question strategic compatibility within the joint venture system throughout the whole of its life, and to make changes if necessary. The strategies which the partners pursue outside the joint venture may also be affected; this can be seen in the adjustments made by both sides in the case of EHPT, which we describe in this section's case study.

We have already sketched the implications of a strategic misfit and the resultant problems of disharmony for strategy development processes in the joint venture system. The vital point is that when disharmonies begin to appear, they should be discussed, not swept under the carpet. It is in the general strategic interest that all parties should try to redefine the strategic mission of the joint venture. In reality, however, people often ignore disharmonies, even though they are aware of them, or treat them as taboo, either due to inertia and inflexibility, or because they dislike conflict. This reaction is understandable, because of the growing pressure to succeed at all levels of management, but it inevitably leads to a situation where the problems continue to grow, resulting eventually in a cataclysmic eruption. When this happens, it is often too late to work towards a new strategic fit, and the joint venture is either dissolved or, more commonly, continued by one of the partners.

The call for a strategic fit springs from the idea that a cooperative venture can only work when it offers both partners a win–win situation. The identification of areas in which the partners can achieve a strategic fit also serves as a basis for deriving strategic principles for the joint venture (Chakravarthy and Lorange, 1991).

A fit exists in any given area when, from the viewpoint of each participant, there is an adequate cooperation basis for a joint venture. Hermann (1988, p. 65) suggests posing the following three questions as a way of deciding whether there is sufficient basis for a joint venture:[1]

- Why should the partners enter into property relations with the joint venture, rather than simply doing business with it?
- Why should the partners set up a joint venture rather than a smaller subsidiary?
- Why should the partners not merge?

---

[1] Hermann (1988, p. 68) also points out (rightly) that the partners must be in agreement not only on strategies and goals, but also on the provision of resources for the joint venture and their respective negotiating positions. Harmony in these areas is essential for the formation of a successful joint venture.

The answers to these questions should clarify a number of issues: first, the advantages of a cooperative venture as against a market transaction; second, the complementarity of the partners or the advantages of scale to be achieved through a joint venture; and third, the advantages of a small independent unit (risk minimization, lower administration costs, greater flexibility) as against a merger between the partner companies.

How can a strategic fit be achieved in practice between the partners? It is useful to make a distinction between two stages: the search for a partner, which also helps a company to clarify what it wants from a prospective partner; and the actual negotiation process, in the course of which the strategic fit is defined.

## Search of a partner

Before a company starts to seek a potential partner for a cooperative venture, it should be able to answer a number of questions to its own satisfaction:

- What are the reasons for embarking on a cooperative venture?
- What, in concrete terms, do we hope to achieve by means of the joint venture?
- What are the attributes which a potential partner must possess?
- How are tasks and roles to be assigned?
- How will the contribution of each participant be decided?
- What level of similarity do we require of a partner in terms of strategy, structure, culture and human resources?
- In what areas are we prepared to make concessions?

Careful answers to these questions will provide a company with a clearer picture of its own expectations and requirements, and its readiness to work towards achieving a strategic fit with another company. It will develop an image of itself and a profile of its requirements of a potential partner; these can then be used as a basis for identifying possible partners and for carrying out negotiations (Figure 4.3).

|               | Company A                                                                   | Company B                                                                   |
|---------------|-----------------------------------------------------------------------------|-----------------------------------------------------------------------------|
| Motives:      | Market channel<br>Product development<br>etc.                               | Market channel<br>Product development<br>etc.                               |
| Outcome<br>expectations: | $X million                                                        | $X million                                                                  |
| Time-frame:   | Long-term/short-term                                                        | Long-term/short-term                                                        |
| Fit with<br>company strategy: | Yes/no                                                      | Yes/no                                                                      |
| Management<br>principle: | Goal-orientation/<br>consensus-orientation<br>formal/informal<br>communications, etc. | Goal-orientation/<br>consensus-orientation<br>formal/informal<br>communications, etc. |

**Figure 4.3** Compatibility assessment

## Negotiating a cooperative venture

During the negotiations, the future partners work out an initial strategic fit and establish a direction for the further development of strategic harmony (or at least compatibility). If the companies have a picture of the overlap between them, this will help them to identify and extend a strategic fit. The first step is to find the area in which a strategic fit seems likely. The partners must then agree on ways in which this area can, will or must be changed. The negotiations serve a number of purposes:

- the partners gain knowledge and understanding of mutual interests;
- each partner gains insight into the specific position of the other;
- areas of strategic fit are defined;
- especially difficult areas of probable conflict are identified; and
- the partners arrive at a joint definition of the direction in which they want the cooperative venture to develop.

The purpose of the negotiations is to define a mission for the joint venture and put it in writing. This is often accomplished in a letter of intent, which is an expression of the strategic fit between the partners.

Working together to define, delimit and document their strategic interests and their respective tasks and contributions gives each partner a feeling for the role which the joint venture will play for the other(s). The joint production of a letter of intent for the venture is a first step towards clarifying issues such as whether the basic strategies of the companies are compatible; whether competition will be a problem; how to avoid unequal benefits or strategic dominance by one partner.

The letter of intent is a first step, but in practice it is seldom sufficient. Time often brings changes both to the shared strategic direction defined at the outset and to the individual strategies which the partners pursue separately. It is therefore vital to keep a constant check on the current state of the strategic fit and to sort out disharmonies with partners as soon as they become apparent.

Joint ventures are continually confronted by uncertainty stemming from the relationship between the partners. Uncertainties and goal conflicts often arise because the partners are pursuing different ends through the joint venture. Another source of uncertainty lies in the fact that the various managers bring different expectations and different levels of personal commitment to the joint venture. The dynamics of change also aggravate goal conflicts. Cooperative relationships never develop in a linear fashion, so changes cannot usually be foreseen.

Goal conflicts between the partners, or between the joint venture and the partners, are probably one of the main problems with which joint ventures have to contend. Even in cases where a business plan has been developed at an early stage, specifying the goals of the partners and the joint venture, their marketing strategy, product planning, financial participation and direction of long-term development, there is still no guarantee of stability. According to Harrigan (1986), goal conflicts can arise between the partners, or between the joint venture and the partners, when the joint venture is affected by forces for change. This often leads to a reconfiguration of the joint venture. It is therefore important to pay careful attention to the strategic compatibility of the companies involved.

Forces for change occur at the following three levels.

At partner level:

- changes in the strategic direction of the partners;

- increase or decrease in the importance of the joint venture for the partners; and
- increase or decrease in the negotiating power of the partners.

At joint venture level:

- lack of success of the joint venture;
- changes in market demand; and
- new strategies adopted by competitors.

Interactions between the partners and the joint venture:

- changes in the need for coordination; and
- changes in autonomy to make decisions.

## Disharmonies and strategy adjustment in joint venture practice: The case of EHPT

EHPT provides a clear example of how strategic dependencies develop between the partners in the joint venture system, and how changes in strategic direction in the system can influence the strategies of the individual partners via the cooperative venture. The main issue is the strategic balance of the whole joint venture system.

### BUSINESS PLAN OF EHPT

The guidelines for EHPT were established in a business plan developed jointly by Ericsson and HP. According to this plan, the partners' aim in creating the joint venture was to exploit the growing market for network management and service management in the telecommunications industry. The strategic goals were set at a 20% share of the network management market and a 10% share of the service management market by 1996. The joint venture was to be based on the competitive advantages which both partners enjoyed in the field of technology. Using existing resources, they planned to work together to create a product based on their complementary technologies. Both companies also hoped to market a brand that would enhance their image and customer trust in their products, both of which are important factors in market success.

The joint venture's main clients were telecommunications companies such as PTT, Deutsche Telekom, etc., and other companies such as Ericsson itself, which add the network management systems to their own network elements and sell them on as complete telecommunications systems. The initial objective of the joint venture was thus to sell to a broad customer base consisting of various telecommunications companies and public suppliers. However, after a year, Ericsson had emerged more or less as the main customer, because the platform which it had developed in the joint venture with HP served as a basis for its own network elements. Faced with this situation, HP tried to open sales channels via other suppliers, using its own sales structure; but this constituted implicit competition for Ericsson, and was therefore an issue of conflict.

HP and Ericsson had previously amassed different kinds of experience in network management. Ericsson had concentrated primarily on the public sector, with TMOS,[2] while HP had concentrated mainly on the private sector. The business plan was based on the assumption that Ericsson was about a year ahead of the competition with TMOS. Ericsson also had a technological advantage in high-quality network elements. HP led the field in open, flexible UNIX computer platforms and in business service management and it also had a service and support organization which was considered to be a particularly important competitive factor in the telecommunications area.

As a first step towards achieving the goals of the joint venture, Ericsson's existing network management technology (TMOS platform) was to be transferred to the UNIX hardware used by HP. The aim was to create an open network management system which would be accessible to a broad customer base, and with which it would be possible to integrate additional applications produced by various telecommunications suppliers. As a result, HP acquired CAP, the

---

[2] TMOS is an integrated network management product assembled from components made by HP, EHPT and Ericsson and sold to customers as a complete system.

most basic technological constituent of TMOS, and planned to develop it further and standardize it. Once the primary goal had been
reached, more HP and Ericsson products were to be integrated, to
build up additional markets.

During EHPT's first year of operation, it emerged that HP also had
an internal network management product, HP Open View, which
proved competitive. Although this product had a somewhat narrower
range of functions than TMOS, it had nevertheless achieved wide
market acceptance by the time the joint venture was a year old,
and it was based on an open UNIX system. This raised the issue
of the future positioning of the two products. HP was no longer
prepared to go on developing CAP, the product acquired for
the joint venture; it wanted instead to base future development
on HP Open View. This raised difficulties about the future strategic
goals of the joint venture. Should EHPT develop a network
management product based on CAP, or should it base its future work
on HP Open View? The original strategy therefore had to be partly
re-examined and a re-evaluation of the business plan seemed
unavoidable.

As this case study on EHPT shows, it is particularly important that the
strategies of the companies should be realigned at regular intervals, or
when goal conflicts arise. Existing goal conflicts can be overcome by
re-evaluating the whole situation. In the case of EHPT, this was subsequently achieved by undertaking a yearly revision of the business plan.
Representatives from the three organizations (HP, Ericsson and EHPT)
took part in this, as in the initial development of the business plan during
the negotiation stage, so that all parties would be sufficiently committed
to identify with the new statement of objectives.

When goal conflicts arise, trust is often already damaged. Reformulating
the business plan provides a basis on which to rebuild trust. During the
exchanges between the partners, existing problems can be discussed and
resolved. Breaches of trust, lack of commitment and questioning  the
sense of the cooperative venture can be serious obstacles to adjusting the
strategies of the partners, especially when goal conflicts are present.
Reformulating the business plan can create fresh commitment. Presenting

the plan as a win–win situation underlines the partners' confidence in the joint venture and reduces any mistrust.

## Developing a strategy for the joint venture

The issue of strategic fit between the partners emphasizes the need to create a win–win situation for the partners. The issue of strategy development for the joint venture places the emphasis on the newly created unit. The question is how to formulate concrete strategic goals for the joint venture based on the strategic fit between the companies. The process of developing a strategy for the joint venture forms the link between the level of the partners and that of the new joint venture (Figure 4.4).

Traditionally, there is a clear grading of responsibility in strategy development. Top management is responsible for developing company strategies, from which are derived strategies for the different divisions, the

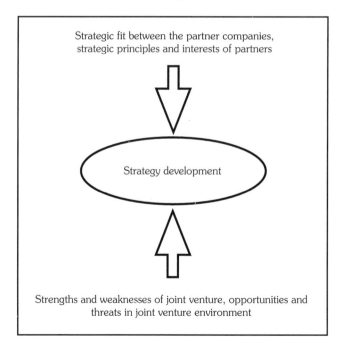

**Figure 4.4** Development of joint venture strategy as a link between the partners and the new entity

strategic business units and finally the individual functions. The process of strategy development usually follows a systematic pattern of successive phases and includes goal setting, environmental analysis, internal analysis, strategy choice and implementation (Figure 4.5).

In view of the difficulties which we called problems of translation, a top-to-bottom procedure of this kind seems less suitable for a joint venture. The development of strategy for the joint venture is not a once-and-for-all affair; it is a continuing process of negotiation between the partners and the joint venture. It is more like a balancing act, in which a delicate and temporary balance is sought between the strategic opportunities of the joint venture on one hand and the demands of the partner companies on the other.

The business plan should form the basis on which strategy for the joint venture is developed. In practice, however, the process in which the partners and the joint venture develop and adjust their strategies is influenced by many factors. Depending on the degree of autonomy granted to the joint venture, the strength of its operational influence, and its importance

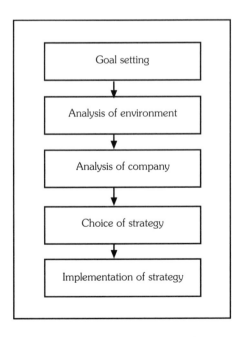

**Figure 4.5**   Classical process of strategy development

in the partners' value-added chain, either the joint venture's viewpoint or that of the partners will dominate and will carry the day in vital questions of strategy interpretation. One could also envisage a form of strategy development for the joint venture in which different kinds of strategic goals would be addressed at the same time. Goals for the overall strategy, finance, marketing products and research and development could be negotiated separately in different committees or project teams (Figure 4.6).

Overall congruence or the weighting of the different objectives would then be the concern of a special supervisory or strategy development committee operating at a superordinate level.

The joint production of a business plan is an important instrument of strategy development for the joint venture. The business plan specifies

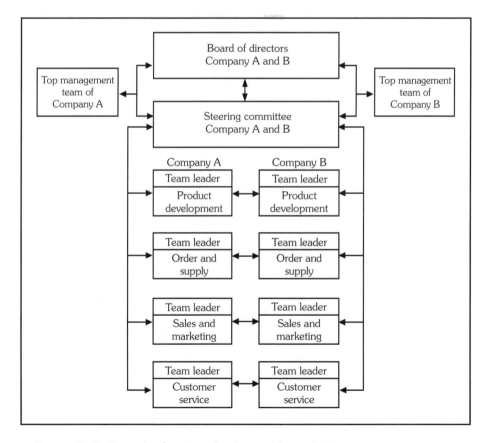

**Figure 4.6**   Example of strategy development by project teams

the common strategic guidelines and the planned development objectives for the joint venture and it documents the outcome of the partners' negotiations on strategy. The joint development of a business plan offers opportunities of inestimable significance for the cohesion of the joint venture system, yet they often go unrecognized.

The following is an example of the contents of a business plan:

- Vision
- Products and services
- Strategic goals
- Development plan
- Customers
- Finance
- Market and distribution
- Potential problems
- Competition
- First year plan.

The structures supporting strategy development processes in the joint venture system, and the ways in which these structures will relate to each other, should be clarified in the formation stage. However, at that stage, adjustment procedures are often treated as less important than setting up a starting position for the joint venture system. The starting position is initially static in nature. The absence of mechanisms and structures for negotiation is felt subsequently, especially when there is a need for the  partners and the joint venture to negotiate adjustments to strategy.

The nature of the structures and systems for strategy development depends mainly on the type of cooperative venture. However, as a general rule, both the joint venture and the partners should always be involved in the process of developing strategy. One of the practical suggestions to be found in the literature is that made by Chakravarthy and Lorange (1991, p. 222 ff.). They suggest a separate supervisory committee for the joint venture, on which both the partner companies would be represented. As time passes and the companies in the joint venture system gain experience and learn to trust each other, the ties which bind the joint venture to the partner companies could gradually be relaxed.

It is difficult to make general statements about methods of strategy development in joint ventures. However, as in other areas, participation should be encouraged, and as many as possible of the people who will be directly affected should be involved as early as possible. The whole joint venture system will obviously benefit if participants at every level learn to understand the system, the relationships within it, and the critical aspects of cooperation between the partners and the joint venture. This costs time and money, so its importance is usually insufficiently recognized; but in many cases, experience has shown that involving the maximum number of employees and raising their level of awareness yields advantages which far outweigh the costs.

The following is a basic guideline for strategy development:

- involve joint venture managers in supervisory committee;
- create interfaces between those involved with the joint venture in different functional areas;
- involve a large number of those who will be affected;
- use methods which involve participation; and
- involve agents at several levels.

## Developing a strategy in the joint venture

We shall now examine strategy processes in the joint venture itself. The discussion centers on the actual demands and problems which confront joint venture management when it tries to implement the strategic goals.

Strategy processes in the joint venture are basically similar to those which take place in any independent company. However, they also involve a whole series of additional problems which are closely related to the particular role of the joint venture within the joint venture system. We have already described in some detail the problems of translating strategic guidelines into practical policies for the joint venture. The management of the joint venture is typically also confronted by problems arising from the issues of coherence of the demands and the adjustment of strategic guidelines to the real situation facing the joint venture. We shall review these problems and their consequences for the joint venture in more detail before offering some general hints for strategy development in the joint venture.

With regard to problems of coherence, the theoretical question is, how far the demands of the various members of the joint venture system can and should be taken into account. In practice, however, the question often does not arise in this form, because the managers of the joint venture has no choice about whether to try to meet this or that expectation. The objectives which the joint venture management must take into account are often revealed through a political process in which certain expectations and demands gain acceptance, even when they have no formal legitimacy according to agreed rules. The real source of coherence problems is the basic uncertainty of joint venture management about which demands should be satisfied. Changing power relations in the joint venture system cause constant change in the relative importance of the various demands and expectations.

Problems of adjustment arise from the fact that the joint venture is caught between its received strategic guidelines on the one hand and the opportunities and risks in its own environment on the other. Even if the actual circumstances of the joint venture are taken into account in the development of strategy for the joint venture system, the environment in which the joint venture finds itself, and its strengths and weaknesses vis-a-vis this environment, are not always given enough weight in the development of strategic principles for the joint venture.

The management of the joint venture faces a particularly difficult situation when new or previously unconsidered market opportunities or development possibilities conflict with the existing strategy, or would tie up resources which were intended for other purposes. Another problem arises when the strategic aims of the joint venture require a course of action which conflicts with the principles of rational economic and strategic management of an independent unit; this opens a gulf between supposedly good joint venture management and the principles of good strategic management of a company.

What can the management of the joint venture do when faced with these difficulties? There are three possible alternatives:

- hang on and wait until the problem solves itself;
- concentrate on the internal objectives of the joint venture; or
- refer the contradictions back to the joint venture system.

It is astonishing how often the first alternative is chosen, even though it is unlikely to bring success either to the joint venture or to the system as a whole. A relatively long time may pass before latent conflicts between the partners erupt, and the inadequacies or practical ineffectiveness of the "official" strategic objectives becomes apparent. It can also happen that by this point, an essentially harmless conflict has grown in scale and significance, until it triggers a series of crises which may even lead to the dissolution of the joint venture.

The second alternative, that is withdrawal or isolation, seems unfavorable in the context of a joint venture system. Admittedly, the management of the joint venture may succeed in terms of the goals which it has set for itself, and the partners too may be satisfied for a time if the independent unit is sufficiently successful, but in the long run, the conflicts will build up and will eventually break out.

This leaves only the third alternative, that is referring perceived contradictions and recognized problems to the appropriate bodies in the joint venture system. This is a solution which can be fair to everyone in the long run. Clearly, it can only be adopted if institutions and procedures for dealing with contradictions were established in the joint venture system at an early stage.

There is one particular danger which deserves brief mention. When conflicts reach a certain level, joint venture systems often tend to turn inwards and concentrate more on their internal functional problems than on their environment and the development of suitable markets. Companies do not, however, form joint ventures with the sole aim of keeping themselves busy. Here, too, a balance must be preserved. Attention must be paid to internal problems, to ensure the smooth working of the whole system; but markets and business objectives must not be neglected as a consequence.

The various processes of strategy development and adjustment which take place at different levels in the joint venture system are interrelated and interdependent. The point of developing strategy for the whole joint venture system is to maintain a continual equilibrium in which the different levels are balanced and complement each other. However, any state of equilibrium can only be transitory. There are repeated shifts of emphasis at all levels; the strategic rationale changes, and the environmental rationale makes new demands. Striving to maintain a strategic equilibrium in the joint venture system is therefore one of the most important tasks for all its members.

## BUILDING AN EQUILIBRIUM

Fuji Xerox, the joint venture between Xerox and Fuji Photo Film established in 1962, has been considered by many as a successful joint venture. Over time, it evolved into a fully integrated operation with activities ranging from research, manufacturing and marketing. In the early 1990s, the joint venture became so successful in terms of revenues that its importance for the partners started to increase.

Initially, the joint venture was intended as a Japanese marketing organization to sell xerographic products. It was, however, set up as a marketing and manufacturing organization. The company grew steadily throughout the sixties and dominated the high-volume segment of the Japanese copier market. In the early seventies Fuji Photo Film transferred its copier plants to Fuji Xerox and became a passive partner. According to the agreement between the two companies, Xerox could use information collected within Fuji Xerox in its own operations. Even technology acquired by Fuji Xerox from outside sources could be freely passed on to Xerox. Fuji Photo Film, on the other hand, could not use information collected within Fuji Xerox in its own operations.

As Fuji Xerox grew, the relationship between the two companies changed. Fuji Photo Film saw the joint venture as a profit-maximizing venture. For this purpose, the partners had established various agreements such as transfer prices, royalties and licences. Over time, these agreements changed. They were viewed as being flexible. This did not, however, undermine the commitment of both companies towards an equitable relationship. The joint venture was seen from both partner's perspective as a profitable company beneficial to both parties. The agreements were guidelines to the relationship and were adapted as the joint venture grew in size.

# CONTINUOUS ADJUSTMENT OF STRATEGY IN THE JOINT VENTURE SYSTEM

We shall now turn our attention to the adjustment and renegotiation of strategy. This is a continuous process which takes place at all levels in the joint venture system. It is not enough to regard strategy development as a once-and-for-all process with a fixed outcome in the shape of an agreed strategy. The essential point to realize is that quite apart from the major strategic projects, questions of strategy arise in many areas of the daily life of the system and observations are made which call into question the agreed strategy and objectives.

There are three distinct elements in the process of strategy adjustment. First, there is strategic controlling in the traditional sense of checking both the implementation of strategy and the premises and assumptions on which the strategic principles are based (e.g. about markets and other environmental developments) and also making changes or additions where necessary. The second element is a process of critical reflection, not only on the outcomes of strategy development processes and attempts at implementation, but also on the processes themselves. This is process learning, and it adds another dimension to the simple process of adaptive learning on which strategic controlling is based (cf. Probst and Büchel, 1997). Learning to adapt only leads to an improvement of the existing content, whereas process learning affects the procedure by which given objectives are achieved.

Our discussion of strategy development at different levels in the joint venture system introduces a learning requirement. Strategic controlling is learning at the lowest level; it involves the adjustment of existing strategies. At a higher level, the processes of strategy development are examined; this constitutes process learning. Events at these two levels lead to a far-reaching extension of strategic thinking. Starting from an awareness that the structure and content of strategic processes at all levels can change over time, we can move on to comprehensive strategic learning within the joint venture system.

**Questions to address**

- How are the goals of the partners being aligned?
- How are the partners' objectives for the joint venture being implemented?
- Who develops the strategy for the joint venture?
- Are project teams involved in strategy development?
- Are the partners working together on a business plan?
- Are the basic principles of strategy development being taken into account?
- How are forces for change in the environment being dealt with?
- What are the options if a partner changes strategic direction?
- What measures are in place to support continuous adjustment of strategy?
- Are existing strategic directions analyzed regularly?

# CHAPTER FIVE

# STRUCTURING AS AN AREA OF JOINT VENTURE MANAGEMENT

Every organization is a social system created for a particular purpose and directed towards the achievement of particular goals leading to the creation of order. To guide the development of an organization, one must analyze its structure and processes as a basis for planning a sequence of actions directed towards the performance of certain tasks. One aspect of structure which the management of a joint venture can influence is the choice of coordinating mechanisms amongst the companies in the joint venture system. In our view, structure not only includes formal organizational structures, but all the other processes and relationships which are found in social systems. In this section, when we talk about structure, we mean all the guiding and coordinating mechanisms which are present in the joint venture system.

## STRUCTURAL PROBLEMS IN THE JOINT VENTURE SYSTEM

If we look at the real world in which joint ventures exist, we see that there is no such thing as an ideal organizational structure which would suit all joint ventures. Nevertheless, managers and management scientists agree that structure is important.

> Managers who plan and negotiate alliances devote considerable time to discussing suitable structures. Were structure not important, managers would probably not accord it precious time. Virtually every manager interviewed in our study believed that the success or failure of alliances hinged on their structures. (Yoshino and Rangan, 1995, p. 79)

This highlights the importance of structures, but we still do not know what the organizational structures should be, and which criteria for choosing structures are most likely to result in a successful joint venture. The basic structure of the joint venture is initially decided by the partners. Responsibilities and property relationships are determined at this level. Once the joint venture has been created, structural decisions are made both at partner level and at joint venture level.

The design of organizational structures involves difficult decisions about mechanisms for coordinating activities. If a joint venture is to be successful, it must be able to adapt and evaluate its own performance in order to make decisions on the use of resources. The organizational structure of a joint venture can be described in terms of three pairs of opposites: (i) differentiation versus integration of activities; (ii) centralization versus decentralization of decision processes; and (iii) standardization versus flexibility of work sequences. We shall use these pairs of opposites to identify the structural factors which are critical in joint venture management. The need to strike a balance between the members of each pair places difficult demands on the structure of joint ventures (Figure 5.1).

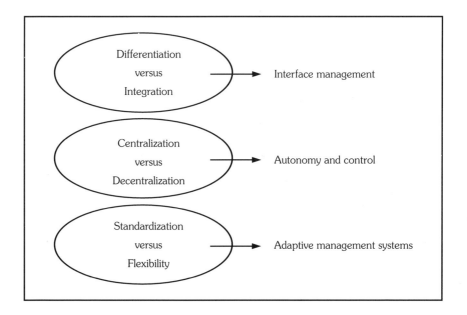

**Figure 5.1**   Structural tensions in the joint venture system

We shall discuss these tensions mainly in relation to the areas of structural management of joint ventures where intervention can produce an equilibrium. To achieve a balance between differentiation and integration of activities, managers must pay careful attention to interface management (Zahra and Elhagrasey, 1994). If a balance is to be reached between centralization and decentralization, levels of control and autonomy must be in equilibrium (Hergert and Morris, 1988; Geringer and Hebert, 1989). Adaptable management systems are needed to achieve a balance between standardization and flexibility. Although we cannot describe a single structure which will suit all joint ventures, we can nevertheless make some suggestions about the best places to intervene.

## BUILDING UP INTERFACES

Interface management is probably the most important factor in the structural management of joint ventures (Lewis, 1990; Yoshino and Rangan, 1995). Interface management in this context means structuring the exchange of information and resources amongst the companies in the joint venture system. It helps to coordinate their activities and supports the common goals. The importance of interfaces varies according to the type of joint venture. The greater the strategic significance of the joint venture in the value-added chain of the partners, the greater the importance of interface management, since coordination calls for an active exchange of information and resources. Especially in the adjustment stage, the joint venture needs to activate the interfaces in order to coordinate its activities with those of the partner companies.

### IMPORTANCE OF INFORMATION FLOW

Ford Motor Company and Mazda Motor Corporation established a joint venture in Thailand, AutoAlliance Company Limited, which manufactures compact pickup trucks for sale through the partners' respective sales network. "From the beginning we were keen on making this relationship more than a mere financial investment," commented one top manager of AutoAlliance Thai. "With our

> people in place, we feel secure in the knowledge that the relation-
> ship will not become a one-way street with information flowing
> from us to a potential competitor. We can rest assured that we can
> monitor the flow of people and information."

Interfaces exist at different levels and in different functional areas. At the strategic level, that is the company leadership, interfaces are needed for establishing the long-term orientation, for setting priorities and for proactive resolution of conflicts.

Interfaces at the strategic level are often committees consisting of members of the various companies. The usual purpose of an interface committee is to smooth out inter-company conflicts. If operational conflicts arise between the partners, or between the partners and the joint venture, the committee provides an official forum in which conflicts can be settled and decisions made.

## ESTABLISHING A WORKING RELATIONSHIP

VW Shanghai is a 50-50 joint venture. VW owns half of the company, and the other half belongs to influential Chinese partners such as the Bank of China and the Chinese Motor Union, the official organization representing the Chinese automotive industry. The two parties are equally represented on the ten-member Board of Directors and the four-member Executive Committee. Do the two parties block each other? "No", says Heinz Bauer, now the VW representative in Peking, but who was present at the negotiations when the joint venture was established. "There is an important clause which stipulates that decisions must be unanimous." The members of the committees must therefore create viable working relationships amongst themselves (*Manager Magazin*, **3**, 1994, p. 172).

In addition to the committees, the companies often have interface managers, who are responsible for the exchange of information between the partners and the joint venture. The interface managers filter out problems and decide whether particular conflicts need to be referred to a committee. However, the use of interface managers to help coordinate activities can be damaging to intercompany relations if they interpret information in a one-sided fashion. They should therefore adopt a neutral position as intermediaries between the organizations.

There are a number of other ways of achieving coordination at the operational level, where there are interfaces between various functional areas and levels in the hierarchy. Some methods include creating teams of members of the partner companies and the joint venture, building up relationships between functional areas and creating functional committees.

## INTERFACES BETWEEN PARTNERS

The most important organ in the alliance between Volvo and Renault is the Joint General Policy Committee, which is chaired alternately by the two new company heads. This committee discusses topics which determine the strategic direction of the company. One stage below this, there are two committees which work at a more detailed and practical level; these are the Joint Car Technical Coordination Committee and the Joint Truck Technical Coordination Committee. They deal with technical questions such as exchange of components or joint purchasing.

The two companies have strictly equal membership of these three top-level committees. However, the 50-50 principle does not apply to the many working groups. The composition of these groups is determined by professional and technical requirements only. The various circles which exist at the operational level include a Joint Quality Management Board, a Joint Design Reference Group and a Joint Personnel Management Committee. About 600 managers from each side are brought together through their work in these groups. For de Seze, manager at Renault, contacts such as these—especially at middle management level—are important for getting to know the culture of the other company.

Source: *Manager Magazin*, **10**, 1992, p. 273

In the course of time, personal contacts develop alongside the official structures. These contacts promote the exchange of information and thus contribute indirectly to the achievement of objectives. Personal contacts usually develop in different areas and at every level. Figure 5.2 shows various levels at which interfaces can exist within the joint venture system.

At each interface, there are three requirements for successful cooperation between the companies. First, their management systems must be compatible. Second, interpersonal relationships must be developed, to support movement of information needed for various functions. Third, management must be guaranteed the support of the partners.

To ensure an effective flow of information, both formal and informal exchanges must be supported. Informal exchange of information often takes place through teams, personal relationships or transfer of personnel. Formal exchanges often depend upon compatible management systems; in their absence, satisfactory exchange of data between companies is unlikely. Compatible systems increase the transparency of information and this promotes trust amongst the companies in the joint venture system.

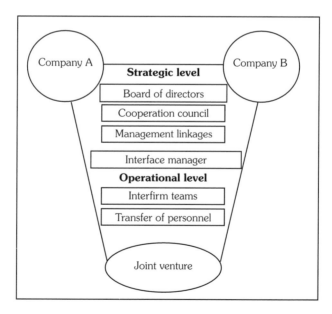

**Figure 5.2**  Interfaces at different levels in the joint venture system

## TRUST VERSUS CONTROL

In a joint venture between a Thai and a foreign partner involving the manufacturing of electronic components in Thailand, the division of the partner's authority was one of the most critical issues. The tenure of president and managing director was rotated between the two partners every year to achieve a balance of control. Although, the areas of responsibility had been defined early—the local partner with a 51% share was responsible for all operations including administration, the foreign partner with a 49% share was responsible for production only. The joint venture was economically successful within a short period of time, yet the division of authority did not work well due to the need for functional coordination. In order to reduce conflicts which emerged, informal meetings inside and outside the workplace were fostered. The Thai partner increased the communication flow between top management, and planned social events for the partners in order to facilitate the relationship beyond the business context. Trust was thereby established between the partners, reducing the need for control.

Interface management is of particular importance in the joint venture itself. Open exchange of information increases trust; transparency of objectives and equal contribution of resources increase the partners' commitment. If the benefits to the companies are obvious, it is easy for them to see the collective sense in the joint venture.

## CONTROL AND AUTONOMY

The formation stage, in which the joint venture is founded by the partners, is followed by the phase where the objectives in the business plan must be translated into action. All attempts at implementation are directed primarily towards the declared objectives, so it is important to consider the role which the joint venture plays for the partner companies. There are many ways in which joint ventures may be classified.

We regard the position of the joint venture in the partners' value-added chains as one of the most important bases for classification, since it is this which chiefly determines the level of coordination needed between the companies and the degree of autonomy which the joint venture enjoys vis-a-vis its founders.

The kinds of coordination mechanisms needed between the joint venture and the partners are a function of the nature of the joint venture. The various types of joint venture differ in their objectives, and in the benefits which they are expected to yield, and the coordination mechanisms must be chosen accordingly. Harrigan (1986) points out that once the venture is founded, the partners must exert control over it, to make sure their goals are realized, while granting it enough autonomy to survive in the market.

Control is important to the partners: it is based on feedback processes which keep them informed about the development of the joint venture, and is thus one of the main ways in which they can make sure that their objectives are being fulfilled. It has been defined in this context as the process of influencing the behavior and output of a third unit (Geringer and Hebert, 1989).

Successful control of the joint venture allows the partners to coordinate its activities internally and prevents the loss of competitive advantage to other companies (Geringer and Hebert, 1989). The structuring of control mechanisms presents particular problems because of differences in objectives, systems and cultures (Killing, 1983). The following discussion underlines the significant part which control plays in the interactions between the partners and the joint venture. It also shows that the question of control only acquires its real significance after the formation stage.

In the literature on organizational structure, autonomy is discussed in relation to the issue of achieving an optimal level of interdependence. This optimal level determines the degree of autonomy of two interdependent units. For a joint venture, autonomy means the freedom to make and implement decisions independently of the partners.

Complete harmonization of decisions is not always possible between two related units because of the limited capacities of the decision makers and the costs of coordination. The greater the autonomy of the units, the more important it is to ensure that their decisions are made in accordance with the superordinate goal system. This presupposes goal congruence, which in turn reduces the need for coordination. Decisions on autonomy are based on the costs of coordination and those of independence. The optimal level of autonomy is that at which objectives can be met while total costs are kept to a minimum.

Autonomy in this sense is a static and cost-oriented concept. However, there are attempts in systems theory literature to extend it by including developmental aspects (Naujoks, 1994). The concept of autonomy includes the opportunities for action and interpretation present in a closed system. The autonomy of a system depends on three factors: potential, freedom and action. Potential may be described as the field of action which an agent possesses by virtue of internal structures and capabilities, and independently of the environment. Freedom is the extent to which an agent can move independently of other agents and other interests; it embraces all relationships with the environment. The third factor, action, means in this context the range of activities amongst which the agent is free to choose.

Since joint ventures are agents operating within systems, their levels of autonomy are extremely variable. The level of autonomy of any joint venture depends on the three factors described above. The potential of the joint venture springs from its core competencies; it depends on the nature of the joint venture and is specific to it. A venture set up to develop a new product has different core competencies from a distribution venture. The potential for autonomy of these two types of joint venture depends on their internal competence to fulfill their set objectives (i.e. product development or distribution). Another element in potential is the development of identity. As a company builds up its internal structure, it becomes distinguishable from its environment, thus gaining its identity. The freedom of the joint venture can be considered from two angles. On the one hand, the joint venture's limited resources create dependency on the partners, thus limiting its freedom. However, its freedom is also determined by perceived environmental uncertainty, which may be regarded either as threatening or as rich in opportunities. The opportunities for action are determined by structural and perceptual factors. These largely determine the degree of autonomy of the joint venture.

The relationship between control and autonomy is an important success factor in managing joint ventures (Killing, 1983). The pattern of control and autonomy depends on two variables: strategic interdependence and environmental uncertainty (Kumar and Seth, 1994). As a rule, the greater the strategic interdependence, the more control the partners exert over the joint venture. The greater the environmental uncertainty, the higher the level of autonomy needed by the joint venture to make independent adjustments to environmental changes. Strategic interdependence is the dependence of two organizations on each other's inputs and outputs. The partners will exert more control over the joint venture if they need its outputs for their own production. The less tightly the joint venture is bound to the partners, that is the lower its dependence on the partners, the higher its autonomy will be. In situations where there is strategic interdependence combined with high environmental uncertainty, a balance must be sought between autonomy and control which will allow the joint venture system to meet its objectives.

The partners' need to control the joint venture and interfere in its decisions increases with (i) the joint venture's strategic significance for the partners; (ii) the value and quantity of the shared resources; and (iii) the degree of transfer between the partners and the joint venture (Harrigan, 1986, p. 71). The most important factor influencing the degree of control which the partners exercise over the joint venture is the need for the joint venture to interact with the partners.

## High control needs

The greater the strategic interdependence between the joint venture and the partner companies, the higher the level of control exercised by the partners. The degree of interdependence is a function of the position of the joint venture in the partners' value-added chains. If the joint venture occupies a strategically significant position, the need for coordination will be relatively high. Control needs are also high if the activities of the partners and those of the joint venture are similar, or if the partners risk losing technology via the joint venture to a third party.

## Low control needs

The partners' need to control the joint venture is low if their only objective is to share risks and costs. The same applies if the joint venture is a diversification strategy for the partners, because its failure would have no direct effect on the partners' core business. Control needs are also lower in a stable environment.

Trust is another factor which reduces the partners' control needs. It may be regarded as a coordination mechanism which, unlike control, is based on the consistency, reliability and predictability of the joint venture's behavior. If the companies in the joint venture system have agreed on common behavior patterns, rules of interpretation and mechanisms for resolving conflicts, they will be more prepared to use trust as a coordinating mechanism.

The joint venture's need for autonomy correlates positively with (i) the speed with which it must react to environmental changes and (ii) the difference between the strategic goals of the partners and those of the joint venture. It correlates negatively with exchange of resources (Harrigan, 1986, p. 72). The more dynamic the environment, the greater the need of the joint venture to be able to react flexibly to change. However, it must continue to coordinate its actions with those of the partners, in order to achieve the agreed objectives. A certain tension therefore exists between the need for autonomy and the need for coordination.

## Low autonomy needs

Coordination between the joint venture and the partners is more important than autonomy when resources are shared and when the joint venture makes an important contribution to the value-added chains of the partners. However, too much control by the partners reduces the joint venture's decision making efficiency and can damage its market competitiveness.

## High autonomy needs

In highly competitive, dynamic industries, the joint venture needs considerable autonomy: it must be adaptable and flexible enough to hold its own in the market, and it must gain legitimacy as an independent organization. Autonomy means freedom of decision in circumstances where the joint venture must make short-term adjustments to the market. The most difficult situations are those in which the joint venture is surrounded by intense competition and must also coordinate its activities closely with those of the partners. Coordination reduces the joint venture's flexibility because of the delays involved in reaching joint decisions. Vertical joint ventures are therefore particularly difficult to structure and direct because on the one hand, they are positioned between the partners in the value-added chain, and on the other, they are working in a new and undefined market. EHPT is a joint venture of this kind.

## AUTONOMY IN EHPT

When EHPT was founded, the intention was to build on the technological competitive advantages of both partners. Using existing resources, they planned to cooperate in developing a product for the telecommunications sector (network management). This product was to be based on the complementary technologies of Ericsson and HP.

The joint venture stood between HP and Ericsson in the value-added chain. HP produced the standard hardware and the joint venture added some telecommunications software. Ericsson then built in customer-specific functions and sold the final product to telecommunications suppliers. The joint venture thus developed a product together with HP, and sold it among others to Ericsson. Ericsson was EHPT's main customer, since EHPT produced the platform for Ericsson's network elements. The joint venture had to put significant effort into coordinating its activities with those of both partners, because it occupied a middle position and depended on both partners for the fulfillment of its objectives. At the same time, it needed enough freedom of decision to adapt to a developing market and to react flexibly to different customer requirements. In this situation, control needs and autonomy needs were both high.

Once the needs for autonomy and control have been assessed, the partners must consider how to exercise control. The following sections contain descriptions of individual control mechanisms.

## Control mechanisms

For the partners, control is the formal mechanism for achieving their objectives. The control structure sets the framework for all processes of negotiation. The partners adopt different kinds of control mechanisms depending on levels of strategic interdependence and environmental uncertainty (Kumar and Seth, 1994).

We may distinguish three kinds of classical control mechanism, namely, process-oriented, content-oriented and context-oriented (Kumar and Seth, 1994).

### Process-oriented control mechanisms

Process-oriented control mechanisms are lateral, integrating mechanisms which influence the planning and decision making processes in the joint venture. The aim of process-oriented control is to increase the exchange of information by creating direct contacts between members of different organizations. Joint ventures build up lateral control mechanisms depending on the need for exchange of information amongst the organizations (Galbraith, 1973). The greater the strategic interdependence of the joint venture and the partners, the more likely it is that lateral forms of control will be used, because such mechanisms are also a means of uniting the companies. They may take the form of multi-organizational teams, temporary project groups or appropriate contact points.

Bodies such as the board of directors or coordinating committees are also a process-oriented form of control. The board of directors consists of members of both the partner organizations and has key control functions (Harrigan, 1986; Schaan, 1988). Members of the board serve as channels of communication and a medium through which information can flow between the joint venture and the partners. Their responsibilities extend beyond ensuring that the objectives of the parent companies are met; they also mediate between the autonomous companies in the system and represent the joint venture *vis-a-vis* its external environment (state, unions, etc.). The higher the level of environmental uncertainty, the greater the need for members of the board of directors to be aware of their external functions. However, where there is a high level of strategic interdependence, they must give priority to coordinating the objectives of the parent companies with the activities of the joint venture.

## Context-oriented control mechanisms

Context-oriented control mechanisms create a link between the partners and the joint venture by providing a framework for achieving the goals of the parent companies. One such control mechanism is the short-term transfer of loyal members of the partner companies into the joint venture. Personnel contracts allow the partners to exert a measure of influence which helps them to ensure fulfillment of their objectives. Loyalty to the partner companies is strengthened by staff who are transferred into the joint venture because they develop social contacts in the new company, and become part of an informal network of people who work in the joint venture while still maintaining their relationships with their former colleagues. This loyalty also increases the partners' influence over the joint venture. However, it often impedes the integration within the joint venture of employee groups of different origin. Transferring employees into the joint venture may make sense to the partner companies as a way of exercising control, but the possible consequences for the joint venture should not be forgotten.

Incentive systems for managers in the joint venture are another form of context-oriented control mechanism (Killing, 1983). If the partners offer incentive systems to joint venture managers, they increase the likelihood that the management of the joint venture will act in their interests. Incentive systems of this kind may be based on quantitative or qualitative measurement of success.

## · PERFORMANCE ASSESSMENT AT EHPT

The aim of EHPT was to sell a large number of network management systems at a profit. Ericsson, however, wanted high-quality network management systems as a basis for its special applications. This meant that there were two criteria for measuring the performance of joint venture managers: the number of network management units sold at a profit (joint venture objective), and the satisfaction of the Ericsson business units with the quality of the product (Ericsson objective). Qualitative criteria for measuring performance might include the ability of a manager to bring together different viewpoints, or the level of motivation shown by joint venture employees. In EHPT, one of the criteria used for judging the performance of joint venture managers was their ability to resolve conflicts.

Communication pathways constitute a third context-oriented control mechanism. The partners can use these pathways by directing into them information useful for promoting their own ends. This creates a danger of selective exchange of information and it often leads in practice to conflicts between different levels. Joint venture managers want access to all relevant information of whatever kind. If the flow of information from the partner companies appears to be selective, this is generally perceived by the joint venture as manipulation: the partners are not putting all their cards on the table. Conflicts then build up which hamper both organizations in the achievement of their objectives and foster suspicion. It is therefore preferable to choose control mechanisms which do not erect extra barriers to trust. We believe that it is more important to act on a basis of trust than to look for methods of control which will erode trust.

### Content-oriented control mechanisms

Content-oriented control mechanisms have to do with the intentions behind control. Partner companies may try to promote their own ends by choosing board members who have a direct interest in secondary or implicit objectives of the joint venture, because they are responsible for those objectives within the partner companies. The partners can exercise control not only over the choice of managers, but also over the way they vote on the board. The greater the number of managers sent by one partner, the greater the probability that the objectives of that partner will be achieved. However, this may eventually cause the other partner to become dissatisfied with the joint venture, because its own objectives are not being met in full. If one partner contributes a large number of managers to the board, this will certainly tend to underline its commitment, but the trust of the other partner may suffer in consequence. The partner companies should therefore be clear with each other about their intentions in appointing managers to the board, so as to avoid misunderstanding and a breakdown of trust.

As well as controlling people, the partners can also control the composition of documents in which the obligations of the companies are set out (Lyles, 1987). The development of a business plan is the main instrument of control, because it involves shared planning of the joint venture's future turnover and making joint decisions on activities and markets (Table 5.1).

The instrument which is probably most used for controlling content, but least discussed, is management systems. They support control through the exchange of certain kinds of information. Compatible management systems, for example order entry systems, accounting systems, financial systems and systems for research, etc., can ensure direct contact between the companies in the joint venture system  on essential aspects of content. The partners can keep track of the operational development of the joint venture and can intervene if necessary.

## Trust before control

To the extent that the partners control the joint venture, they reduce its autonomy. It is therefore useful to consider alternative coordination mechanisms which do not limit the joint venture's freedom and  flexibility. Formal control mechanisms are naturally important, but they are not the only means of directing a joint venture and they can be a source of mistrust.

| Type of control | Control mechanisms |
|---|---|
| Process-oriented control<br><br><br>Context-oriented control<br><br><br>Content-oriented control | – decisions by board of directors<br>– appointments to planning groups<br>– choice of teams<br>– short-term employment contracts<br>– incentive systems<br>– communication pathways<br>– appointments to board of directors<br>– composition of binding documents<br>– exchange of information via management systems |

**Table 5.1** Types of control and control mechanisms

## MANAGEMENT SYSTEMS

Management as an activity means designing, directing and developing a whole system. The purpose of management systems in this context is to make it possible to organize and mold the joint venture. Management systems are part of the structural management of the joint venture system. They are systems for planning and monitoring and for conveying information. They exist for the purposes of aligning goals, exchanging information and making adjustments. Management systems help to standardize and coordinate sequences of events within the joint venture, and between the joint venture and the partners. Management systems provide a supporting framework within which relationships can be recognized and instruments, methods and principles can be classified.

Management systems are part of the infrastructure of an organization and create order by means of their stabilizing function. According to Lorange and Roos (1992), management systems should serve four functions: (i) provide an information base for setting objectives; (ii) implement objectives; (iii) provide budget planning; and (iv) monitor progress.

Management systems are an information base in that they serve as a data bank both for the joint venture and for the partners. When decisions need to be adapted or strategies reformulated, information is needed about the business environment and about the partners. Exchanging information supports analysis and adjustment of the strategic direction of the joint venture and its structural implementation.

Management systems which serve the implementation of objectives should span different functions and should have a short-term perspective. One way of implementing objectives is to set up projects of limited duration. When choosing a project team to implement strategic goals, care should be taken to include members with appropriate responsibilities from each company in the joint venture system.

Budget planning serves (i) to consolidate the strategic plans of functional areas within the joint venture and (ii) to consolidate the plans of the different companies within the joint venture system. It may be carried out at joint venture level or at the level of the entire joint venture system. In the interests of the functioning of the system as a whole, the most important activity is the consolidation of the plans of all the member companies. The consolidation process usually reveals any resource deficits or capacity problems which may be present and allows adjustments to be made. According to Lorange and Roos (1992), there are three kinds of resource deficits: human resource, technological and financial deficits. With regard to human resources, it is important to find employees who will be capable of realizing the plans. To avoid technological deficits, the partners should provide the necessary technologies, with support staff if necessary. The partners might carry out market trials of products, or provide laboratory time, or give sales support. To avoid financial deficits, firm guarantees should be obtained of the funds promised by the partners and the necessary internal resources.

The most important element in a management system is probably progress monitoring. It is often pointed out that the financial systems of the joint venture should be compatible with those of the partners; the question is, what level of resources is needed to bring this about?

## ADAPTABLE MANAGEMENT SYSTEMS IN EHPT

EHPT, the Ericsson-Hewlett-Packard joint venture, took over its financial management system from Ericsson, because it (EHPT) emerged from one of Ericsson's business units. The expense involved in producing compatible systems would have been so great that the

> partners and the joint venture agreed to adapt the existing Ericsson management system according to a few important criteria. EHPT and HP did, however, work together to develop additional yardsticks for comparing research and development.

Management systems should also (i) monitor critical underlying assumptions; (ii) scan the environment; (iii) monitor strategic programs; (iv) assess competitor and customer responses; and (v) monitor strategic budget expenditures (Lorange and Roos, 1992, p. 115). Monitoring assumptions means analyzing the objectives and reassessing whether the joint venture is developing in the right direction. It can also serve as an early warning system; the monitoring of assumptions about growth rate will provide us with an example. Existing growth forecasts can be analyzed with reference to life-cycle forecasts, analyses of product competition or changes in distribution. Progress monitoring can then lead to adjustments in strategy to prevent potential divergence of the companies in the joint venture system.

The second function of management systems is to scan the business environment. Joint ventures are particularly prone to the consequences of failing to do this, because they are preoccupied with relationships or conflicts between the companies in the joint venture system. As in interface management, mixed committees should be set up to analyze data on the environment, so that external as well as internal information can be processed. In EHPT, a special staff department called "Business Development" was created, to analyze relevant environmental changes.

Reactions from customers and competitors can also indicate a need to make changes in company strategy. A reassessment of the environment, the customers and the competition can lead to a reassignment of responsibilities amongst the companies in the joint venture system.

The scope and degree of differentiation of management systems depends on the nature and objectives of the joint venture. The greater the importance of the joint venture to the partners, the more important the structuring of the information flow, and the greater the need for the companies to have compatible management systems. The importance of the flow of information through management systems can change over time. In the formation stage and at the beginning of the adjustment stage, management systems are especially important, because coordination needs are usually high. As time passes, the joint venture often gains more autonomy, which reduces the need for a continuous exchange of information.

Joint ventures rarely exhibit ideal structures; nevertheless, a few useful points can be made about organizing their structural management. To establish a successful joint venture system and guide its development, one needs to be aware of the tensions inherent in such a system. Managers should aim to achieve a balance between differentiation and integration, between centralization and decentralization, and between standardization and flexibility. We have considered three areas which need to be structured according to the demands of the situation. The first of these was interface management, the main purposes of which are to structure the flow of information and resources, and to coordinate the activities of the joint venture and the partners. The second is control, which is the partners' most important mechanism for achieving their objectives, though it must be set against the autonomy which the joint venture needs for independent market survival. Finally, management systems serve planning and monitoring functions, and enable companies to make adjustments. All these aspects of the structural management of joint ventures can be regarded as guidance mechanisms which steer the joint venture system towards achieving its objectives.

## Questions to address

- Does the joint venture system contain mechanisms for guidance and coordination?
- Have the organizations in the joint venture system agreed on coordination mechanisms?
- Have interfaces been created between the organizations?
- At what level are these interfaces? What are their functions?
- How great is the strategic interdependence between the organizations?
- Is control by the partners necessary?
- How uncertain is the environment of the joint venture?

- Does the joint venture have enough autonomy to make short-term adjustments to environmental changes?
- Does the joint venture have adaptable management systems?
- Have the management systems of the organizations been harmonized?
- Is there a regular check on the partners' assumptions about the direction which the joint venture is taking?
- Are analyses made of the environment? Are competitor and customer reactions recorded?
- Is the progress of the joint venture checked at regular intervals?

# CHAPTER SIX

# CULTURAL AWARENESS AS AN AREA OF JOINT VENTURE MANAGEMENT

There is now a formidable volume of publications on corporate culture. The first major surge came in the early 1980s (Schein, 1985). In the 1990s, there was a revival of interest in culture in connection to the issue of organizational learning. However, despite the enormous number of existing publications—or perhaps because of it—there is still a lack of clarity about the meaning of the term. The term "organizational culture" is often used in such a way as to embrace all aspects of life in organizations; for this very reason, it often explains nothing.

In the academic literature and in business manuals, the term "culture" is often used interchangeably with other terms such as "company style", "corporate culture", "organizational culture" and "company culture". Cultures may be "bureaucratic" or "open"; universities have them and so do multinational organizations. There is often an implicit assumption that culture is a "soft" factor which might be used as a way of dealing with danger and uncertainty, a new and different instrument of management still shrouded in myths. In our view, however, a purely instrumental view of culture is unhelpful and unpromising. Given the complexity of culture, and the interpretative nature of definitions, it is unlikely to be fully susceptible to control. It would therefore be difficult, if not impossible, to manage culture from the outside, treating it out of context as a separate phenomenon. We do not therefore regard development of culture as one of the functions of joint venture management; we prefer to take a more cautious line and approach the issue as one of cultural awareness in management. The practical consequences of this approach will become clear in the course of this chapter.

The limited extent to which culture can be manipulated in joint venture systems will be discussed in more detail below. First, however, we shall describe the different levels at which culture may be said to exist. We shall also show how culture-based problems in joint venture management often affect several levels and can also be addressed at several levels.

Culture-related problems are extremely diverse, and there is a strong temptation to elevate all problems which do not fall clearly into another category to the status of "cultural difficulties". Culture is a fuzzy concept, so the variety of cultural problems which may arise in a joint venture system is hardly surprising. The following set of questions may help us to develop a more systematic approach:

- What do we mean by organizational culture, national culture and joint venture culture?
- How can these cultures be diagnosed?
- What problems are likely to arise when different cultures collide?
- How can such difficulties be resolved? Is it possible to shape culture, or at least to set the parameters within which the organizational, national or joint venture culture will develop?

## THE MANY FACES OF CULTURE IN JOINT VENTURE MANAGEMENT

Our first step in attempting to understand culture is to distinguish three types, namely organizational culture, joint venture culture and national culture. These terms all occur frequently in the literature. We shall also consider the relationships amongst them.

The culture of an organization has many different dimensions. Schein's (1985) definition of culture as a system of commonly shared values, norms and basic assumptions provides us with a lowest common denominator. Viewed from this angle, culture is a tool for molding a company, like strategy or structure. However, a company does not simply have a culture; it is a culture. It is a relatively closed system of ideas, with a specific pool of knowledge made manifest partly in symbols and partly in artifacts.

Culture can thus be further differentiated into a material level consisting of symbols and artifacts, an evaluative level consisting of values and norms, and a conceptual–cognitive level consisting of unconscious basic assumptions (Figure 6.1).

At the material level, we find all the visible forms of organizational culture, that is artifacts and behavior patterns. Examples include architecture, furnishing, status symbols, documents or a typical style of dress. At the evaluative level, culture encompasses the customs, norms and taboos which exist within the company. It therefore has important coordinating and integrating functions. Finally, at the cognitive level, we find the "basic assumptions", which are taken for granted by employees and which shape their behavior. They are simply "the way things are done". In other words, they are a set of unconscious assumptions held by members of the organization about relationships with the environment and about the way they see the "reality" of the organization. These assumptions therefore mold both external relationships and internal processes, and they exert a lasting influence on perception, thinking, feeling and behavior. Fundamental assumptions

| Levels | Features | Examples |
|---|---|---|
| Artifacts | Visible, but often undecipherable | Architecture, office layout, art, titles, jokes, slang |
| Values and norms | Higher level of awareness discussable depending on degree of institutionalization | Leadership style, attitudes, ethics, behaviors |
| Basic assumptions | Taken for granted as self-evident, invisible, unconscious | Picture of human nature, thought patterns, knowledge |

**Figure 6.1** Levels of organizational culture
Source: Based on Schein, E. (1985) *Organizational Culture and Leadership: A Dynamic View*, San Francisco: Jossey-Bass, p. 17

take shape over time, by a process of trial and error. Once they have developed, they are difficult to change and can only be modified through radical relearning processes.

The material level of culture, that is the artifacts, is also called the "superficial structure". This is relatively easy to study using traditional sociological methods. The fundamental assumptions, however, are the "deep structure" and are usually insufficiently understood. It is doubtful how far targeted diagnosis or intervention is possible at this level. Later in this chapter, we shall introduce the concept of "culturally aware joint venture management" and this will help us to find a middle ground between accepting culture as one of life's immutables and believing that radical change is possible.

Schein's (1985) division of organizational culture into three levels is particularly suited to our purposes because of its openness: it can be applied to industry, organizations or individual employees.

## Emergence of joint venture culture

We now turn to a closer examination of the culture of joint ventures. By this we mean the new culture which develops in a joint venture when the cultures of the two partners clash. If a joint venture is to develop an independent culture, the first thing it needs is time. The employees from each of the partner companies need to become familiar with the culture of the other company, and learn to understand it, before the first moves towards integration can take effect. Staff often have an inner resistance to change. They are inclined to believe that the company culture from which they themselves have come is the better and more successful one. Many employees therefore develop certain mechanisms for perceiving and judging other cultures. These take the form of stereotypes, which serve to reduce complexity and regulate behavior. They simplify perception of the unfamiliar and also narrow it drastically. In time, patterns of behavior developed on this basis become so strongly internalized that the individual is no longer aware of them. Unconscious constructions then become the prevailing interpretation of reality.

If two completely different cultures collide in a joint venture, the previously unconscious "theories of action" of their members are challenged

(Argyris and Schön, 1978). Symbols, rituals and world views previously supposed to be universally valid become ambiguous and uncertainty develops on both sides. After a while, "shadow cultures" often develop and offer initially covert alternative patterns of interpretation. If the contradiction is forced into the open, conflicts are likely and they cannot be solved simply by deciding on a particular kind of new culture. The slowly emerging culture of the joint venture exhibits all the typical visible and invisible features of an independent organizational culture, which cannot be controlled deductively.

The multiplicity of factors, which influences the development of an independent joint venture culture, creates particular problems for management. The culture of the joint venture is bound into an overall cultural context which contains a number of different levels. These are the organizational cultures of the partner companies, the different cultures which individual employees bring into the joint venture system, and the prevailing national culture(s).

Individual cultures are brought into the joint venture system by employees who come from a wide variety of subcultures. They may be from different branches of industry, or different ethnic groups, and they have different professional and social backgrounds. Even where employees from different subcultures adopt a pragmatic approach and are prepared to adapt, there are still bound to be conflicting viewpoints and differences of opinion and these have to be resolved. We talk about the strategies or achievements of institutions, that is of the joint venture or the partner companies, but we should not forget that actions are performed by people, not organizations, and that we must give due weight to their values and norms.

When we consider the different functions which organizational culture performs, we realize the importance of trying to understand cultural phenomena at all levels in the joint venture system, whether they spring from the different cultures of the partners or the emerging culture of the joint venture. According to Ulrich (1984, p. 312 ff.) culture fulfills a number of functions:

- Integration: Culture serves to create a general consensus on fundamental issues and facilitates decision making during crises;
- Coordination: Shared values and norms can help to coordinate

actions, because they exclude some alternatives from the outset. Culture thus eliminates the need to make new decisions for every case, and can substitute for structural and human resources management;

• Motivation: The change of values and the emphasis on the individual are increasingly responsible for crises of meaning, both in society in general and in the workplace. The division of work in big companies adds to this effect. Culture imparts meaning and satisfies basic needs; it increases motivation within the company and legitimizes external actions; and

• Identification: Culture offers ways of identifying with the organization and creates a "we-feeling".

The functions of culture in fostering motivation and identification are particularly important in the very early stages of joint venture development. They can be vital in ensuring a good start. They are subsequently supported by the coordinating and integrating functions of culture. During this stage, the partner companies must be prepared to allow the joint venture to develop a separate identity, and the management of the joint venture must be careful to perform its symbolic functions. "Management by wandering around", increasing direct communication with employees and an open-door policy can help to establish an independent culture in the joint venture.

The following case study shows how harmony between the organizational cultures of the partners can contribute to the success of the venture and to the development of a separate joint venture culture. Wörner (1992) showed the establishment of cultural harmony between Bosch and Siemens.

## CULTURAL HARMONY BETWEEN PARTNERS

In the 1970s, Robert Bosch Ltd and Siemens Ltd founded a joint venture, called Bosch-Siemens Household Appliances Ltd (BSHG). The partners participated on a 50:50 basis. Their main strategic aim was to join forces in the household appliances industry by combining their potential and avoiding duplication. Bosch and Siemens had realized there were going to be strong pressures towards rationalization in the household appliances industry because of its fragmented supply structure and the increasing saturation of the market. They recognized that in the long run, the only suppliers who would be able to achieve economies of scale and thus remain competitive would be technically innovative companies of a certain minimum size. BSHG in its present form is the result of a continuous process of interaction which has lasted more than two decades. As a joint venture in a traditional world market, BSHG faced the challenging prospect of integrating the different cultures of the partner companies into a separate joint venture culture, while preserving the specific brand identities and presenting them in a credible and convincing fashion to the outside world.

In spite of the many differences between Bosch and Siemens, there are nevertheless some remarkable similarities and parallels between their histories and company cultures. Both partners are traditional German industrial companies. They are well established in the fields of electrical engineering and electronics, and they are active on world markets. The images which the companies have of themselves were largely shaped by the beliefs of their founders, Robert Bosch and Werner von Siemens. Both companies have a declared policy of innovation and of striving for technological leadership. For both, customer benefit has been the driving force behind technical development, and the reason for their commitment to the highest quality standards. In their dealings with the public and other companies operating in the same markets, both Bosch and Siemens cultivate an image of helpfulness combined with discretion.

BSHG has maintained the business principles established by its parent companies and has been able to project them convincingly and enduringly in its own product areas. The BSHG brands are based on technology which is common to Bosch and Siemens; this is why strategic innovations are introduced by both main brands simultaneously. However, the two companies project slightly different images reflecting their major fields of activity (Bosch: car electrics, electronics and electric tools; Siemens: plant and systems technology, electronics, computers). Nevertheless there is an overall harmony

> between the cultures of the two companies which has been a significant factor in the success of the joint venture.

# The influence of national culture

We turn now to the much discussed topic of national culture. In a multinational joint venture, the intercultural dimension is most obvious when allowances must be made for specific aspects of local culture. In a situation of this kind, a joint venture faces the challenge of harmonizing goals and values despite an added complication in the shape of national or local cultural factors. National cultures are an important influence on the development of joint ventures, and raise a number of important questions; however, this does not mean that they are the paramount factor in joint venture success. In practice, they are an extra limiting variable, which management must take into account. The different levels of culture, that is individual, organizational or national, do not exist in isolation; they are always linked together.

The strength of the influence exerted by national cultural characteristics is shown in a number of studies published in the 1980s (see Hofstede, 1980). A particular aim of these studies was to find out whether company culture or national culture was more likely to predominate in large, multinational companies. The result was surprising: even in big companies like IBM, which have a unitary worldwide image and relatively strong cultural integration, national cultural differences have an important impact.

We shall examine some aspects of multicultural joint venture management, illustrating our arguments by reference to cultural features of joint ventures within an American–Japanese joint venture.

## CULTURAL PROBLEMS

The Showa–Packard joint venture was launched in the summer of 1977 after several Japanese companies had approached the American food company, Packard, to start licensing their products in Japan. Initially, the joint venture was to produce and market breakfast cereal and instant coffee. The products were to be marketed under the joint brands of Packard and Showa. The joint venture agreement stated that there would be an even representation on the Board of Directors. Showa was going to staff the joint venture and nominate the President, while the American company was going to fill the position of Executive Vice President.

After a short period of time, the President of the joint venture died and had to be replaced. Showa nominated a replacement to the joint venture which was not deemed suitable by the American company. According to Japanese management practices, senior people who had served the company well and had been a member of the Board were rotated into new positions affiliated with the parent company in order to vacate the Board position for someone else. Although the person may not be the best for the position in the affiliated company, his service to the company is honored until retirement.

For Packard such practices were unacceptable in a joint venture. Instead, they proposed a junior Showa employee as a potential candidate. In response, Showa's management indicated that one of the Packard members of the Board of the joint venture was personally not fully integrated into the Japanese environment. As a result, the two parent companies had to negotiate over the most senior positions.

Hofstede's (1980) attempts to describe and compare national cultures is one of the most well-known approaches and is well suited to an examination of national culture in joint venture development. According to Hofstede, national cultures may be compared in terms of four dimensions: power distance, uncertainty avoidance, individualism/collectivism and masculinity/feminity.

## Power distance

Power distance refers to the different ways in which authority, influence and power are exercised in institutions. The more authority used by key decision makers to convince employees, the greater the power distance.

In organizations, hierarchical forms and opportunities for participation in important decision making usually vary between countries.

## Uncertainty avoidance

Uncertainty avoidance is the extent to which a society feels threatened by uncertain or ambiguous situations, and how it uses formal rules and programs to avoid them. The need to avoid uncertainty is reflected in the organization's mechanisms for formalizing and standardizing procedures, as well as its time horizon. A strong tendency to formalize and standardize is usually a sign that a society prefers to avoid uncertainty.

## Individualism/collectivism

The individualism/collectivism dimension is a measure of regard for the needs and goals of individuals versus social norms and state provision. This is expressed in different countries by individual job design, for example, as against a group payment system.

## Masculinity/femininity

The difference between masculinity and femininity is the difference between a rational, aggressive and materialistic orientation (masculine) and an emotional, human approach to work (feminine).

When measured on these four dimensions, countries tend to fall into clusters. This gives an impression of levels of cultural proximity, and suggests specific aspects of culture which may affect joint ventures in particular countries. Power distance seems most pronounced in Malaysia and India, uncertainty avoidance in France and Korea, and individualism in Germany, France and North America. Masculinity is particularly evident in Japan.

In the context of joint venture management, it should be noted that different cultural dimensions are important in different developmental stages (Figure 6.2). In the early stages of negotiation and agreement,

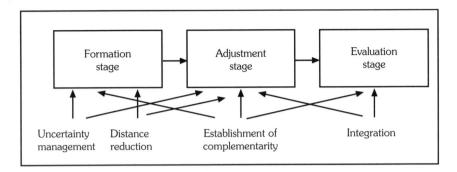

**Figure 6.2**   Joint venture development and multicultural management
Source: Adapted from Swierczek, F. and Hirsch, G. (1994) Joint Ventures in Asia and Multicultural Management, In: *European Management Journal*, **12**, pp. 197–209

differences in uncertainty management are especially important. When faced with uncertainty, the Chinese take the view that fate decides; Europeans, however, like to draw up clear strategies for the future and try to anticipate uncertainty.

An important factor in the negotiation phase is the position in the hierarchy of the managers engaged in setting up the joint venture. The central offices of European companies tend to send third- or fourth-level managers to China, although their key qualifications are not usually in strategic management. The lack of formal equality between them and their Chinese contacts runs counter to the Chinese tradition of "making a deal with a friend". There is also the danger that the Western managers will adopt a patronizing, know-all style of management.

The following remarks made by a Chinese employee about his experiences of Western management style are a typical example:

> They [the Western partners] taught me everything that they knew about the pharmaceuticals industry, but they took away my self-esteem. Their management development program was successful, if you were a minor functionary—a *chamcha*. As soon as they started trying to change some cultural peculiarity, they started to accuse one of all kinds of things. They seemed incapable of understanding that in the long term, it would have been better for their firm to manage the subsidiary according to the local pattern, rather than setting themselves up as a foreign delegation. (Moran, 1993)

Differences in individuality versus collectivity have the greatest effect during the implementation phase. The development of the joint venture is eased if all the managers are equally involved in decision making, and if the Western managers accept the principle of group consensus. Western managers should also respect the family-like system of "management by relationships" (*guanxi*), which gives high priority to maintaining informal contacts.

In the final stage of joint venture development, that is decision and control, different cultures will tend to use different measures of success. For the Asian partners, success lies in the amount of successful learning which has taken place, irrespective of the duration of the joint venture. European companies on the other hand look for the fulfillment of objectives.

The following anecdote elaborated by Serapio and Cascio (1996) shows that differences in management styles can also be revealed in attitudes to ending a joint venture.

## PROBLEMS OF TERMINATION

In 1991, Sover S.P.A., a small Italian spectacles manufacturer, suggested to their partner in China that their cooperative arrangement should be dissolved. Amongst other things, it accused the Chinese partner, Suzhou No. 1 Factory, of making pirate copies of the joint designs. The Chinese partner was vehemently opposed to dissolution. Since the agreement of all management was needed, Sover was in a difficult position. It asked the Chinese Foreign Economic Relations and Trade Commission for help. The response was an official recommendation to continue with the cooperative venture; the reason given was that "if a son is ill, you don't just turn your back on him".

Cultural factors often play a crucial part in the performance of joint ventures. It is therefore essential to adopt a multicultural management approach to ensure sensitive planning and structuring of the joint venture, and to do justice to the different levels of culture in the joint venture system. Westerners who do business in China often say that the present style of management in China does not correspond to "normal" Western business practice. However, it is a mistake to try to solve business problems in China using only Western management concepts. It is important to look at objects and events through Chinese eyes, and try to find common cultural ground. This can often be achieved simply by trying to understand the different rules of communication. If you know how your partner communicates, and what information may be concealed behind a particular style of communication, you have already taken the first step towards successful cooperation.

## CULTURAL DIAGNOSIS: HOW CAN WE IDENTIFY DIFFERENT CULTURES?

If we are to resolve the cultural problems in a joint venture, we must first be able to identify them. This involves a comprehensive analysis of the organizational and national cultures.

The first stage is to describe the existing culture of each partner and to use the descriptions as a basis for formulating a desired culture for the joint venture. There are usually two possible ways of obtaining a description of the existing culture. One involves direct recording of values, thought patterns and norms; the other is to make an indirect analysis of employees' utterances, behavior patterns and forms of expression.

Once the existing cultures of the partner companies have been described, the second step is to compare their cultural profiles and try to visualize a desirable culture for the shared enterprise. One possibility is to take the existing cultures and try to align the features which are judged to be extremely negative or extremely positive. The existing cultures can then be compared with the desired culture and a list of practical measures for adaptation can be compiled. These measures may include regular performance of symbolic actions, that is creating norms; setting an example, that is modeling norms; and giving explicit recognition, that is strengthening norms. A range of human resource policies can also be designed to influence cultural fit (Figure 6.3).

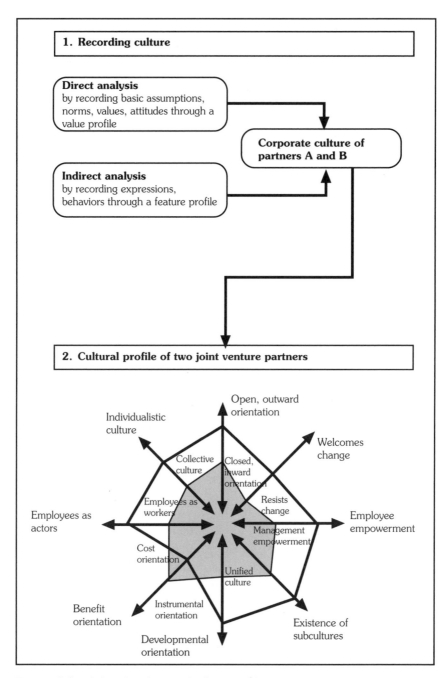

**Figure 6.3**   Cultural analysis and culture profiling
Source: Adapted from Bronder and Pritzel (1992) and Bleicher (1992)

# CULTURAL DIFFERENCES

In a joint venture between a Vietnamese (60%) and a European partner (40%) in the lubricant industry, the cultural differences were part of the reason for emerging conflicts. Differences between the two partners arose in project management as the following examples show:

### Planning
While the Vietnamese tended to be more general and ambiguous in planning, the European counterpart was specific and clear. The more specific a plan, the easier it becomes to criticize someone. In order to avoid "losing face" the Vietnamese tended to leave the plan at a higher level of abstraction and did not assign clear responsibility.

### Implementation
The European partner seemed to follow up on plans more precisely. For the Vietnamese a plan seemed to be less committing. As one manager said: "A plan is only a plan, the action depends on facts."

### Communication
One of the European managers said: "in some cases saying 'yes' by Vietnamese means 'that is alright' but it does not have the affirmative meaning that it has in the West." The Vietnamese seemed reluctant to say "no" because they feared "losing face" if others knew that something had not been understood.

### Time
Within a Vietnamese context, meetings were long and frequent. Since there was a need to be within a group and reduce uncertainty, people needed to be informed. According to one Vietnamese manager: "the meeting is also a place to rest" which was in sharp contrast to the West where "time is money".

### Rules and procedures
Although assigning responsibilities for each functional area was

necessary to satisfy the needs of Vietnamese managers, they tended to break rules and responsibilities more frequently than Western managers. Changes to assigned responsibilities seemed to be difficult to implement within a Vietnamese context since most changes seemed to be viewed as a synonym for aggressive behavior.

**Team**

The use of teams was not viewed very favorably within the Vietnamese context. This was due to the fact that a team creates situations where one person may work more than others, and no clear responsibilities are defined. Internal competition between employees was not sufficient to motivate employees within the team (Table 6.1).

| Cultural differences | Level of severity | Stated by |
|---|---|---|
| Reluctance of Vietnamese to say "no" | Medium | Foreigners |
| Relationship-based problem solving | Medium | Both |
| Vietnamese resist changes | Low | Foreigners |
| Different focus in human resource management, e.g. promotion, compensation | High | Both |
| Different viewpoints in evaluating performance | Low | Both |
| Differences in disclosing data | Low | Both |
| Difficulty in keeping Vietnamese loyal and motivated | Medium | Foreigners |
| Time consuming and consensus-based decision making process by Vietnamese | Medium | Foreigners |
| Vietnamese managers are ambitious planners, do not like to adhere to plans, and do not control budgets | Medium | Both |

**Table 6.1**   Stated cultural differences

If the cultural analyses show major differences between the partners' own organizational cultures, or between the types of culture which they desire for the joint venture, the tension usually results in one of a number of possible reactions. These are cultural pluralism, cultural fusion, cultural development, cultural adjustment, cultural imperialism and cultural resistance. Bronder (1992, p. 218) shows typical patterns of reactions to culture clashes.

## Patterns of reaction to culture clashes

### Cultural pluralism

The different cultures continue to exist separately. There is no noticeable rapprochement; there may even be a stronger delimitation. This need not always be a bad thing; if the tension is severe, it can be a successful way out, if for example national teams work on separate tasks.

### Cultural fusion

The different cultures fuse to form a new, unified culture into which the characteristics of all partners are absorbed. If a joint venture develops an independent culture, it disengages itself from its founding partners and this is widely regarded as necessary for its success.

### Cultural development

The joint venture develops a new, independent cultural profile. For this to happen, the employees must be willing and able, and the partner companies must exert low levels of control and influence, thus giving the joint venture space to develop its own culture. A staffing policy of bringing people in from outside can support the development of a new culture.

### Cultural adjustment

Complete fusion of cultures is not always necessary. It can be equally acceptable to achieve harmony in critical areas, that is where conflict is likely, while the cultures continue to exist separately. This kind of adjustment often takes the form of explicit or implicit "rules of play", which impose a code of behavior in particular areas.

## Cultural imperialism

The company culture of one of the partners prevails. This can slant the cooperative venture towards one partner rather than the other. It may lead to mistrust and misunderstandings, and even to the dissolution of the joint venture.

## Cultural resistance

There may be clear resistance within the cooperative venture to the cultures which meet in it. This is an extreme reaction in which the employee groups from the partners refuse to accept the culture of the other partner and therefore cooperation is severly hindered.

It can be extremely difficult to deal with different cultures in a joint venture, even when cultural aspects have been explicitly covered in the early discussions. The lengthy and difficult process by which EHPT developed a separate joint venture culture is a good example.

## DEVELOPMENT OF CULTURE IN EHPT

When EHPT was founded, the motto was "1+1=3". The high expectations which the founder companies and their employees brought to the joint venture provided a basis for the development of a culture. It was repeatedly stressed that the competencies and synergies of the two parent companies were to be united in a new common culture in the joint venture. At the beginning of the project, management insisted that both sides show great similarity in terms of culture.

As time passed, however, it became clear that the differences were greater than had been supposed. They became obvious when former employees of HP and Ericsson had to work together in EHPT, or when work was performed jointly by HP and EHPT. The employees revealed some of these cultural differences which affected management practices outlined in Table 6.2.

| HP | Ericsson |
|---|---|
| results-oriented | process-oriented |
| high-risk acceptance | low-risk acceptance |
| market-oriented | technology- and project-oriented |
| short-term view | long-term view |
| global company | international company |

**Table 6.2**   Cultural differences

The management of EHPT deliberately recruited HP employees in order to acquire HP knowledge and skills. This gave Ericsson employees the feeling that HP employees were the ones who knew it all and did it better. The HP employees in turn felt that they could not change anything, because nobody would listen to them.

The differences between the company cultures was not communicated to the two groups of employees, so their efforts to work together on a daily basis constantly threw up new areas of conflict. A program was finally set up for the joint venture in which cultural differences were discussed in intercultural seminars. As a result of this program, and the continuing daily contact between the employee groups, EHPT began to develop an independent culture.

In the last few sections of this chapter, we have examined the different levels of culture in the joint venture system, possible ways of describing them and the various patterns according to which an independent joint venture culture may develop. There remains the fundamental question of whether culture can be actively created. We shall now consider how far cultural aspects of joint ventures are open to deliberate intervention and, if so, by what means.

# CULTURAL MANAGEMENT VERSUS CULTURALLY AWARE MANAGEMENT IN JOINT VENTURES

Both theoreticians and business managers often seem to assume that once culture has been diagnosed, it can be molded and manipulated almost at will. This is by no means necessarily the case, because of the complexity of the phenomenon which we call culture and its dependence on context. For these reasons, and to dissociate ourselves from any assumption that culture is completely malleable, we shall summarize in the following set of propositions, the concept of culturally aware joint venture management.

> *Culture cannot be changed from outside, or without the intensive involvement of all participants and all those who will be affected.*

Culture is something which is actively acquired and lived. It is a characteristic of an entire company, and it arises through interactions amongst all the members of the system and between the system and its environment. It is therefore possible to influence culture, but not to impose it systematically.

> *Culture develops through the interplay of self-organization and organization by others.*

Central to our analysis of culture is our view of a company as a self-organizing, evolving social system (Probst, 1987). In the course of time, this system elaborates a specific code which guides people's actions. The code contains norms and values which influences and determines internal and external relationships. The company culture is a result of systemic self-organization and structured interventions; these interventions can be symbolic or material. Culture exists as a system of meaning in the minds of the employees; it is created by subjective perceptions and interpretations, and is ultimately the result of a shared construction of reality. Reality in organizations is therefore not something which has been prescribed by management, but rather the outcome of individual and collective processes of explanation, interpretation, structuring and negotiation. Thus "all company activities are—at least potentially—influences which shape culture. To put it another way, everything which happens in a system has cultural implications, and creates culture or changes it" (Klimecki and Probst, 1990, p. 60).

> *Manipulating culture cannot amount to more than manipulating contexts.*

It follows from the first two propositions that a change in culture which is successful from a management viewpoint can only be attempted by preparing a context which will promote the desired culture. This requires a harmonious concept which fosters cultural change at both material and symbolic levels.

A comprehensive manipulation of context would embrace all spheres in which the perceptions, behaviors and thought patterns of employees are molded. Especially important are contexts in which employees are prepared to express their culture. The following activities offer opportunities for influencing culture: (i) consensus-oriented management and participative decision making; (ii) appropriate incentive systems; (iii) design of documents and use of symbols; and (iv) the use of human resource development.

## Consensus-oriented management of joint ventures

According to Ulrich (1984, p. 319), consensus-oriented joint venture management requires dialogue involving all those amongst whom a "community of meaning" is to be created; their wishes should be explored in a process of open and undistorted dialogue aimed at reaching consensus. In practical terms, this means that the positive potential of culture can only be exploited when the employees of the joint venture have built up a set of basic assumptions about the how and the why of the joint venture. Agreement on objectives and how to achieve them should be established at the outset, and basic values and behaviors should be analyzed and harmonized. These processes are greatly facilitated if the employees in the joint venture share learning and other experiences, and thus take a conscious and active part in shaping an independent culture.

Consensus-oriented management is only possible if certain basic conditions are met which facilitate open dialogue. These include communication paths which bypass the hierarchical structures between the joint venture and the partners, and within the joint venture itself. Other possibilities include open committees, forums or project groups which span different hierarchical levels; an agreed joint venture constitution in which the dialogue principle is embedded; partly autonomous work groups; and, as a general principle, the use of teams to solve problems.

## Incentive-oriented management of joint ventures

Incentive systems can be used to shape culture because they create a set of long-term guidelines which stabilize expectations and help employees to orientate their behavior. Theoretically, incentives may be material or non-material, individual or collective. They may be used to strengthen an existing culture or to change it. The very existence or non-existence of incentive systems, or the announcement of their introduction, is in itself symbolic.

## Document design and use of symbols

Redesigning documents and symbols, perhaps for the purpose of writing a mission statement, or for producing the company's own guidelines or publications, offers the joint venture an opportunity to differentiate itself from the partner companies. Developing a mission can be a step towards creating an independent philosophy. Mission statements bring into the open guidelines for action which were previously present in implicit form. Like incentive systems, they stabilize expectations. Publications such as management information documents, business and social reports, newsletters and articles in specialist journals can strengthen the "we-feeling" in the joint venture. The production of internal publications can also stimulate further development of the joint venture culture.

The following points may serve as guidelines for culturally aware management of joint ventures:

- company cultures can only be manipulated to a limited extent;
- development of culture is always a long-term process;
- manipulating culture is an uncertain business: actions inspired by a particular set of intentions can have unintended consequences;
- the interdependencies between different culture-related factors must be thoroughly analyzed and considered; and
- culturally aware joint venture management rests essentially on a collective process of creating awareness of shared values and assumptions, encouraging their expression and strengthening the will to apply them.

From these guidelines we can derive three basic principles which we regard as essential to cultural awareness in joint venture management:

- positive view of mistakes;
- transparency of communication; and
- institutionalization of self-organizing processes.

## Positive view of mistakes

Mistakes are not simply written off as losses, but are regarded as opportunities for learning and cooperation, as in the Japanese management tradition (the Japanese term for this is *kaizen*). Working together must offer people a chance to learn as they go along, and this applies to mistakes too, since in the early stages of a joint venture, there are no ready answers; they have to be found by trial and error. Mistakes should be in principle permissible and regarded as opportunities to learn or to unlearn. An essential task of joint venture managers is to encourage the development of a culture in which mistakes are openly addressed, people can analyze and criticize their own behavior, and solutions which at first sight seem unacceptable can be considered.

## Transparency of communication

The prevailing culture in a joint venture exerts a strong influence on the manner of communication as well as its content. The normal atmosphere in the company should be one of open communication; people should not feel inhibited about having ideas and expressing them. Even those who maintain that they have nothing to say should be encouraged to talk and have a chance to contribute their own ideas to the shared development process. Open communication can counteract mistrust and suspicion right from the beginning. If all joint venture employees are involved, day-to-day decisions at every level can be made transparent. If the joint venture has a culture of open and transparent learning and communication, joint negotiations and the sharing of experiences become the norm and thus make a substantial contribution to the identity of the joint venture.

## Institutionalization of self-organizing processes

If we concede that culture is only "manageable" to a limited extent, then we shall need to seek a new style of management which makes room for creativity and self-organization, rather than using traditional instruments of control and influence. Joint venture managers become "facilitators" (Probst, 1987); their role is limited to offering structural aids and interpretations, thus helping to make the complex reality of the joint venture a little more comprehensible and easier to handle.

In summary, culture can provide a starting point for the successful management of joint ventures. However, it is amenable to "molding" by interventionist methods only within narrow limits. The visible elements of culture can often be changed, but it is questionable whether this has much effect on the deeper structures. Attempts to impose culture from outside seem doomed to failure; the only alternative seems to be a more modest, culturally aware form of joint venture management which accepts its own limits and recognizes that all members of the organization are themselves responsible for the way they interpret and evaluate their situation, while at the same time taking advantage of opportunities to set parameters, such as structures for communication and decision making.

## Questions to address

- Which of the problems connected with the joint venture are due to cultural factors? Are these really due to culture or could they spring from strategic, structural or staffing problems?
- Which "layers" of culture are involved in individual problems? Is the problem traceable to the values of individuals, the culture of the partner companies or the national culture?
- In which management areas are the cultural problems apparent?
- Is it possible to draw up a profile showing where the cultures converge and where they diverge?
- Have cultural problems been tackled by direct methods or by manipulating the context?
- What opportunities are there for manipulating the context of particular problems?
- Are cultural problems discussed openly, without the implicit assumption that one of the cultures is superior?
- Are all those who are affected included in the discussion of cultural problems?
- Do decision procedures, incentive systems, symbols and documentation work in the "right" direction?
- To what extent do all the organizations in the system take a positive view of errors, practice open communication and facilitate self-organization?

# CHAPTER SEVEN

# HUMAN RESOURCES AS AN AREA OF JOINT VENTURE MANAGEMENT

We shall now consider the development of human resource systems; this is the last of the four main areas in which joint venture management can exert an influence. It is no longer disputed that the "human factor" plays a decisive part in the success of companies. Nevertheless, it often happens that personnel issues receive too little attention in the formation of joint ventures.

Empirical studies of dissatisfaction and instability in joint ventures have found that in many companies, the issues involved in human resource management are not discussed until it is too late, and problems have turned into manifest conflicts. Many conflicts in different areas of the joint venture can be traced back to insufficient attention having been paid to staffing issues during the formation stage (Pucik, 1988). Human resource policies are often not decided by the partners, but left to those who will be responsible for them in the joint venture. At best, the partners may provide a patchwork of solutions to a variety of acute problems.

We must therefore consider all the different functions of human resource management in the joint venture system. First, we shall describe some difficulties which are specific to joint ventures. We shall then turn our attention to the structuring of individual human resource functions; recruitment and selection, assessment and pay systems, human resource development and career opportunities. In the final section, we shall discuss the reintegration of employees into the partner companies.

# HUMAN RESOURCE PROBLEMS IN THE JOINT VENTURE SYSTEM

Human resource management is generally understood to include all tasks which have to do with staff issues in a company. In a slightly different formulation, human resource management includes all staff-related decisions which influence the effectiveness of a company (Milkovich and Boudreau, 1991). Human resource management in a joint venture system differs in two ways from "traditional" human resource management. First, there is an exchange of staff amongst several units, that is between the partners and the joint venture. Second, the joint venture itself contains groups of employees of different origins.

The movement of employees between the partners and the joint venture plays a crucial part in the success of the collaboration. The greater the movement of staff, the easier it can be for the companies to coordinate their activities. However, the fact that the staff comes from different backgrounds and has been molded by different organizational cultures can increase the potential for conflict in the joint venture system. Other aggravating factors are the loyalty which many employees feel to their "home" organization, and their unwillingness to disengage themselves from their previous routines. The difficulties which different groups of employees may have in getting along together works against the need for coordination between the partner companies; this is a serious problem for human resource management in the joint venture system.

## DIFFERENT EMPLOYEE GROUPS

In a joint venture in the garment industry in Myanmar, the foreign partner is from Hong Kong and the local partner is the government. Within such a context the differences between types of employees working in the joint venture are especially visible. The local managers get posted to the joint venture from the government. Due to their work experience within similar factories in Myanmar and their high level of education (frequently in foreign countries), they are valued for their knowledge. As government employees, they, however, get government salaries which are fairly low. The partner from Hong Kong frequently assigns young, mid-career staff. These foreign managers frequently have a lower level of education and receive a salary superior to their counterparts within the joint venture. As a result, conflicts emerge between the local and foreign group due to perceived inequities.

The loyalty problem and the different cultural experiences of the various employee groups creates potential for personnel-related conflicts of various kinds. It is important that joint venture managers should be aware of this. One important source of conflict is the uncertainty which is unavoidably present in joint ventures. The project style of working, undefined duration of the work, and the lack of communication and transparency with regard to the objectives of the joint venture often add to the difficulties of integrating the employees into the new company. Uncertainty may also aggravate basically harmless conflicts, which then escalate and may jeopardize the whole joint venture.

## DEVELOPING A SENSE OF LOYALTY

According to a foreign partner in Vietnam, the biggest problem in managing the Vietnamese staff was developing a sense of loyalty to the joint venture. Since loyalty cannot be bought, it had to be earned by being sensitive to local needs. Within the Vietnamese context, the labor contract which guarantees a wide range of benefits was a useful tool for solving labor problems and creating employee trust and a perception of fairness. Yet in addition, it was necessary to focus on the welfare of employees by considering their personal situations.

The presence of different employee groups makes it difficult to create a unitary human resource policy for the joint venture. The partner companies from which the different groups originate usually have different human resource practices. Furthermore, the joint venture must try to establish a human resource policy of its own, suited to its own objectives, and this will most likely differ from those of the partners.

The various groups which are present in a typical joint venture may be classified as in Figure 7.1. Their heterogeneity often leads to a situation in which a number of human resource practices run parallel in the joint venture. Different human resource management practices are there to meet the needs of different groups, but they can lead to conflicts, for example, when people doing the same work do not receive the same pay. Local employees are often paid what is customary in their country, whereas an employee who is assigned to the joint venture for a limited period continues to be paid by one of the partner companies. There are also different assessment criteria for long-term joint venture employees as against short-term assignees.

The main problems affecting human resource management in the joint venture system include:

- conflict between the need to coordinate different human resource practices;
- uncertainty in the joint venture increases the likelihood of conflict;
- small differences are perceived as being more important than they are;
- presence of groups of employees who come from different backgrounds and stay for different periods of time makes it difficult to create a unitary human resource policy; and
- obvious differences in human resource policies affecting different groups can create serious conflicts and frustrations.

Human resource management in joint venture systems usually involves finding answers to the following questions (cf. Lorange and Roos, 1992):

- How will suitable staff be chosen for the joint venture, and how can good employees in the partner companies be motivated to move to the joint venture?
- How will the partner companies fill key positions? What are the criteria for making appointments?
- What systems of pay, incentives and assessment will be used in the joint venture?
- How will human resource development be organized, and what career opportunities will be open to the employees in the joint venture?

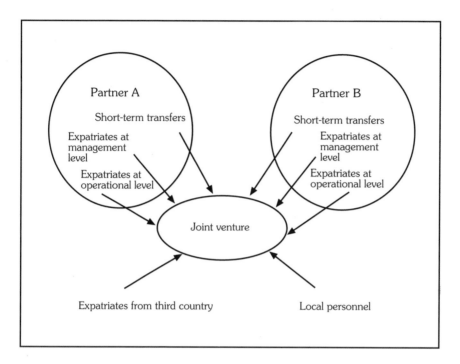

**Figure 7.1** Different employee groups in the joint venture
Source: Adapted from Zeira, Y. and Shenkar, O. (1990) Interactive Parent Characteristics: Implications for Management and Human Resources in International Joint Ventures, In: *Management International Review*, Special Issue, pp. 7–22

- How can employees from the joint venture be reintegrated into the partner companies, and what are the basic issues affecting the transfer and reintegration of employees?

# HUMAN RESOURCE PLANNING, RECRUITMENT AND SELECTION

Finding suitable human resources is one of the most difficult tasks in establishing a joint venture and also one of the most important. Joint venture staff are usually recruited by the partner companies. Employees are therefore sent by two separate organizations.

A common problem is that the partners do not always offer their best employees. There are several possible reasons for this. First, the partners may try to keep their best staff in their own organizations. Second, the partners may set too low a value on the joint venture and think it not worth their while to offer their best people. Third, communication may be so poor that qualified employees who might be interested never realize that the opportunity exists to move to the joint venture.

This situation constitutes a serious pitfall for the joint venture. No matter how good its strategy or its structure, these are useless unless implemented by suitable people. The strategic decision to create a joint venture demands a certain level of commitment from the partners, not least with regard to human resources.

Strategic human resource management can provide a way of harmonizing the strategy of the joint venture with the personnel decisions of both partner companies. It involves aligning the planning of company strategy with the planning of human resources. In a joint venture system, strategic human resource management is primarily a matter of achieving a convergence between the human resource planning of the partners and that of the joint venture. At the very beginning, in the formation stage, the partners should develop joint venture strategies for selection, assessment, pay and human resource development. This will help to limit potential conflicts arising from the partners' different human resources practices.

Human resource issues often receive too little attention in the early stages of negotiation which precede the formation of a joint venture (Pucik, 1988). This could perhaps be avoided if human resource managers from both founder companies and the future human resource manager of the joint venture were present at the negotiations. This would focus more attention on personnel decisions in time to avoid some of the difficulties.

Strategic decisions on selection involve a number of steps. First, the partners and the joint venture should analyze the joint venture objectives to determine what skills and competencies are needed to meet the objectives. This provides a basis for deciding where employees should be recruited and how many are needed. The analysis of skills and competencies can then be used to create job profiles for the positions to be filled. Lorange and Roos (1992) suggest that communication skills and the ability to work in teams should be given at least as much emphasis as special professional competencies, otherwise the danger of conflict which is always serious in joint ventures may increase even further.

Cauley de la Sierra (1995) suggests that employees should be recruited from the staff who were present at the negotiations between the partners. They are already familiar with the strategic direction of the joint venture and they have had an opportunity to make personal contacts with the staff of the partner company.

If staff are not prepared to move from the partner companies into the joint venture, its strategy will fail. They must therefore be offered incentives and career opportunities to make the move attractive. Opportunities and infrastructure are usually better in a multinational company, so incentives to move to the joint venture might take the form of higher positions, short assignments, greater entrepreneurial freedom or personal convenience. The creation of incentives can lead to internal difficulties, so it is a good idea to recruit external employees as well, to avoid setting high expectations which cannot subsequently be fulfilled.

Appointments to positions of leadership within the joint venture are a delicate matter. Key positions in the joint venture are often allocated according to the level of capital investment by the partners, regardless of the competencies which the positions demand. This is a pity because good appointments to leadership positions can be extremely helpful.

## KEY MANAGEMENT POSITIONS

The joint venture VW Shanghai has found an ideal pattern for allocating posts. The managing director and head of the company is Chinese. His role is mainly to represent the company, and he establishes and maintains contacts with officials. The second most senior Chinese is responsible for human resources. The two Germans hold the key positions on the board of directors, as head of finance and head of production.

It is worth giving a good deal of thought to key appointments, to take advantage of the complementary skills of the partners. Yoshino and Rangan (1995) go a step further and suggest that all leading positions should be filled in parallel by managers from both partner companies. The advantage of double appointments is that the partners would have to negotiate plans, objectives and use of resources on a continuous basis within the joint venture. The disadvantage is that parallel occupation of posts can result in power struggles and in wasted time and resources. Whether double appointments make sense can only be decided in the light of the specific circumstances.

The most demanding positions in a joint venture are without doubt the management positions. Three main qualities are suggested in the literature as being the most important: flexibility, interpersonal skills and the ability to inspire trust over long periods (Yoshino and Rangan, 1995). In the following extract, the managing director of a joint venture describes his job:

> This is one of those jobs for which a job description is meaningless. To begin with, the job is ambiguous, and so is the situation one must manage. One never knows what to expect day to day, but at the same time one must try to anticipate long-term trends and developments. In the course of a day, I deal with issues ranging from the extremely mundane to the very strategic. I must be able to shift my thinking quickly from immediate to long-term issues. A fun part of the job is that there are very few ready-made answers. I have to be creative in finding solutions, often on an ad hoc basis, to many of the problems I face. (Yoshino and Rangan, 1995, p. 144)

According to Yoshino and Rangan, a manager in a joint venture needs all the skills possessed by the board of directors of any other company, but lacks the corresponding authority to make independent decisions. For a joint venture manager, managing relationships and convincing people are vital parts of the job. The position of managing director of a joint venture can serve as a learning arena and a probationary period for someone who may later be appointed to the board of one of the partner companies.

## HUMAN RESOURCE SELECTION

When the EHPT joint venture was founded, the majority of the employees were taken over from a former Ericsson business unit. The Ericsson employees received a contract from EHPT which provided for a move without change in conditions. All were given the choice of staying with Ericsson, but 95% of the employees of the Ericsson business unit decided to move to the joint venture. They were given a guarantee that they could move back to Ericsson within two years.

In order to make HP skills and experience available to EHPT, it was agreed that more HP employees should be recruited. The management wanted EHPT to take at least 10% of its employees from HP. It was stated in the contract that two of the highest management positions must be filled from HP. The director of the joint venture and the holders of all other management positions were to be appointed by Ericsson.

Although the plan to recruit HP employees was not in dispute, it nevertheless proved difficult in practice. One reason was that HP employees were better paid than Ericsson employees. Another was that few were prepared to move to another company which they considered less prestigious without a guarantee that they could move back again. The outcome was that  HP employees who were prepared to move were often offered better conditions, a two-year contract, and a guarantee that they could return.  Once the first problems emerged in the relationship between HP and EHPT, it became even more difficult to transfer HP employees into the joint venture, because HP managers advised their people not to move and often made them better offers within HP.

The result was a clear majority of Ericsson employees in the joint venture. There was no ready flow of HP skills and experience into the joint venture. The joint venture had grown from an Ericsson business unit, so the organizational culture changed little. It also meant that Ericsson had almost complete control of personnel decisions. Pay rises, promotions and management development were arranged entirely by the Ericsson human resource department. Differences in pay between the different employee groups caused envy, which hampered daily cooperation.

Both groups of employees had contracts which permitted them to return to the parent companies, so given the cultural difficulties, there was a danger that they would leave EHPT over minor dissatisfactions with the joint venture. This was already happening by the end of the first year. The consequences were all the more

> serious because the joint venture depended primarily on the knowledge and skills of its employees.

This case study shows that the development of a consistent human resource policy during the formation stage is crucial not only to the functioning of the joint venture, but also for avoiding difficulties in later stages of development. The provision of suitable personnel is also a token of the partners' commitment, which is a deciding factor in the long-term success of the joint venture. If one of the partners seems less than completely willing to transfer competent employees into the joint venture, the commitment of the other partner may decrease over time.

## ASSIGNMENT OF EMPLOYEES TO THE JOINT VENTURE

In order to build a positive working relationship between the partners, the Mazda-Ford joint venture in Thailand was set up totally independent of the parent companies. Managers assigned from the two parents do not report to their parent companies. They are fully responsible towards the joint venture. In the future, most of the important positions are to be filled by Thai nationals which do not represent Mazda or Ford.

# HUMAN RESOURCE ASSESSMENT AND COMPENSATION

As in human resource selection, there is generally a lack of strategic alignment between the partners and the joint venture on human resource assessment and pay systems. The importance of negotiating these issues during the formation stage cannot be overestimated. It is worth stressing once again that human resource management systems exert a major influence on the culture of the joint venture, thus setting the scene for the learning processes which take place within the joint venture system. If, for example, the managing director of the joint venture receives a one-sided assessment, based on his or her success in meeting the objectives of one of the partners rather than on his or her ability to form an integrated company, a culture of mistrust is likely to develop.

The partner companies usually have different human resource systems, so the joint venture will do best to develop its own system, adapted to its own circumstances. Taking over the human resource system of one of the partners can create a barrier to developing a specific joint venture identity. The joint venture should therefore seek its own strategic direction in managing its personnel. Since the choice of appropriate human resource management systems depends on the nature of the joint venture and the reasons for its existence, it is difficult to do more than formulate a few general principles. The following case study shows some of the difficulties in finding a coherent joint venture human resource system.

## PROMOTION OF EMPLOYEES

Promotion of employees in a Malaysia–Myanmar joint venture in the business of fruit and vegetable canning was a key issue where the partners had different outlooks. According to one of the foreign directors: "As a market orientation, we are tracing for productivity and ability. If someone has the ability, he has to get a higher salary." According to a Myanmar manager: "As a government servant, we cannot decide as we like, we have to follow the government labor laws and regulations. Workers who have many years of services, have to be considered for promotion. If junior people show superior performance to senior people and they are promoted that means creating a difficult management situation."

Three factors are important in the assessment of joint venture employees: the level at which the assessment is made, the criteria used and the consequences. The level of the assessment is a question of who is making it. When assessing senior and middle managers, care should be taken to avoid a one-sided, biased evaluation by one of the partners. It is not uncommon for each partner to evaluate those employees whom it has transferred to the joint venture, and of whom it has already formed a picture before the evaluation takes place. Lorange and Roos (1992) suggest that managers should be assessed by a committee made up of representatives of the joint venture and both partner companies; the committee would also be responsible for ensuring feedback. It is also worth considering a committee of this kind to evaluate other employees in the joint venture, since here too there can be difficulties when the person being assessed and the person making the assessment come from different partner companies.

With regard to criteria, employees should be assessed not only for technical competence, but also for intercultural skills such as the ability to work in teams, solve conflicts, etc. Two further criteria should be used when assessing joint venture managers: these are skilled in analyzing the environment and long-term orientation. Joint ventures often run into problems because they concentrate on internal relationships, and not enough on environmental changes, hence the need for managers who are skilled in monitoring outside developments. Managers should be assessed not only according to the short-term objectives, but also according to long-term, learning-oriented objectives.

The impact of human resource assessments on the pay system must also be taken into account. A link between assessment and pay is an effective way of influencing behavior. In joint ventures, it has far-reaching consequences, because it creates the incentive to meet the objectives which were set in the early stages.

The presence of different groups of employees in the joint venture makes it difficult to establish a unitary system of pay and incentives. The difficulty increases in proportion to the difference between the pay systems of the partner companies. Since the various groups were accustomed to different pay systems before transfer, the attempt to standardize levels of pay can result in everyone pushing for the highest rates. However, it often happens that the joint venture is not prepared to meet this level, while the employees on the other hand are not prepared to work below their previous rate unless other incentives are offered. The aim in aligning pay policies must be to achieve perceived equality between the different groups. Those who accept a lower level of pay within the joint venture might be compensated by career incentives.

The most important feature of the pay policy, however, is that it should be linked to the strategy of the joint venture. The stability of the joint venture can be increased by basing management incentive systems on the concrete objectives arising from the business plan.

This case study shows the difficulties which arise from an unequal pay structure. In this case, the pay system made it difficult for the joint venture to establish its own cultural identity.

---

## CONFLICTS OVER PAY POLICY

One of the worst problems with which EHPT had to contend was the difference in levels of pay between employees from the two partner companies. Since most of the employees who came from HP had only moved to the joint venture for two years, they continued to be paid by their parent company, with the addition of a foreign assignment allowance (usually even higher). The Ericsson employees, however, were paid by the joint venture, at levels similar to those they had experienced while working for Ericsson. This resulted in pay differences of up to 50% for the same job. The joint venture tried to keep the difference from being generally known, but once the employees had established personal contacts amongst themselves, those who came from Ericsson started to feel "inferior" and envious.

The pay differences were a source of inter-group conflict and hampered the integration of employees into the joint venture. Employees from Ericsson felt that those from HP were more highly valued. HP employees were more closely linked to their parent company and the bond was strengthened by the higher rates of pay.

---

# HUMAN RESOURCE DEVELOPMENT AND CAREER PROSPECTS

The type of human resource development provided depends on its purpose and on the groups of employees for whom it is intended. Its purpose may be either to help employees to gain qualifications as individuals, or to train them for the purposes of the organization. It may be aimed at managers or at operational staff. In joint ventures, there is a problem with respect to human resource development because the long-term existence of the company may not be guaranteed.

For senior and middle managers who were transferred to the joint venture from the partners, the question of their future career development arises at the time of the transfer. According to Lorange and Roos (1992), they must often decide after only a short time in the joint venture whether they want to pursue a career there or in one of the partner companies.

Many companies have worldwide human resource and career development plans which groups of employees follow over periods of years. Employees who move from a partner company to the joint venture may fall out of this system. On the other hand, a short period in the joint venture may be regarded as a development opportunity which improves a manager's career chances. How such a transfer is handled in practice depends on the human resource policy of the company. When a manager makes a move of this kind, its significance and possible consequences should be made clear to him or her.

It is usually a good thing for operational staff to have access to the human resource development opportunities of both partner companies. This helps to build up a culture of trust between the partners, and provides opportunities for each to learn from the other. It is especially valuable in joint ventures which were formed to take advantage of complementarities, because neither group of employees will have the full range of necessary skills. Decisions therefore have to be made about the skills in which employees need further training and who will provide that training. There are three main possibilities. First, the joint venture may make use of the human resource development programs of the partner companies. Second, it may develop its own. Third, it may use external advisers. The simplest solution is to use the provisions of the partner companies, but doing so may bind the joint venture more closely to the partners and critical employee resources may be lost. It therefore seems advisable for the joint venture to provide its own human resource development programs in core skills.

## EMPLOYEE DEVELOPMENT

There was little human resource development provided for management in the EHPT joint venture. The two partner companies, HP and Ericsson, identified the managers who were important for their own company and followed their careers. The partner companies had primary responsibility for training these managers. This was meant to ensure that these managers could return to the partner companies should the joint venture be dissolved.

At first, only Ericsson offered employee training, in the form of seminars. After a year, it was decided that previous employees of both Ericsson and HP could attend seminars in either company. The joint venture did not set up its own seminars and did not employ external advisers.

# REINTEGRATING EMPLOYEES INTO THE PARTNER COMPANIES

For the partner companies, reintegration is a critical issue in human resource management. At the very beginning, during the formation stage, the partners have to decide what will happen to joint venture employees if the venture is dissolved. The partners do not usually give transferred employees a long-term guarantee that they can return. In the case of EHPT, the Ericsson employees were given a two-year return guarantee, but after that, they were part of the joint venture. A policy of this kind can result in the joint venture suffering a massive loss of important human resources at the end of the stipulated time. Another danger is that employees will remain loyal to their previous company throughout this period. To avoid conflicts of loyalty, the partners must convey to their employees that loyalty to the joint venture comes first, because otherwise there will be problems of trust which could threaten the very existence of the joint venture.

When a joint venture is dissolved, reintegrating the employees can bring advantages to the parent companies. There may be initial adjustment problems when employees return from the "freedom" of the joint venture, but the knowledge which they have acquired is an important resource. Returning employees bring with them the fruits of their experience and add to the company's knowledge about the other partner. The reintegration of people returning from the joint venture should not be viewed as a burdensome task, because they are bearers of knowledge and bring advantages to the company.

In the cooperative association between the Banque Nationale de Paris (BNP) and the Dresdner Bank employees gained experience for a time in the partner company and then returned with it to their original organization. The partner company or joint venture became a learning arena where employees accumulated knowledge which they then made available to their "home" company.

To summarize, human resource management plays a vital part in the success of joint ventures. Human resource policies shape the behavior of the employees. Human resource issues should therefore receive due attention at the beginning, in the formation stage. If the strategic direction of the joint venture's future human resource policy is clearly established and harmonized with the human resource policies of the partners, the chances of the joint venture succeeding are greatly enhanced.

## Questions to address

- Is human resource management an important issue in the negotiations between the partner companies?
- Do the human resource managers of both partner companies and future joint venture employees take part in the negotiations?
- Is a strategic human resource policy being developed for the joint venture and aligned with the human resource strategies of the partner companies?
- How are employees recruited for the joint venture?
- What incentives and guarantees are offered to future joint venture employees?
- Do these employees retain access to the human resource and career development programs of the partner companies from which they come?

- What different employee groups does the joint venture have?
- What are the particular problems which might arise amongst these groups?
- How are appointments made to leadership positions in the joint venture? Do political, symbolic or technical considerations predominate?
- Does the joint venture have different human resource policies running in parallel? What conflicts are implicit in this situation? How can they be avoided?
- Is there sufficient transparency in the joint venture with regard to the different human resource policies, pay systems, development opportunities, etc.?
- Have concrete measures been planned for reintegrating employees from the joint venture?
- What will be done to ensure that the partners make optimal use of the experiences of employees returning from the joint venture?

# CHAPTER EIGHT

# SENSEMAKING, TRUST AND COMMITMENT AS BASES OF JOINT VENTURE MANAGEMENT

Strategy, structure, culture and human resources are important areas in the management of joint ventures, but they are not the whole story. We believe that there are three further factors which lie at the heart of all joint venture activity. These are trust, commitment and sensemaking. Together they form the glue on which the cohesion of joint venture management depends.

Trust is the most important requirement for the management of joint ventures, because it helps to reduce complexity. Trust is an expectation for the future, built up through personal relationships. This expectation reduces uncertainty, thus enabling us to act in the present. Commitment is about the need for balanced contributions from all members of the joint venture system. Finally, sensemaking provides the reason for the existence of the joint venture and for the participation of the other companies; it affects all levels, processes and areas of development. All three factors are necessary for the success of a joint venture and support its stability over time.

Sensemaking, trust and commitment are concepts which have a strong intuitive appeal and which constitute a growing focus of interest in the specialist literature.[1] We shall discuss all three factors individually, because they are basic to any joint venture relationship, although they cannot be located as isolated, specific features within a company or joint venture. Sense, trust and commitment are significant because people

---

[1]See, for example, Dwyer, Schurr and Oh, 1987; Anderson and Narus, 1990; Mohr and Spekman, 1994; Cullen and Johnson, 1995; Gundlach, Achrol and Mentzer, 1995; Korsgaard, Schweiger and Sapienza, 1995; Madhok, 1995. On sensemaking, see especially Weick, 1995.

do not follow the rules of strict economic rationality when setting up joint ventures.

If sense, trust and commitment are important, then advice on how to organize joint ventures should be based on a closer analysis of their functions and the conditions in which they flourish. We need to find out what influences their early development and show how they affect the success of the joint venture. Such is the purpose of the following discussion.

## SENSEMAKING AS A BASIS FOR JOINT VENTURE MANAGEMENT

The establishment of a joint venture creates a new situation in which there is a fundamental need for sensemaking. The partner companies, which often continue to compete in other areas, are confronted by a novel set of circumstances in which the accustomed rules do not apply. Differing norms, strategies and cultures collide within the newly created entity company and this causes initial uncertainty. Existing structures are no longer valid and new ones are not yet in place. The formal creation of a new company is not enough to ensure that it will run smoothly; it must also find and develop a new identity. Sensemaking means creating an identity, and reducing ambiguity and complexity sufficiently to facilitate action.

By means of a process of organizing, ambivalence and uncertainty are transformed into comprehensible structures which provide a source of meaning to joint venture managers in their daily management tasks (Weick, 1995). This constitutes a fundamental affirmation of the existence of the joint venture and permits further processes of development and learning to take place. We shall elaborate on these points in the following sections. Before doing so, however, we need to ask ourselves what we mean by "sense".

First, sense means that something is comprehensible. It is human nature to look for explanations, in order to reduce ambiguity in unfamiliar situations, and to create certainty and order through subjective interpretation. The urge to find sense in situations is so strong that we continue to use old patterns of action even in circumstances where they are no longer successful.

Sociologists also ascribe an order-creating function to sense or identity. Sensemaking in social situations involves choosing meaningful alternatives from a large number of possibilities. It is therefore a continuous process of bringing possibilities for the future into the present. In the context of joint ventures, sense, like trust, is not an individual matter, but primarily a social construct. Our interest is therefore in the various facets of sensemaking in the joint venture. This is especially relevant to the initial formation stage, because sense legitimizes the venture and so all parties must be made aware of it. Sense brings together scattered facts and unfamiliar events, and makes complex situations easier to understand. Companies and joint ventures only come into being as a result of sense, because people do not discover something which already exists: they first invent the reality (of the joint venture) in their own heads (Weick, 1995). If we develop this idea further, we shall gain a clearer picture of the essential function of constructing identity.

## Sensemaking creates identity

New management strategies such as downsizing, lean management and joint ventures force companies to make difficult adjustments, since they can result in loss of traditions and a radically changed outlook. Especially during the formation and early adjustment stage, the managers of a joint venture find themselves in unfamiliar territory where traditional patterns and habits no longer work and where they have no frame of reference.

If this temporary loss of orientation is not handled properly, the result may be an identity crisis, or, even worse, failure to develop a new unit with an independent identity. In this situation, the function of sensemaking is to engender a separate identity for the joint venture which distinguishes it from the partners. From a systems theory point of view, the function of sense in creating identity emerges in the definition of systems as "sense-constituting and sense-constituted patterns". A context of sense is created when different people relate their actions, giving rise to an identifiable system, that is a basis on which people can act "in the name of the joint venture". This can result in an increased "we-feeling". The joint venture thus distinguishes itself from its environment by building up its own frame of reference, which may be a specific repertoire of symbols, or a particular form of language or a pattern of interpretations. It is only when symbolic components are formed that the new company becomes a truly independent unit, and not a more or less forced collaboration between the managers of two companies, determined from the beginning by the prescribed goals of the joint venture.

Sensemaking is difficult in situations:

- which are unusually difficult to understand, and which are characterized by high levels of ambiguity;
- which are completely unfamiliar, and appear to have no order or structure ("I have never been here before. I have no idea where I am. I don't even know who can help me.");
- where there is a lack of group cohesion, and no accepted leading personality; and
- where sensemaking involves questioning one's own identity.

Browning, Beyer and Shetler (1995) describe the case of a cooperation called SEMATECH which exhibits a number of interesting features of sensemaking.

## SEMATECH: PROBLEMS OF SENSEMAKING IN THE EARLY STAGES OF COOPERATION

SEMATECH (Semiconductor Manufacturing Technology), founded in 1987, is a consortium of US semiconductor manufacturers and the American Government. Fourteen companies entered the consortium in order to combine resources, stabilize and increase their market shares and improve their deteriorating competitive positions. According to the mission statement, the goal of SEMATECH was to enable the US semiconductor industry to achieve a leading position in the world market by the middle of the 1990s. This goal was to be achieved by means of three strategies: improving the industrial infrastructure, improving the manufacturing process and improving the management of existing manufacturing plants.

During the initial phase of the cooperation, an organizational structure was developed sequentially. This established some order in a situation which had previously been unstructured and confusing. As a first step, general coordinating mechanisms such as a board of directors and a technical advisory committee were created to decide on overall objectives. As work progressed, further units were created according to need, for example special task forces or research groups to tackle new problems. In this way, meaning was established within distinct groups and this furthered the development of the whole cooperative venture.

However, the creation of the various bodies was not an entirely smooth process and SEMATECH suffered serious initial difficulties. For about a year, unsuccessful attempts were made to find a suitable Chief Executive Officer (CEO). This ended with the appointment of Bob Noyce, a charismatic personality who was respected both by the employees and by the industry as a whole. The presence of an accepted leading personality made it easier for people to plan and monitor their actions according to recognized principles, and thus to realize that there was a shared purpose behind them.

There was a further problem in the shape of continuing disputes between Bob Noyce and Paul Castrucci, the Chief Operations Officer (COO) selected by the board of directors. Noyce had not met Castrucci before accepting the position of CEO and the disagreements between them led to Castrucci's resignation. Two years later, Noyce, whose personality had made a significant contribution to the cohesion of the cooperation, died. A few months later, the employees had to adapt to a new leader recruited from outside. However, they were able to cope with this fresh uncertainty because they continued to follow proven strategies, rather than looking for a new identity.

In spite of many initial difficulties, SEMATECH achieved good results. All three initial objectives were met, and at the beginning of 1992, instead of a further fall in market share, the first increase was recorded. A situation which had been incomprehensible in the initial phase was now structured and clarified. Close collaboration within small specialist teams provided a basis for collective sensemaking, and the presence of an accepted leader provided cohesion for the cooperative venture as a whole. Another sign of

success was that after five years, 11 of the original 14 founder companies affirmed their continuing commitment.
SEMATECH'S founding companies:
- Advanced Micro Devices
- AT&T Microelectronics
- Digital Equipment Corp.
- Harris Corp.
- Hewlett-Packard
- IBM
- Intel
- LSI Logic
- Micron Technology
- Motorola
- National Semiconductor
- NCR
- Rockwell International
- Texas Instruments

When people are dealing with new and unaccustomed structures, as in the creation of a new cooperative unit, there is a particular danger that sense will not be found, or that if it is found, it will rapidly be lost again.

Many of the issues which we discussed earlier can be identified in the account of the formation of SEMATECH. The reason for the major ambiguities was that SEMATECH was founded with the unstructured aim of revitalizing the American semiconductor industry. Nobody knew beforehand how this might be accomplished, so experimentation with unfamiliar instruments and methods was explicitly encouraged. Continuous change in procedure was essential to success. This meant that the process of developing the cooperation was essentially a process of change. Since SEMATECH was a new company, there was no previous experience to fall back on. Uncertainty and instability were the norm.

It is instructive to consider the steps in the sensemaking process which SEMATECH underwent. Cooperative behavior replaced the previous free competition for all participants, so they were obliged to rethink their competitive ethos. Strict property principles had to make way for a cooperative mentality. In the absence of coordinating mechanisms, the initial structural disorder was more conducive to loss of sense than to sensemaking.

The first step towards creating structure came with the appointment of a CEO who was accepted by the employees, but the effects were not lasting. Appointments to other management positions did not follow a policy which was comprehensible to the employees. Senior managers sometimes had only a few people under them, whereas at lower levels, the reverse was often true. This caused a great deal of ambiguity with regard to personal identity and status, especially since formal organization charts were missing and employees wrote their own job descriptions. There was also uncertainty about staff recruitment, since people were chosen because they were willing to move rather than according to objective personnel rotation needs.

A further point was that widely differing company cultures came into contact in the cooperative venture. As a first step towards integration, SEMATECH composed a reference list of abbreviations and technical terms. Since it was initially planned that the cooperation would only last five years, there was justifiable doubt about the need for a major cultural change. On the other hand, SEMATECH had a demanding set of objectives and an essentially cooperative rationale which could only be put into practice by managers who were aware of cultural factors. Bob Noyce was a manager of this kind. On his first day, he allegedly took off his tie, to show that the company was to have a hard-working and informal atmosphere. A further measure which supported sensemaking during the initial phase of SEMATECH's existence was the encouragement of awareness of continual change. The motto, "If it isn't competitive, it has to change" bound all the participating companies into a kind of common destiny: the only options were joint survival or the disintegration of the industry.

The subsequent success of SEMATECH owed a great deal to the fact that each of the participating companies was bound to the others in this way. The contribution of materials and ideas by some partners stimulated the others and promoted sensemaking, which in this case took the form of cooperation as a behavioral norm. The contributions also led to the growth of trust between the organizations; this was expressed in the expectation that the other partners would also contribute. However, the will to cooperate was not in itself sufficient. Supporting measures had to be taken to enable sensemaking to proceed through the medium of open communication. This was difficult at the beginning for SEMATECH, because of the high level of awareness of individual property relations and the problem was only solved by the gradual development of readiness to share with regard to production procedures.

A final point worth mentioning is the importance of structures which have a stabilizing effect. The institutionalization of regular meetings meant that adjustments could be made to the common goals, the direction of technological development and the structuring of the new organization. One objective was to find a structure to facilitate coordination with suppliers. The formal structural measures which were ultimately adopted left room for any unplanned and unusual ideas which might arise. This is important in encouraging sensemaking; it also underlines the fact that sense cannot be prescribed, but must be found and interpreted in subjectively experienced situations.

It follows from this that the task of joint venture managers is to offer meaningful alternatives which are practicable and do not conflict with the previous outlook, since this would cause uncertainty in decision making. Instruments aimed at "creating" sense—a function which is still ascribed to company culture—are likely to fail, because sense cannot be created by administrative means, especially if people are aware that the attempt is being made. Sense-oriented joint venture management must therefore be understood as a way of creating opportunities to find sense, by offering aids to understanding and structuring complex problems and situations. Better still, it can mean setting an active example which clearly shows that sensemaking is possible. This means that all those involved must be prepared to regard sensemaking as a learning process.

## Sensemaking as a learning process

Sensemaking serves to structure ambiguous situations and thus to absorb uncertainty, as happened in the case of SEMATECH. Sensemaking can be interpreted as an organizational learning process where immediate experience is influential on the development of cognitive structures. Kolb (1984) conceives of experiential learning as a cycle with four phases; in the case of joint ventures, it may be interpreted as shown in Figure 8.1.

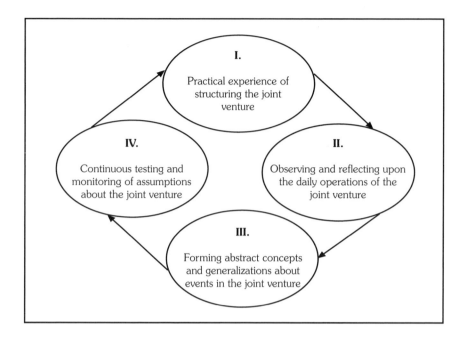

**Figure 8.1** Experiential learning as a sensemaking process
Source: Adapted from Wolfe, D.M. and Kolb, D.A. (1979) Career Development, Personal Growth, and Experiential Learning. In: Kolb, D., Rubin, J. and McIntyre, J. (eds) *Organizational Psychology*, Englewood Cliffs, New Jersey: Prentice-Hall, p. 539

This process view of sensemaking in the joint venture is useful because it allows us to trace the gradual process of building up order or certainty. Weick (1995a), in his book on the social psychology of organizing, points out that an organization never exists as such but consists of related events and relationships which are structured in a systematic way. The fundamental process of sensemaking in joint ventures can thus be seen as a process of finding order, that is forming collective patterns of interpretation.

Organized action presupposes a sufficient knowledge of its necessary conditions and likely effects. This knowledge is not usually easy to acquire when one is faced with sense in varying and contradictory manifestations. The model shown in Figure 8.1 is a first step towards tracing the process of sensemaking by focusing on action.

Some suggestions which Weick (1995) formulated for individuals are also relevant to joint ventures. Three examples are shown.

*When faced with disorder, don't panic!*

People often think of joint ventures as ordered, rational units. In reality, uncertainty is unavoidable and is usually perceived as a catastrophe. It need not be so, if ambivalence is viewed as a necessary corrective to stability.

*Chaotic action is better than organized inaction!*

Sense often appears only after action has taken place (retrospective sensemaking); this means that experience of the reality of a joint venture is the only material available for making "interpretations". In a disorderly situation, action increases the chance that joint venture managers will find out what it is that they are doing and what they really want.

*There is no such thing as a clear, unambiguous solution!*

In complex situations, it is often impossible to trace particular effects back to specific causes. If people understand that there will be continuous change in the joint venture, they can readjust to constantly changing situations.

## TRUST AS A BASIS FOR JOINT VENTURE MANAGEMENT

For some time now, trust has been regarded as an extremely significant factor in organizations in general and in joint ventures in particular. In his recent management best-seller *Liberation Management*, Peters (1992) argues that trust is the missing "Factor X" in company activity. Its importance has also been underlined by Arrow (1980), who regards trust as an effective lubricant for market-coordinated processes. Mutual trust can be a valuable adjunct to other forms of control in dealing with the opportunistic behavior which takes place in relation to joint ventures.

In the context of joint ventures, trust stabilizes the relationships between organizations, reduces the need for complex contractual agreements, permits open exchange of information and reduces transaction costs (Fishman and Levinthal, 1991; Bromiley and Cummings, 1993). In short, trust supports the formation, coordination, handling and, not least, the success of joint ventures.

We shall now examine more closely the functions of trust and the way in which trust develops. We shall distinguish between personal trust which exists between particular joint venture managers, and trust as a collective feature of the system which unites the partner companies and the joint venture. We shall then consider the factors which influence trust at both levels and make some suggestions for "trust-oriented joint venture management".

## Functions of trust

Trust is an attitude of expectation. Faced with an uncertain situation, one assumes that one's opposite will act in a way which will be acceptable. This is the essence of trust. It is an elementary fact of social life, because people can never make decisions in the light of total certainty. In spite of all our attempts at rational planning, we cannot base our actions on foresight of their effects. Successful action involves absorbing uncertainties, because we do not have complete control over future circumstances. Trust offers a way of bridging this time gap, since it is "granted as an advance on success and on time and reversal" (Luhmann, 1989). If we take trust as a "risky advance", we anticipate the future. We act as though the future were certain and we could overcome the time gap.

---

### WITHDRAWAL OF THE FOREIGN PARTNER AFTER THE ESTABLISHMENT OF TRUST

Yingkou Offset Duplicator is a Sino-foreign joint venture established by Yingkou Offset Duplicator Complex factory and Tarzan Industrial Holdings Ltd Hong Kong producing modern office equipment. Although the board of directors is evenly split between the Chinese and Hong Kong partners, the Chinese partner controls the operational activities of the company. Once the day-to-day operations were running successfully, the Hong Kong partner decided to withdraw from active decision making. The partner only participates in the long-term planning (5–10 years) and the board of director meetings which are held once a year or whenever necessary. Once the basis for trust had been established between the partners, the foreign party withdrew from actively managing the joint venture in the belief that his objectives for the joint venture would be met by the partners.

A further function of trust is to reduce complexity. Trust does this by bringing future circumstances into the present, thus reducing the complexity of future alternatives to something which is manageable now. However, even though it reduces the number of future alternatives, the act of trusting someone cannot be equated with credulity; it usually contains an element of rational decision and thus an expectation of influencing success.

Trust may be shown for a number of completely different reasons:

- A trusts B because he or she perceives his or her behavior as genuine and honest;
- A believes that B has good intentions, because B appears to be considerate;
- A has no reason to suppose that B intends to manipulate him or her; and
- A relies on B because a breach of trust would incur serious disadvantages for B.

These statements contain widely different reasons for trusting; at a later stage, we shall be able to derive measures from them for promoting trust within joint ventures.

## The process of building trust

Trust can be built at two levels in joint ventures: first, as personal trust between joint venture managers; second, as institutional or systemic trust between the partner companies. Out of the possible sources of personal trust, three are especially relevant here: personal qualities, situational factors and the pattern of interactions between the partners (Figure 8.2).

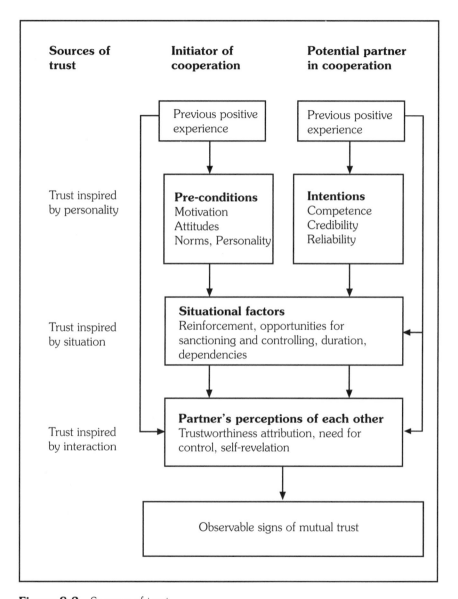

**Figure 8.2** Sources of trust
Source: Adapted from Petermann, F. (1985) *Psychologie des Vertrauens*, Salzburg: Müller, p. 47

First, the process of building trust is determined by personal qualities such as attitudes, reliability, values, competence and fairness. Furthermore, in the special circumstances of a cooperative venture, an important part is played by structural factors, such as opportunities for control and sanction, and by the processes of perception, attribution and self-revelation which are determined by interactions between employees. These three sources of trust depend on previous experiences and also influence subsequent strategies.

---

### BUILDING TRUST THROUGH ALTERNATELY HOSTED NEGOTIATIONS SESSIONS

The Thai Maxwell Electric Co Ltd joint venture was established by a group of leading Thai industrialists and entrepreneurs from Japan, Taiwan, Singapore and Indonesia to manufacture and distribute transformers. Since a number of partners were involved, the most crucial aspect was trust. In order to build trust, each partner alternately hosted a negotiation session prior to reaching a joint venture agreement. This provided the opportunity to meet and understand each other, which played a key role in the process of negotiation. One manager said:

> Every partner wants to make sure that the investment will make profit, and the profit will be shared fairly. Here, only trust can bind the partners together and the trust has to be developed over time.

---

Trust is usually shown in observable ways such as readiness to make material and non-material advances to the joint venture, to provide information or to make the results of research available. The building of trust between joint venture managers is usually a gradual process, which was described many years ago as the "self-heightening cycle of trust" (Golembiewski and McConkie, 1975). It is especially important to generate trust in the early joint venture formation stage because otherwise mistrust emerges and develops in an equally spiral manner.

Direct and indirect reasons for the development of trust have been identified by Rössl (1994). There are direct reasons for trusting people who increase their own risks without being asked to do so, for example by agreeing to self-imposed penalties for breaches of contract; who had reason to fear external consequences, for example if they would suffer serious damage as a result of a breach of faith; or who feared losing their own share of the advantages of synergy, which are part of the benefits of cooperation. These direct reasons for trusting are usually accompanied by indirect or supporting factors which in themselves do not inspire trust, but which set the scene for its development. These include the familiarity which develops from a broad information base and adequate opportunities to exercise control. Trust is also fostered by references to the existing mutual dependencies and by communications in which the cooperative intent is clearly expressed. Indications that a particular person has cooperated with others in the past also encourages trust.

Trust at the second level, that is institutional or interorganizational trust, is interpreted here as trustworthiness. It is therefore a quality which can be directly deduced from certain features or actions of a partner company.

## Factors which influence interorganizational trust

When considering the issue of trust in joint ventures, we must look not only at personal factors, but also at possible structural influences. One factor which encourages trust is the existence of intercompany communication structures which permit openness. If, for example, objectives agreed in joint discussions are communicated both within and between the organizations, trust is involved in two ways: first, the decision to publicize the partners' expectations and the objectives chosen for the joint venture is based on trust; and second, publicizing itself creates trust. Another structural factor which influences the development of trust is the number of different kinds of subject matter exchanged within the joint venture system. These may include products and services as well as information or emotional reactions. The more similar the material exchanged, the more likely it is that trust will develop. The duration of the cooperative relationship is also a significant factor in the development of both interpersonal and interorganizational trust. If companies cooperate with each other over a significant period of time, they develop shared values and norms, and these make a higher level of trust possible. Trust is also more likely to develop where there is a balance between autonomy and control.

We need to know whether and how far it is possible to set the conditions within which trust will develop, that is whether we can influence it directly. This brings us to the issue of whether trust can be "created", or whether the function of a manager consists essentially in "trust-conscious management". A German study by Bierhoff (1987) of employees within an organization gives us some indication of the conditions in which trust develops. Trust increases in proportion to:

- consistency of behavior: consistent behavior is more predictable and reliable;
- consistent keeping of promises, so that good intentions, fairness and loyalty are visible in actions;
- integrity, in the sense of recognizable honesty;
- discretion, that is trustworthiness in keeping secrets;
- open discussion of ideas and opinions;
- level of competence to perform tasks; and
- readiness to listen to ideas and opinions, that is a "willing ear".

The fact that we can identify variables which influence the development of trust might tempt us to overestimate the extent to which it can be controlled and cause us to make the unjustified assumption that it can be deliberately created. It seems more advisable in fact to aim not at "trust management", but at "trust-conscious management" of joint ventures. This would involve examining the trustworthiness of others and monitoring the reasons for trusting. This may seem to suggest that trust is "organizable"; in reality, however, it is primarily the outcome of successful sharing and cooperating. It is therefore pointless to look for instruments for managing trust in joint ventures. A much more promising approach is to examine every management activity from the point of view of trust.

This creates special challenges, because trust usually depends on the managers working in the joint venture rather than on the links between the partner companies. Furthermore, managers' ratings of existing levels of trust tend to be higher than ratings made by other employees (cf.

Butler, 1991). This suggests a possible difference between upward-directed trust and downward-directed trust. Downward-directed trust may be greater because the managers have had a hand in choosing their subordinates and the power of their positions makes them less sensitive about trust. It is probably more difficult to develop trust from a weaker position than from a stronger one, particularly when the power of stronger positions is protected by formal hierarchies. It is therefore all the more important that management should try to ensure continuity of tenure of key positions.

## BUILDING TRUST DURING NEGOTIATIONS IN AN ASIAN TRAVEL JOINT VENTURE

Kuoni Travel Holding Ltd, a key European player in business and leisure travel, and the Peninsular and Oriental Steam Navigation Company (P&O), a British multinational shipping and property group, jointly created an Asian travel joint venture. As of January 1997, Kuoni acquired a 50% equity share in P&O Travel Ltd, an Asian subsidiary of P&O. The joint venture is to trade under its present name—Key Asia Travel Group. Key Asia Travel Ltd is based in Hong Kong and also has operations in Singapore and Bangkok. The firm is one of the leading travel organizations in the region and generates an annual turnover of approximately US$90 million with a staff of 210.

The joint venture combines the local know-how of P&O Travel Ltd and Kuoni's worldwide experience in the travel business. The goal of the joint venture is that Key Asia Travel shall become a leading and well reputed wholesaler in Asia Pacific. The business focus lies in the area of tour operating as well as cruise expeditions. The joint venture intends to expand according to opportunities into China, Malaysia, Singapore, Indonesia and the Philippines.

During the negotiations, the two parties were able to build a relationship of mutual understanding. At the beginning, the parties signed a letter of intent, received information about each other's companies and initiated management meetings. This led to the establishment of a "Heads of Agreement" which was the foundation of later negotiations. Within this agreement, the maximum purchase price for the Kuoni equity share, the conditions of the purchase agreement, the assignment of management positions and exit mechanisms were specified. Once this agreement was internally reviewed within both parties' organizations, the two parties met to negotiate potential deal breakers. Once consent was reached regarding the most important issues of negotiation, a due diligence process was initiated and the business plan was finalized resulting in the signing of the agreement.

The negotiations lasted nine months, which was longer than expected. They were, however, crucial. During the negotiations, both parties were able to develop an understanding for the most important issues of the other partner. The three most important aspects during the negotiations were the trademark agreement, the appointment of management positions and the exit mechanisms. According to the agreement, the P&O trademark will be preserved and Kuoni appoints the chairman of the board of directors. In order to guarantee a long-term perspective of the joint venture, exit mechanisms were negotiated which make it mutually beneficial to uphold the joint venture in the present form. Both parties have "call options" which allow them to exit the joint venture in cases of deadlock or breach. These options are expected to help reinforce each partner's commitment to the joint venture and create a deterrent for an early exit. Within the agreement, the business plan against which the joint venture is expected to perform was laid out for three years. This business plan is reviewed on a regular basis to guarantee commitment by both partners.

According to the Chairman and Vice-Chairman of P&O Asia Travel Ltd, the time-consuming process of negotiations helped in building trust and reduced the amount of conflict which potentially emerges if crucial factors have not been discussed early on. Negotiations are frequently essential for the establishment of trust in a joint venture and help during the implementation of the business.

# COMMITMENT AS A BASIS FOR JOINT VENTURE MANAGEMENT

Founding a cooperation usually means establishing a psychological relationship between the partners. This happens through the building of commitment, which reduces opportunistic or self-seeking behavior on the part of the partners. Commitment leads partners to make short-term sacrifices in the interests of a long-term collaboration. Like trust, commitment is especially important to joint ventures, because it is part of the "input" side of the relationship, and may thus offer a way of influencing the likelihood of success.

Commitment is a subjectively experienced bond with a particular organization, situation or partner. It is expressed in appropriate actions. The action component distinguishes commitment from trust, which is simply an attitude of expectation.

The following are signs of commitment to joint ventures:

- partner companies move their best employees into the joint venture.
- partners make explicit and cost-effective decisions on providing employee training;
- development of joint venture strategies which would be of no further use if the cooperation ended;
- partners contribute special resources to the joint venture, e.g. technologies; and
- the managing director can be appointed by either partner.

Mutual commitment between two joint venture partners is reflected in values and actions which are aimed at prolonging the relationship, or which express acceptance of common or agreed goals and readiness to put resources into the venture. Commitment mostly involves temporary sacrifice, for example in terms of appointing the managing director of the joint venture. However, sacrifice has strategic significance, since it is made in expectation of future benefit.

Commitment therefore has an enduring temporal aspect. Specific behaviors must exhibit a certain constancy in order to contribute to the long-term functioning of the joint venture relationship. We shall mainly be concerned with the conditions which favor the development of commitment and the contribution which commitment can make to the success of the joint venture.

## Conditions for the development of commitment

A company is likely to show commitment only where there is an expectation of future gain. The contribution made by one's partner is also important because if it is perceived as "fair" or "equal", it increases one's own motivation to show commitment. If the pattern of investment is one-sided, it might perhaps be changed in subsequent negotiations, but these are often useless because it is too late to equalize the investments. This is typical for vertical joint ventures, where, for example, a supplier who produces specialized machinery specifically for a joint venture and contributes customer-specific know-how, has a competitive advantage in the market because he or she has a guaranteed sales outlet. However, he or she is in a weak negotiating position with regard to the joint venture, because if the venture is dissolved, his or her investments will be largely worthless. They are therefore dependent on follow-up orders from the joint venture, and thus on its continued survival.

One-sided commitment exists where investments cannot be revoked. The more specific the resources invested, the more vulnerable the investor, and therefore the higher the level of commitment that he or she puts into the business relationship. The specificity of resources can take many different forms (e.g. Williamson 1985, p. 95 ff.). One example would be if joint venture partners make agreements on location, but moves turn out later to be extremely costly or impossible. This is particularly likely to happen if the joint venture option is to be replaced by subsidiaries when the company enters a new market. Another example of a specific investment is the harmonization of interfaces, for example by setting up particular network communication systems or by coordinating logistics. Other examples include the provision of special products or services for a joint venture, or the development of knowledge specific to the business (e.g. through training events internal to the joint venture) which lose their value outside this particular cooperative relationship.

The contributions made by both sides are much more significant for the development and preservation of commitment. Interpersonal behavior and, in the case of joint ventures, intercompany behavior are based on a continuous process of give and take, in which neither side wishes to bear more of the cost than the other and each side wishes to profit from the situation as much as possible. This statement is based on two of the points which were made earlier: first, all actions within the joint venture are shaped by expectations; and second, there must be a subjective feeling of fairness and equality with regard to contribution of resources and future gain.

In the context of joint ventures, it is often impossible to ascribe commitment to particular causes and it cannot be generated in isolation. Commitment depends not only on psychological factors such as expectation and perceived equality of contribution, but also on a number of other strategic and operational variables.

## Influences on commitment

What are the other parameters which influence the development of commitment in joint ventures? A recent study of international joint ventures offers some preliminary answers to this question (cf. Anderson and Weitz, 1992; Cullen and Johnson, 1995). The factors which were studied are shown in Figure 8.3.

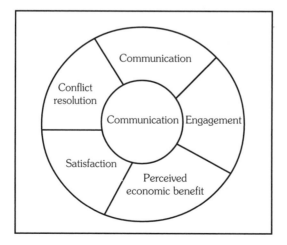

**Figure 8.3** Influences on commitment

## Conflict management and commitment

Incompatible goals, ineffective communication between the partner companies and dissatisfaction with the distribution of scarce resources lead to conflicts in intercompany relationships. Conflicts hinder the development of norms, fair exchange and the mutual trust which is necessary for a lasting relationship. Even if the venture is economically successful, the satisfaction of the partners will decrease as the level of conflict rises. Conflicts bring high economic and social costs, and thus reduce commitment. Effective management of conflict, on the other hand, fosters the development of commitment.

The wide scope for conflicts which could jeopardize commitment, and thus the success of the joint venture, makes it imperative to set up efficient and effective conflict resolution mechanisms in the joint venture. Better still, these mechanisms should be agreed at the stage of the initial contract. In the interests of both prevention and cure, management should aim to identify conflicts at the lowest possible stage of escalation and to channel them appropriately. Conflict resolution is hampered by the tendency to deal with relationship conflicts at a purely practical level, for fear of losing face. This means attempting the impossible, that is rationalizing the irrational (feelings, embarrassment) and trying to convince one's opponent by means of "logical" arguments. This approach to dealing with conflicts is a part of Western tradition, but we should not allow it to obscure the fact that the development of commitment depends heavily on harmonious relationships.

## Commitment and expressed satisfaction

General and openly expressed satisfaction with the joint venture and the partner companies is a close correlate of commitment. The level of satisfaction depends not only on economic considerations but also on factors such as opportunities to exchange technology, gain market access, transfer organizational knowledge and take part in organizational learning. Indicators of satisfaction include the quota of top managers who stay in joint ventures, a high level of willingness to contribute and a readiness to justify the joint venture to the outside world. Outward expressions of satisfaction therefore frequently correspond to internal levels of commitment. If commitment is low, one might look for dissatisfaction with the work situation, for example people not being given enough responsibility or joint venture managers not receiving enough recognition from the partner companies.

## Commitment and engagement

The complexity of control mechanisms in joint ventures is often mentioned in the literature (e.g. Geringer and Hebert, 1989). Control mechanisms such as the pattern of property relations and appointments to key positions play a decisive part in the development of commitment. It seems likely, for example, that the psychological pressure to show commitment increases with engagement in the operational functioning of the joint venture and power of decision over it. Commitment can also make it easier to rationalize earlier actions, using arguments such as: "We appoint the managers of the joint venture, so of course we have a high level of commitment here."

## Commitment and perceived economic benefit

We have already suggested that a positive perception of the cost–benefit relationship is a necessary condition for commitment. To this may be added the expectation of future benefit which the joint venture can provide. An examination of bookkeeping figures such as turnover, profit or return on investment is not enough, because future results are largely ignored. When assessing economic benefit, therefore, explicit mention should be made of probable future developments. This can result in high commitment to the joint venture even if current economic benefit is low.

## HEDGING AS A MECHANISM FOR INCREASING PARTNER COMMITMENT

The joint venture between Mazda and Ford in Thailand tried to guarantee commitment over time by defining the economic exposure of both partners in the joint venture agreement. Both benefits and risks were analyzed and proportionately distributed according to the financial participation. Since the currency in which the joint venture operates is the Thai baht, both Mazda and Ford are exposed to currency fluctuations, yet the pegging of the Thai baht to the US dollar has made Mazda more vulnerable to fluctuations than Ford. Therefore, the joint venture agreed on a hedging strategy whereby:

- half of the products will be sold in Thailand out of which 70% will be sourced locally; and
- Mazda's exposure will be covered by guaranteeing sourcing of 30% from Japan.

After the floatation of the baht, both partners were exposed to currency fluctuations. As a result, a new joint arrangement had to be negotiated.

## Commitment and open communication

Communication is important for securing mutual advantages. The more open the communication, the higher will be the level of commitment. To guarantee commitment, communication must perform four functions: the guidance function (instruction and feedback), the information function (reduction of uncertainty), the socialization function (communicating a "we-feeling") and the coordination function (harmonization, clarification of dependencies).

In summary, we can say that the development of commitment can be directly influenced by successful conflict management, satisfaction, perceived economic benefit, engagement and style of communication. The level of commitment which is believed to exist is essentially a matter of

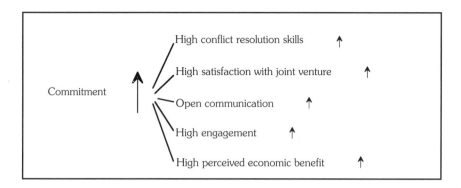

**Figure 8.4**   Conditions for high level of commitment

subjective perception. If, for example, the contribution of a partner company is no longer seen as adequate, tensions arise which might be tackled
in a variety of ways (Figure 8.4).

Based on Feldman and Arnold (1983, p. 117), there exist three groups
of reactions to differences in level of commitment, namely reactions by
the managers of the joint venture itself, reactions by the joint venture
partners and measures taken by outside groups or authorities.

If a joint venture manager believes that one of the partners is less
committed to the relationship, he or she may reduce their own company's
commitment, thus changing the cost–benefit ratio. Similarly, if a partner

Reactions of joint venture managers include:

- changing the cost–benefit ratio;
- changing the criteria for comparison;
- concentrating on advantages;
- expressing dissatisfaction openly; and
- dissolving the joint venture.

Reactions of joint venture partners include:

- complaining; and
- looking for alternative partners.

Reactions from the environment include:

- exercise of power by stakeholders; and
- social, political and economic sanctions.

**Table 8.1**   Joint venture reactions

in an otherwise fair relationship displays an even higher level of commitment, one may increase one's own commitment in proportion. Further ways of stabilizing the situation include changing the criteria for comparison (e.g. by comparing with previous joint venture partners) or re-evaluating the existing relationship by concentrating on the positive aspects of the joint venture. This means that problems and imbalances are ignored and the advantages of the cooperative venture are emphasized.

A second group of reactions to unequal commitment consists of the measures which may be adopted by the joint venture partners, for example looking for alternative partners (Table 8.1). If your joint venture partner is interested in continuing the cooperation, but he or she complains and looks around for another partner, perhaps you should take this as a hint that you need to do something about it. You might respond to the increasing costs of his or her input to the joint venture by giving a higher "reward" or attempting to reduce costs.

Finally, the environment can be a source of stabilizing mechanisms. If, for example, a joint venture was created under the influence of important external stakeholders, their position of power will be a relevant factor in its survival. There may also be other circumstances in the environment which make the dissolution of the joint venture unattractive, as happens with many politically motivated joint ventures in Asia. In addition to their economic function, they often serve to advertise national interests, so there is a certain resistance to dissolving them. If the external factors are seen as important, they may foster the development of commitment.

All the behaviors which we have described are "normal" reactions to a subjectively experienced imbalance; their aim is to achieve balanced contributions and expectations. The management of a joint venture only has two options. One is to compare the present partner with previous ones; this may shed a more favorable light on the level of commitment of the present partner. The other, better way to prolong the joint venture to the lasting satisfaction of both sides is to engage in a process of continuing discussion and rapprochement of different viewpoints. This is consistent with Hirschman's (1970) recommendation that "voice" is preferable to "exit". The only way to establish a basis for long-term commitment in a joint venture is to always be ready to discuss ("voice") rather than walk out ("exit").

## Sensemaking

| Functions of sensemaking | • generates identity and distinguishes the joint venture from the environment<br>• creates the conditions for development and learning<br>• safeguards existence by creating certainty and order |
|---|---|
| Sensemaking is easier | • if there is an accepted leading group<br>• the higher the level of cohesion<br>• the fewer the defensive routines, or the more they are dismantled<br>• the safer one's own identity<br>• the more familiar and comprehensible the situation |

## Trust

| Functions of trust | • stabilizes relationships<br>• bridges time differences<br>• permits more open exchange of information<br>• reduces complexity |
|---|---|
| Trust increases with | • consistency of behavior<br>• task-specific motivation<br>• discretion<br>• honesty<br>• length of relationship<br>• frequency and openness of communication<br>• balance between autonomy and dependence |

## Commitment

| Functions of commitment | • creates a psychological basis for a relationship between the partners<br>• reduces opportunism<br>• sets limits of tolerance<br>• supports long-term orientation of joint ventures<br>• includes readiness to commit resources to the joint venture<br>• strengthens sense of obligation |
|---|---|
| Commitment increases with | • perceived equality of contributed resources<br>• success in managing conflicts<br>• communication and expressed satisfaction<br>• property share and number of joint venture partners at director level<br>• control over decisions<br>• perceived economic benefit |

**Table 8.2** Characteristics of sensemaking, trust and commitment

# SENSEMAKING, TRUST AND COMMITMENT AS BASES FOR COOPERATION

Sense, trust and commitment are vital to the management of joint ventures. We made this statement at the beginning of the chapter, and we shall conclude with a brief summary of our arguments. We identified trust as the most important condition for cooperation, because it helps to reduce complexity in the joint venture situation and lays foundations for future action by "engagement in the here and now". Measures can be taken at both personal and structural levels to promote trust and they help to transform a diffuse atmosphere of trust into a controlled, if not fully controllable, relationship. Commitment is another basic factor; it exists if both partners contribute material resources and ideas, and is thus a major influence on the success of the joint venture. The conditions which encourage commitment can be influenced by the managers of the joint venture, by the joint venture partners and by environmental factors. Sensemaking, with which we began our discussion, is responsible for the existence of joint ventures and it affects all levels, processes and areas of joint venture management activity.

We offer a summary of the main functions of sense, trust and commitment, and the main influences on their development. Table 8.2 is intended as an aid to reflection, not an all-purpose "how-to-do" checklist.

---

### Questions to address

- How can the participants work together to master unfamiliar situations?
- How do the partners make sense of the new situation?
- Can the partner be trusted?
- What factors hinder the establishment of a relationship based on trust?
- How can trust be shown?
- What is the level of the partner's commitment?
- Is the relationship characterized by open exchange of information?

- What level of readiness is there to put more resources into the joint venture?
- Are the partners' contributions to the joint venture economically and symbolically equal?
- How can existing shortcomings in trust and commitment be tackled?

# CHAPTER NINE

# MEASURING SUCCESS IN THE JOINT VENTURE SYSTEM

Success and failure are vital issues for joint ventures. Measurement of success is essential, perhaps even more so than in the case of other forms of enterprise. There are various reasons for this, first, the fact that the joint venture is part of a cooperative arrangement with different partners, and second, that it usually exists as a kind of project. The partner companies need to make joint analyses of the success of the venture because they usually have different expectations, and if only one partner is dissatisfied, this can threaten the existence of the whole arrangement.

In this chapter, we shall consider the different viewpoints from which success can be evaluated, and the different levels in the joint venture system at which it can be measured. Measurement of success is important not only for the purpose of evaluating the business results; it is also essential from the management point of view, because without it, there is no feedback on which to base adjustment or to correct previous decisions.

Although a great deal has been written about success and failure, the question of how to recognize them has hardly received any attention at all. How do we decide whether a joint venture is succeeding or failing? What criteria can we use? Our discussion will shed light on the following questions:

- What criteria are appropriate for assessing the success or failure of joint ventures?
- What does success mean at different levels in the joint venture system and does it mean different things to different people?
- How can success be judged in practice and what are the problems?
- How might we judge the success of the whole joint venture system?

Success is often regarded as an absolute, as something which either is or isn't. In fact, success and failure are relative matters and can only be evaluated according to specific criteria and measures. Something which seems successful from one point of view often looks like a failure from another.

If two partner companies use different measures to evaluate their joint venture, they may reach totally different conclusions. The fact that one partner considers the venture successful is no guarantee that the other partner will also be satisfied with it. If, for example, one of the partner companies hopes that the venture will build up its potential for long-term success, while the other wants to make better use of its production facilities during a recession, the difference will certainly show up when the time arrives to judge the success of the joint venture, even if it has not done so before. Evaluations also tend to differ depending on whether they are made by the partners or by the managers of the joint venture itself. It is often the case that a joint venture appears successful in its own right, but the partners are not satisfied with it.

## SUCCESS MEASUREMENT IN EHPT

When the EHPT joint venture was created, the partners developed a business plan in which they set out their objectives for the new company. This plan contained not only the financial objectives (desired market share, turnover, margin), but also qualitative aims, for example "to be the no.1 quality supplier of applications and services for networks and service management systems to operators of multivendor telecom networks".

The business plan covered eight areas:

- EHPT goals;
- strategic objectives of the joint venture;
- customers, markets and sales channels;
- competition;
- products, services and research and development planning;
- finance;
- potential problems; and

- operational planning for the first year.

The success of the joint venture was to be measured in relation to each area.

The two partners also had other goals which they were pursuing though the joint venture. These were not put in writing and only emerged as time went by. Various hidden agendas came to light, especially during periods when one of the partners was dissatisfied with the joint venture. A major difficulty which hampered success measurement was the fact that written criteria existed only for a part of the joint venture's activities.

The diversity and the relative nature of the various possible success criteria derive from two factors. First, there are many different kinds of success, for example economic or strategic. Second, the level of analysis is important, especially when judging success in joint venture systems. Different criteria are used depending on whether success is being judged by the management of the joint venture or by one of the joint venture partners. In more general terms, we can say that measurement of success in the joint venture system is characterized by multiple dependencies: different concepts of success are relevant depending on the viewpoint of the observer, the chosen level of analysis and the particular questions to which answers are being sought. For these reasons alone, every company should try to define its concepts of success and failure ever more closely. It must decide which interests and objectives should be taken into account, what time-scale applies (long- or short-term), and at what level the assessment is to be made.

There are obviously many different dimensions which can be used to measure the success or failure of joint ventures and joint venture systems. The first distinction to be made is that between the various levels of analysis. It makes a great deal of difference whether the joint venture is regarded as a single unit, that is as an independent company, or from the point of view of one of the partners. In the second case, the emphasis is on the goals of the partner company, whereas in the first case, the objectives and functioning of the joint venture itself are more important. The time-scale is also relevant. Different measures are appropriate depending on whether the cooperative relationship is intended as a short- or a long-term arrangement, for example whether the aim is to make more use of production capacity, acquire know-how or build up competitive advantages. There are also different ways of realizing objectives, for example of increasing the number of new products, and these have different implications over time. The number of new products might be increased quickly by buying patents and market-ready developments, but measures such as these might not have lasting effects. Alternatively, the same goal might be reached by increasing the innovative power of the company's own research and development department; this would take some time to achieve, but the effects would be substantial and lasting.

These introductory remarks are intended to show that there is no single valid concept of success which we can apply either to companies in general or joint ventures in particular. On the contrary, success can be measured in terms of many different dimensions. The practical issue is, what to measure in any given situation. The variety of possible definitions of success, and their relative nature, can lead to grave misunderstandings if the basis for making success judgments in a particular case is not specified clearly and in detail.

## DIFFERENT CONCEPTS OF SUCCESS IN THE JOINT VENTURE SYSTEM

People often try to apply the same measures of success to joint ventures as they would use for traditional organizations. This is understandable: they fall back on methods which they have used previously because they are familiar with them and know how to evaluate the results. However, traditional measures are often one-sided financial criteria such as profit, productivity, turnover or other short-term criteria which relate to the past. These statistics are admittedly relatively easy to determine and to compare, but they do not provide an adequate basis on which to evaluate a joint venture; indeed, they cover only a small part of what is needed for a comprehensive assessment of the joint venture system. A full assessment must take into account a variety of aspects, which we shall try to identify in the rest of this chapter. First, however, we shall describe the special problems involved and the different viewpoints on measuring success in the joint venture system. We shall then consider the different levels of assessment.

## Problems of success measurement in the joint venture system

There are three factors which make it difficult to judge the success of joint ventures (cf. Baird, Lyles and Reger, 1993). The first obstacle is the co-operative context. A cooperative venture involves different levels, different partners and complex often contradictory interests, to a much greater extent than in a single company. The assessment of success in a joint venture system must always take into account the interests of the various partners, so the popular notion that success can be measured without regard for particular interests is not sustainable. Second, the objectives for the joint venture are often not defined clearly enough, and where this is the case, it will obviously be difficult to decide whether they have been met. Third, many joint ventures face especially high levels of uncertainty with regard to technologies, products or markets. This further reduces the meaning and validity of short-term, quantitative indices of success and puts obstacles in the way of a traditional success measurement based on stable company performance. From the point of view of the partners, joint ventures are often an option for carrying out basic research and gaining market access, that is they are a strategy or instrument for keeping certain possibilities open and reducing the risk of missing important market or technological developments.

The cooperative context, the large number of forms which joint ventures may take and the variety of reasons for creating them are all factors which make it extremely difficult to create general success measures for joint ventures. It is not simply a question of choosing the "correct" success criteria and the best dimensions to measure; the different angles from which success can be viewed and the different levels of analysis must also be taken into account.

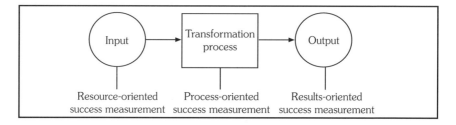

**Figure 9.1**   Theoretical approaches for measuring success

## Theoretical and practical perspectives on success measurement

In the literature, we find several different approaches to assessing the success or failure of an organization. Daft (1992) describes three major approaches, according to which success is measured by results, processes or the ability of an organization to acquire certain scarce resources (Figure 9.1).

More recent approaches extend this by including different interests and linking them together (stakeholder concepts) (e.g. Connolly, Conlon and Deutsch, 1980; Tusi, 1990). They also focus on the extent to which the success measures used in an organization are an expression of its basic values, or are linked to the particular type of company or to particular stages in its life-cycle (e.g. Quinn and Rohrbaugh, 1983).

### Results-oriented success measurement

This measurement is based on output dimensions, that is on dimensions related to the goals of the transformation process. The success of a joint venture is measured in terms of whether, or how far, certain objectives are met. The most important of these are usually profitability, growth and market share, but other aims are also significant, for example quality objectives, number of new products, research findings, stability and satisfaction. Since there are usually different and competing interests and aims in joint ventures, the practical question here, as in other approaches to success measurement, is how to negotiate which goals will be used in the evaluation and how they will be measured.

## *Process-oriented success measurement*

This measurement is based not on specified output goals, but on an evaluation of the company's internal transformation processes. There are two distinct approaches. The first focuses on internal economic efficiency, that is the relationship between resources and output. According to the second, a company is successful if, for example it has a strong culture and a positive company "climate", if loyalty and team spirit prevail and there is a high level of trust between employees and management.

The output and process dimensions are usually closely related. It is often the particular characteristics and strengths of the transformation processes which enable a company to be successful in terms of results. In practice, however, the qualitative aspects of internal company processes have rarely been taken into account.

## *Resource-oriented success measurement*

This measurement is based on the company's ability to obtain scarce resources from the environment. This approach is used primarily when output is difficult to define and evaluate. A classic example is a research cooperation, which is generally considered successful if it is equipped to an above-average standard. Other resource-oriented criteria include the number of well-known and respected professors in a university, the number of internal applications which a department receives, or the negotiating power which a company has *vis-a-vis* its suppliers.

## *Multidimensional success measurement*

Multidimensional approaches attempt to do justice to the multiplicity of interests and objectives which exist in business contexts, and to include the different levels of company performance by considering resources, processes and results. This is a realistic way to approach a company as a system of plural interests, but the end result is often less meaningful. An advantage of multidimensional approaches is that they reveal more clearly the contradictions and goal conflicts in joint ventures and therefore provide a good basis for a comprehensive assessment.

If we examine more closely the variety of methods which are used to measure the success of joint ventures, we can distinguish a number of different content-oriented approaches. The traditional methods of evaluating the success of cooperative ventures are all based on economic, strategic or behavioral perspectives (cf. Probst and Büchel, 1994). Today, we can add another approach, namely the learning perspective.

## The economic perspective

Economic approaches are in principle output-oriented; their purpose is to decide whether the cooperative venture is increasing the value of the partner companies. The economic approach to success judgments is based on the theory of financial and capital markets and involves examining variables such as return on invested capital, net yearly profit and the development of free cash flows. The factors which underlie the economic results, and the ways in which the results are achieved, are of lesser importance from this point of view. The essential criterion for evaluating a joint venture is whether better results might have been obtained from alternative forms of investment. Typical criteria for economic assessment include decrease in unit costs through better use of production capacity (degression of fixed overheads) or increase in turnover as a result of a sales cooperation in a growing market. Economic success indicators are often retrospective and they are usually quantitative in nature.

## The strategic perspective

From the strategic point of view, the important criteria are company size, product-market combinations, market share, competitive position, advantages based on research results and a strong position on the distribution and procurement markets. A further criterion is the extent to which the cooperation yields synergies between the partners or between the joint venture and one of the partners. The economic approach, described above, is based on the assumption that the financial results of the joint venture are of primary importance to the partners, and that the capital market can be used as an "objective" measure of the profitability of invested capital. The strategic approach, however, places greater emphasis on core competencies and on the strategic focus which each company has adopted or wishes to develop.

The joint venture is judged essentially according to its contribution in these areas. Like the economic perspective, the strategic perspective is primarily output-oriented; the differences are that from the strategic point of view, the "output" of the joint venture is defined differently; the orientation is me-dium- to long-term; and there is a clearer emphasis from the beginning on the significance of the joint venture for the competitive position of a partner company. Typical criteria are the safeguarding of particular resources, ac-cess to a new kind of technology, or increasing the company's competitive strength by using the special know-how of a partner. Strategic indicators are always forward-looking and are usually difficult to quantify.

## The behavioral perspective

The emphasis here is on the behavior of the participants in their cooperative relationship. Essential success indicators include the development of a separate culture and identity, the ability to deal with conflicts and continued survival versus premature dissolution of the joint venture. Other aspects which are taken into account are the factors which trigger crises and conflicts, and indications of the presence in the joint venture system of the three basic factors discussed in Chapter 8, namely trust, commitment and sensemaking. Whereas the economic and strategic perspectives are primarily output-oriented, the behavioral perspective is concerned with the processes within the joint venture system. Examples of behavior-oriented measures are the cultural compatibility of the partner companies, the frequency and intensity of conflicts, and mechanisms for making decisions and resolving conflicts within the cooperation. Some of the dimensions are quantifiable, but most behavioral indicators can only be assessed in qualitative terms.

In company practice, combined standards are often applied and they are discussed in some of the literature on success measurement in joint venture systems (Baird, Lyles and Reger, 1983; Probst and Büchel, 1994). The idea is simple: the larger the number of techniques used, the more comprehensive the resulting picture. On the whole, this is a valid argument, but it leaves out two important points. First, the different approaches are not mutually independent, as the simple expedient of grouping them might suggest. Output, for example, always depends in some way on processes within the joint venture system. Processes and results always determine each other. A complete and comprehensive evaluation of success must therefore take into account the interdependencies between the different perspectives.

Using different measures together gives rise to a second, more serious problem, and one which is by no means rare in company practice. We have already stated that the dimensions which are used in different approaches vary in specificity and quantifiability, and in the ease with which the information can be obtained and aggregated. In these circumstances, there is a temptation to place increasing reliance on the indicators which are easiest to measure. This typically leads to a situation in which retrospective, short-term economic measures prevail. It is therefore important to have a framework within which the different approaches can be clearly related to each other, so that none of them are lost.

## Learning as an additional perspective on success

Taken together, the traditional approaches allow us to make relatively comprehensive assessments of the success or failure of cooperative ventures. However, they omit an aspect in which both company managers and business theoreticians are now showing an increasing interest (Helleloid and Simonin, 1993; Probst and Büchel, 1994). This is the concept of learning. We shall offer only a brief outline here of how joint venture systems might be analyzed and assessed from the learning angle, since Chapter 10 contains a detailed treatment of this issue.

If we take learning into account, indicators such as an increase in market share or the premature ending of a cooperation are not the only ways to judge success or failure. Much more important are factors such as whether a company consistently reviews its own weaknesses and strengths and its prevailing patterns of activity, whether it acquires "implicit knowledge", and whether it increases its ability to learn; these are also genuine forms of progress which companies can make through cooperative arrangements. From the learning angle, the criterion of success is an ability to institute successful learning processes, thereby building up lasting key competencies.

When we formulate objectives and the ways in which they are to be met, learning is always implied; the traditional approach, however, does not emphasize it. This is the first difference between the traditional approach to success and a learning approach. The learning perspective focuses awareness on the learning processes which lead to the achievement of traditional goals. It does not exclude traditional approaches or render them superfluous. It simply involves a shift of attention from results and behaviors per se to conscious reflection on the creation of knowledge.

The learning perspective also allows completely new goals to be set for cooperations, of a kind which could not be formulated from a traditional point of view. "Learning goals" such as acquiring knowledge or increasing the ability to resolve conflicts are not part of the traditional approach and can only play a part in success measurement if a learning approach is adopted.

The learning view of success and failure is at present in its infancy. Initial approaches are based on examining the extent to which the general conditions for learning, such as communication, transparency and integration, are present in the cooperative relationship. Second, they involve considering how far the strategy, structure, culture and human resource policies support or hinder learning processes (cf. Prange, Probst and Rüling, 1996; Probst and Büchel, 1997). The learning perspective combines a results-oriented approach with a process approach, since it takes into account on the one hand the acquisition of knowledge and the attainment of learning goals, and on the other, the learning processes which support these ends. Indicators of learning are largely qualitative in nature. There are as yet no comprehensive methods for evaluating "learning success" in cooperations.

Table 9.1 contains an overview of the different approaches to success measurement.

## MEASURING SUCCESS AT DIFFERENT LEVELS

Distinguishing between the different levels at which success or failure can be determined is a useful first step towards developing a practical assessment procedure. We shall therefore describe success judgments as made by the management of the joint venture and as made by the partner companies; then we shall consider how the success of the joint venture system as a whole might be evaluated (Figure 9.2).

| Types of success perspective | Examples of main variables | Focus | Time scale | Indicators |
|---|---|---|---|---|
| Economic perspective | ROI, cash flows | Results/output | Short-term, essentially retrospective | Quantitative indicators |
| Strategic perspective | Competitive position, market power | Results/output, possibly resources | Long-term, forward-looking | Qualitative and quantitative indicators |
| Behavioral perspective | Identity, stability, decision making, conflict management | Processes | Medium-term, present- and future-oriented | Qualitative indicators |
| Learning perspective | Knowledge, learning processes, problem solving potential | Results/outputs and processes | Medium- to long-term, forward-looking | Qualitative indicators |

**Table 9.1**   Approaches to success judgments in joint venture systems

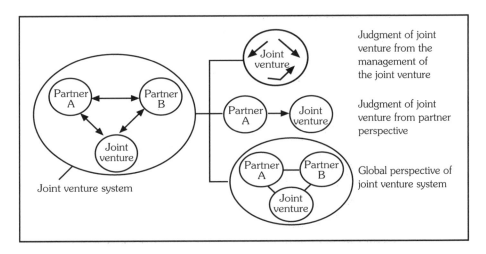

**Figure 9.2**   Levels of success measurement in the joint venture system

## Assessing the joint venture

Deciding whether something is a success or a failure is a management problem which follows implementation. There are three main questions to which the managers of a joint venture need to find answers. First, they must consider how far the joint venture fulfills the objectives of the partners. Second, they must consider the joint venture as an independent company and assess how well it is being managed as a separate enterprise. This is especially important when a joint venture is setting up its own market relationships and entering into direct competition with independent companies. Third, they must evaluate the internal processes of the joint venture, to see whether the company "works", that is how far existing structures and processes result in smooth functioning and how conflicts are solved. In other words, they must examine the important mechanisms for making decisions.

### Assessment according to the joint venture objectives

The first question looks simple: are the set objectives being met or not? In practice, however, it is often as difficult to decide whether objectives have been met as it was to meet them in the first place. Joint ventures often have objectives which are not clearly formulated or which require further interpretation.

The objectives must be defined and recorded as clearly as possible, otherwise the joint venture cannot be judged by its results. This brings us back to the old dilemma: on the one hand, the objectives should be as precise and specific as possible; on the other, the independent company should be allowed room to maneuver to enable it to make the best use of its independence. As was the case with strategy development in the joint venture system, it is important to formulate specific goals, but they should then be discussed regularly at all levels, so that they can be adjusted if necessary. Nevertheless, there will still be serious difficulties in judging success on the basis of goal attainment. The following reasons are frequently mentioned:

- the success judgment is in principle retrospective, that is it is based on whether or to what extent a particular existing objective has been met;

- the partners often set different objectives, which makes it difficult for the joint venture to arrive at a clear formulation of its own goals; and
- a success judgment of this kind is based on only a relatively small part of the content of the joint venture, namely, its specified objectives.

For the joint venture managers to make a reliable assessment, they need to do more than consider the extent to which particular objectives have been met. They must also examine the joint venture as an independent company.

## Assessing the joint venture as a "stand-alone"

It is particularly important to assess the joint venture as a separate unit, because autonomy is a significant feature of this particular form of cooperation. In other words, the joint venture differs from other forms of cooperation precisely in that it involves the creation of an independent unit. A joint venture should therefore be judged as though it were an autonomous company. The reasons why the partners decided on a cooperative venture are not important in this context. Economic and strategic aspects may be included, but the results which the joint venture produces are evaluated according to more general principles and criteria.

Another aspect of this is that joint venture managers should be assessed on their performance as company leaders. If they recognize and take advantage of opportunities, systematically reduce costs, etc., this suggests that the joint venture is being well run as an enterprise in its own right.

The practical issue is to decide which dimensions to use for making assessments. Unlike the criteria for assessment by goal attainment, the criteria for assessing the joint venture as an independent company cannot be derived from the business plan. The problem is often solved by choosing various economic and strategic criteria which permit comparison of the joint venture with other similarly positioned joint ventures, or with other alternatives on the financial and capital markets which carry a similar degree of risk.

## Decision-making and conflict management in the joint venture

Managing joint ventures means steering a course between the demands and objectives of the partners and the task of running the joint venture as an independent unit. As we have already seen in the context of strategy development, there can be a good deal of conflict between the goals which the partners pursue on their own account, their common objectives for the joint venture, and the specific strategies and goals that the management of the joint venture develops for itself.

These conflicts are inherent in the nature of joint ventures and need not be viewed in an entirely negative light. Indeed, the tensions between the different levels in the system and the different objectives of its members can lead to repeated discussion of particular issues, and this may result in adjustments which take into account relevant changes in environmental conditions or in the expectations of different parties. Decision making processes and mechanisms for resolving conflicts are therefore of great significance in the joint venture. They should be carefully assessed for the extent to which they can accommodate the multiplicity of interests in the joint venture system and contribute to resolving potential conflicts.

If joint venture managers examine the procedures for making decisions and solving conflicts, they may find important clues to potential problems. They will see whether they need to introduce new decision making or conflict resolving procedures, or whether existing ones need adapting. The precise form which these procedures takes depends very much on the circumstances of the individual joint venture.

Assessments of success at joint venture level should be carried out in three stages (Figure 9.3). First, the joint venture should be evaluated in relation to its given objectives. The objectives reveal the extent to which the joint venture is dependent on the partner companies. In the second stage, the joint venture should be considered as an independent unit. This highlights its special characteristic, namely, its autonomy within the joint venture system. In the third stage, the joint venture's mechanisms for making decisions and dealing with conflicts are examined; it is important to consider whether definite rules and procedures exist for these vital processes, and if so, whether they conflict with basic structural rules.

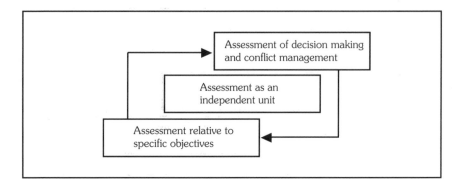

**Figure 9.3**   Stages in assessment of the joint venture

## Assessing the joint venture from the partners' viewpoint

At this level, success is evaluated according to the contribution which the joint venture makes to the success of a partner company. The view taken by each partner is especially significant to the joint venture because it is this which ultimately determines whether or not a partner wishes to prolong an existing cooperation. This is not a matter of how the internal processes of the joint venture work, or how they might be improved. The only deciding factor is whether the results of the joint venture correspond to the expectations of a partner company and whether the venture is therefore strategically meaningful to that company. An assessment of management processes within the joint venture has little significance for the partners. More important are the economic and strategic perspectives; these are based on different dimensions and geared to different time-scales, but they are essentially results-oriented.

It often happens that even though a joint venture appears successful in itself, at least one of the partner companies is dissatisfied, as was the case with EHPT. This is an important reason for assessing the joint venture from the points of view of the partners.

## ASSESSMENT OF EHPT FROM DIFFERENT VIEWPOINTS

By the end of the first year, there were clear differences between the various assessments of the joint venture. EHPT had met all the financial objectives set down in the business plan, but the partners were not equally satisfied with it.

EHPT was supplying Ericsson with the technological platform which it needed. Since the new company was profitable, and was manufacturing products of the desired quality, Ericsson judged it to be successful. From the point of view of HP, however, it was less so. CAP, the product which HP had acquired for the joint venture, was not taken over internally and the initial plan to develop a joint product based on CAP was not carried out. EHPT more or less owned the product, although HP had the rights to it. The HP employees did not identify with the product. Furthermore, HP achieved success with a network management product of its own and this threw further doubt on the joint development through EHPT of a competing product. Ericsson preferred the joint product, while HP favored further development of its own product. HP's expectations in relation to CAP had already been disappointing and Ericsson was skeptical about the HP product. There was thus a danger that HP would withdraw from the joint venture.

A situation of this kind, as outlined in the above case study, typically arises when a joint venture is economically successful, well managed and effective in the market in its own right, but its financial results do not help the partners to reach their strategic goals.

The first step in assessing a joint venture from the point of view of a partner company is to evaluate its performance against the objectives with which the partner entered the cooperation. The assessment is thus made according to the demands which one partner places upon the joint venture. The second step is to look for more general benefits which the joint venture brings to that partner; it may make additional contributions or offer benefits which the partner had not foreseen and therefore could not expect. This broader view of the joint venture's contribution to the success of the partner company stimulates a process of reflection which can reveal unforeseen advantages and disadvantages and which may cause existing objectives to be questioned or supplemented.

The practical side of making an assessment from the partner angle can be problematic. The partners often fail to provide clear definitions of the goals with which they entered the cooperation and which could be used to evaluate success. It is often not even clear who is responsible for specifying these goals. Even within the partner companies, there are often goal conflicts which make it difficult to say exactly what the company's interests or objectives are.

To assess a joint venture from the partners' viewpoint:

- develop an internal list of the partners' requirements *vis-a-vis* the joint venture;
- use this as a basis to determine their concrete objectives, specifying the form and time-scale of each;
- use the list of objectives as a basis for the first step in evaluating success from the partners' viewpoints; and
- check the list at regular intervals.

Our previous distinction between economic, strategic, behavioral and learning perspectives on success can also be made from the partners' point of view. We shall now examine briefly the contributions which the joint venture might make to success in these areas, and how its contributions might be assessed. We believe that the different ways of judging success should not be considered separately, but treated as part of an overall picture.

## Different views of success taken by joint venture partners

From an economic viewpoint, the joint venture contributes to the financial success of the partner company through distribution of profits, dividends or products manufactured jointly by a partner company and the joint venture. When making success judgments, the returns from the joint venture should be set against the expenditure incurred by the partner. Equally significant are the profitability figures, which allow the partner company to compare the return on the capital invested in the joint venture with alternative investment opportunities or projects. In addition to the figures for a particular period, the contribution made by the cooperation to increasing the value of the partner company should be examined.

From the strategic viewpoint, the important factor is the joint venture's role in improving the partner's competitive position and strength. There are many ways in which competitive position can be improved; examples include products, markets, additional outputs, business organization, costs of production and materials, brand image and technology. In our experience, there is a strong temptation to include in "strategic benefit" anything which cannot be described, measured or explained in other ways. It is important, therefore, to show exactly why a particular contribution should be regarded as strategic. If possible, the improvement in competitive position should be clearly described. There are a range of aids and methods for analyzing competitive position and these are widely used in company practice. They include instruments such as portfolio analysis, industry analysis, etc.

The joint venture is also important to the partners from a learning viewpoint. A picture of the benefits which a joint venture brings to a partner company is not complete without the opportunities which the new unit offers for acquiring knowledge.

We can only make a proper evaluation of the joint venture's total contribution if we combine all three viewpoints. The assessment will be distorted if we limit ourselves to economics, or if we concentrate on strategy while ignoring short-term economic factors. This does not mean, of course, that we cannot choose to apply a particular emphasis. However, we would suggest that where a certain emphasis is chosen, the assessment should always be supplemented by discussing the contributions made by the joint venture in other areas.

## Success and failure in the joint venture system

Neither company managers nor academics have paid much attention as yet to the need for an overall evaluation of the entire joint venture system. When we discussed the evaluation of success from the partners' viewpoint, we considered the value of the joint venture to individual partners. Here, we are concerned with the balance and potential for development of the whole cooperative structure. This takes us beyond the internal processes of the joint venture and what the partners think of it.

There are obvious reasons for considering the success of a joint venture at the level of the whole system. Joint ventures are a form of collaboration between companies which go beyond relationships mediated entirely by the market. Companies which interact in the market are parties in exchange, and in extreme cases, their involvement may be limited to one transaction. In joint ventures, however, the relationships between the companies go much further. In any form of cooperation, a vital factor is the ability of the participants to create a win–win situation in which everyone can be satisfied. Other important factors are the extent to which the joint venture system succeeds in developing its own identity and the cultural integration of the different partners.

Over and above the objectives of the partner companies, there is also a kind of ideal image of the whole cooperative system. As time passes, the system may move closer to this ideal. Various principles derive from the concept of a superordinate ideal:

- The different objectives of the partner companies can be examined and harmonized in the light of the overall goals of the system. The argument here is that the system as a whole has a purpose which provides a superordinate source of stability and harmony in the joint venture system, and can serve as a guideline for the individual companies. An ideal state of cooperation can hardly be expected to develop in the first few months, but all parties should ask themselves from time to time whether the strategies which they are pursuing individually in relation to the joint venture are helping or hindering the development of the factors which are basic to any cooperative venture, that is trust, commitment and sensemaking.
- The shared process of building and exploiting synergies is a vital factor. For the health of the whole system, it is important to create win–win situations in many areas, so that one partner does not profit at the expense of the others.
- Attainment of goals by individual companies does not necessarily lead to the success of the whole system. However, the whole system must be successful if the individual companies are to go on cooperating

successfully. The cooperation can only survive over a long period if success and failure are discussed in terms of the whole system. Individual partners can certainly profit at the expense of the others for a limited period, but in the medium term, this kind of behavior threatens the cooperation and leads either to its dissolution or to a decrease in the commitment of the other partners.

- Since there is no authority which supervises the whole system, each participant must be in a position to understand the system and to take account of different viewpoints. An understanding of the whole system is important for its development. Steps must therefore be taken to ensure that anyone is in a position to see his or her own decisions and observations from the point of view of the whole.

## MULTIDIMENSIONAL APPROACHES TO SUCCESS MEASUREMENT

We shall now bring together the different levels at which success judgments can be made. We have already shown the inadequacy of picking out individual levels or viewpoints when trying to form a complete picture of the success of a cooperation. On the other hand, it is neither feasible nor meaningful to work systematically through all possible levels and viewpoints. We need to gather as much information as possible, but we also need a practicable method for routine use in joint ventures. We shall therefore try to offer some practical suggestions on how to measure success.

### Requirements for methods of measuring success in joint venture systems

The requirements which a method of measuring success in joint venture systems must satisfy are easily described: the measurement must be comprehensive in content, practicable and adaptable (Figure 9.4).

Success judgments should take account of input, output and process dimensions. The aim is to obtain a comprehensive picture of the

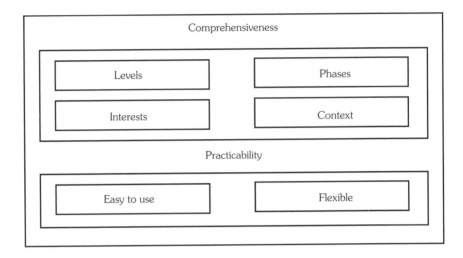

**Figure 9.4**   Requirements for methods of success measurement in joint venture systems

transformation process, together with the relationships between the joint venture, the partner companies and the environment of the whole system. "Comprehensive content" means primarily that the assessment should cover different levels, stages, interests and contexts.

From the practical angle, ease of use and adaptability are particularly important. No matter how ingenious the method, it is useless if it is impracticable. The chosen success indicators must also be reconsidered from time to time in relation to all the criteria we have suggested and changed if necessary. There must be a process of repeated analysis if people are to learn how to make better success judgments. It is precisely because measures of success are not absolute and immutable, but vary with different interests and contexts, that they must be re-examined periodically. As time passes, a company gains experience with different methods of success measurement, and the advantages and disadvantages of various measures are discussed. The company is then able to develop its own assessment system, suited to its own circumstances.

It should always be remembered that a success judgment is an interpretation made by people. An assessment should therefore never be made by a single external agent, but should be developed jointly and discussed by the different parties in the joint venture system. The assessment should always be more than a simple "marking" process. Its aim is to give the various parties an opportunity to obtain feedback on their own behavior and to make improvements in consequence.

The full list of requirements will only be met in exceptional cases. However, the following questions should be answered in every assessment:

- At what level is success being judged?
- What is the current stage of development of the joint venture system, and what is its environment?
- What interests will the judgment take into account?
- Are the terms and variables clearly defined, and will the indicators used really yield the desired information?
- How well can this method of measurement be used in practice?
- How can we make sure that the method of evaluation is constantly re-negotiated and re-analyzed?

## Situational choice of evaluation criteria

We shall now turn to the literature and describe a theoretical approach to choosing measures of success for use in a specific situation. This approach was developed by Anderson (1990) as a result of a survey. The various success measures are distinguished not according to different views of success, that is economic, strategic, behavioral or learning; here, the distinction is made according to whether they measure input or output variables (Figure 9.5). As we have shown, success can be measured at different points in the transformation process, for example using short-term output variables such as profit and cash flow, or longer term variables such as innovation or safeguarding resources.

Either input or output variables may be more suitable for evaluating success, depending on the function of the joint venture, its type or situation. This approach is not based on a particular definition of success; instead, variables are chosen because they are the most meaningful in the circumstances.

For purposes of success measurement, the current situation in the joint venture can be described in terms of two dimensions: first, the transparency of the production process, that is knowledge of how certain input

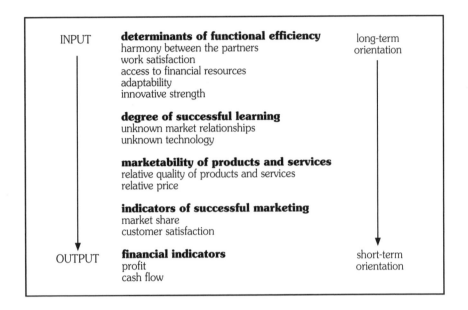

**Figure 9.5**   Criteria of joint venture success along an input-output continuum
Source: Based on Anderson, E. (1990) Two Firms, One Frontier: On Assessing Joint
Venture Performance, In: *Sloan Management Review*, Winter, pp. 19–30

factors result in a particular output; second, the completeness and exactness with which the outputs of the joint venture can be determined. These two dimensions are independent of each other, for example there are situations in which the outputs can be measured, but it is not clear how particular input factors contributed to them. In other situations, the outputs can be measured, and it is also clear how they were produced.

The different kinds of situation can be shown in a matrix which in principle can be used to find a suitable success criterion for any set of circumstances (Figure 9.6). The basic concept is simple: the more difficult it is to give an exact and complete description of output criteria, the more important it is to consider input variables. This might well be the case in research and development (R&D) joint ventures, or ventures created to explore new business areas or acquire knowledge. When on the other hand the output variables can be clearly measured, but the person making the assessment is not sure how the input variables contribute to their production, then success should be judged mainly on the basis of output variables.

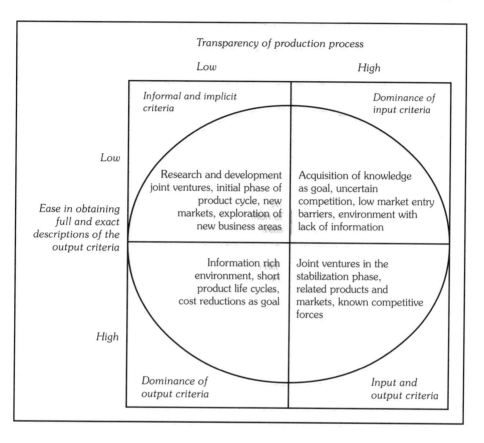

**Figure 9.6** Joint venture assessment criteria
Source: Adapted from Anderson, E. (1990) Two Firms, One Frontier: On Assessing
Joint Venture Performance, In: *Sloan Management Review*, Winter, pp. 19–30

The practical advantages of this matrix model are obvious. For every
joint venture or every success evaluation, it should, ideally, be possible to
use the matrix to derive appropriate assessment criteria. However, in the
light of our discussion of the requirements to be met by methods of measuring success in the joint venture system, the procedure of choosing criteria to
suit the situation is open to criticism. The greatest danger is that if situational
criteria are chosen, the approach will not reflect the complexity of the joint
venture system. Important input variables will only be included if there are
no output data available, or, vice versa, output data will always be preferred
if they are on hand.

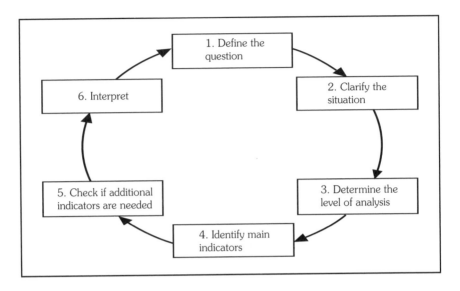

**Figure 9.7**   Six steps in evaluating joint venture success

## Process of success evaluation

We shall now present a simple diagram as an aid to making success judgments. A success evaluation is an attempt to answer a specific question; the quality of the answer may vary, that is it may or may not be complete, and the dimensions on which it is based may or may not be relevant. When evaluating the success of a joint venture system, sufficient attention should be paid to clarifying the question, analyzing the situation in which the judgment is to be made, determining the most important viewpoints and levels of analysis, and discussing additional success indicators at other levels. Every method of evaluating success must be comprehensive in content and easy to use. To ensure that these requirements are met as far as possible, we suggest following the six steps shown in Figure 9.7.

The first step is to define the question which the success evaluation has to answer; this clarifies what it is that needs to be measured. In the second step, the current position of the joint venture must be analyzed. Important factors include the nature of the joint venture, the current stage of development of the cooperation and the environment in which it exists. The third step is to decide on the level of analysis and the fourth is to define the success indicators to be used at this level. The fifth step involves examining the relationship between the success indicators at the main level and additional success indicators at other levels; this extends the range of indicators. In the sixth step, the individual criteria are applied, interpreted and documented.

At each stage, there are a number of important questions which should be asked.

## 1. Defining the question

What is the issue? What are the limits of the area to be assessed? For whom is the success evaluation being made? What is its purpose? What information is needed, and what answers must be given if the judgment is to fulfill its purpose?

## 2. Analyzing the situation in which the evaluation is to be made

What is the structure of the joint venture system? What is the relationship between the partners in respect of the aspect of the joint venture to be assessed? Where does the joint venture stand in relation to the value-added chains of the partners? What is the strategic mission of the joint venture? What are the strategic aims of each partner in the cooperation? How does the joint venture stand in relation to its procurement and sales markets? What level of integration is there between the partners in the cooperation? At what points in the cooperative structure do conflicts arise?

## 3. Choosing the main level of analysis

Is the joint venture to be judged as an independent unit, or from the partners' viewpoint? Should the whole joint venture system be included? Where should the emphasis of the evaluation lie? What are the critical aspects?

## 4. Choosing relevant success indicators at the main level of analysis

What is meant by success in this context? What definition of success (economic, strategic, behavioral, learning) will best serve the purpose of the evaluation?

## 5. Choosing additional success indicators

What contribution can the other definitions of success make? Are there aspects which might have been overlooked? What kind of evaluation would be obtained if different criteria (e.g. learning) were used? How do the events to be evaluated look at a different level? What would the evaluation be like if the position of the other partner, the newly created company, or the whole system were included?

## 6. Interpretation and documentation

How can the individual success indicators be determined and measured? What do the results really tell us? What conclusions can we draw from combinations of different criteria? Are the results obtained at different levels or from different viewpoints contradictory? Where are there weak points, and where could things be improved? What areas should be especially closely observed in future? To whom might the results of the success evaluation be interesting and helpful?

We believe that the most important purpose of success evaluation is to identify weak areas and opportunities for improvement. The success judgment itself is only the first step; the important part is, what happens to the results. If they end up in a drawer, they were not worth the trouble. If, however, they are used constructively, as a basis for reflection on any level in the joint venture system, they will have served their main purpose.

### Questions to address

- For whom is the success evaluation being made?
- What is its purpose?
- What information is needed for it to serve its purpose?
- What is the situation in which the joint venture system is being judged?
- Is the joint venture being judged as an independent unit or from the point of view of a partner?

- What is meant by success?
- Which definition of success—economic, strategic, behavioral, or learning—best serves the purpose of the evaluation?
- How can the individual success indicators be measured?
- What would the evaluation be if the position of the other partner, the new company, or the whole system were included?
- Are evaluations made at different levels or from different viewpoints contradictory?
- What conclusions can be drawn from a combination of different criteria?

# CHAPTER TEN

# KNOWLEDGE AND LEARNING IN THE JOINT VENTURE SYSTEM

As Badaracco (1991) points out, the number of researchers has increased considerably during the past decades and with them corporate research and development (R&D) expenditures as well as the number of scientific journals. In like manner, the overall body of knowledge seems to expand at an accelerating pace. In this situation, companies need to ensure their access to strategically relevant knowledge if they want to beat their competition. Knowledge becomes a strategic asset, or, as Drucker (1993, p. 42) puts it: "Knowledge is the only meaningful resource today. The traditional 'factors of production' have not disappeared, but they have become secondary." Knowledge is more and more considered a vital ingredient in competitive success and will probably continue to be so.

As the competition for knowledge intensifies, companies must give more thought to ways of acquiring knowledge resources which they need. The possibility of using cooperative strategies, especially joint ventures, as instruments for gaining knowledge is increasingly discussed in the business press and in the academic literature (Lyles, 1987; Inkpen, 1995). We shall now take up that discussion, and ask what it really means to create a joint venture for the purpose of learning or acquiring knowledge. We shall address the following questions:

- How can joint ventures help a company to gain knowledge?
- What does it mean to regard a joint venture as an instrument of learning?
- What do we mean by "learning in the joint venture system"?
- At what levels in the joint venture system does learning take place?
- Once knowledge is acquired, how can it be transferred?
- How can barriers to knowledge creation be dismantled?

- How can a win–win learning situation be created for the whole joint venture system?

## THE IMPORTANCE OF A LEARNING APPROACH

Knowledge is not permanent; it is not a resource which, once acquired, can always be drawn upon in unlimited fashion. Knowledge can only be used within certain time limits; it quickly ages and becomes useless. We must free ourselves from a traditional, static view of knowledge and concentrate instead on learning processes which emphasize the dynamic aspect of acquiring knowledge. The important thing is not to collect knowledge and hoard it indefinitely, but to gain access to relevant knowledge and to create new knowledge—in other words, to learn. A learning-oriented company must continuously improve its products and services. It is always worth trying out something new and every experience should be seen as an opportunity for learning. According to this view, increasing the company's ability to solve problems and to take action is as important as acquiring explicit or codifiable knowledge. An increase in these abilities may be termed "implicit" knowledge and it can be distinguished in a number of ways from "explicit" knowledge (Nonaka and Takeuchi, 1995).

### Types of knowledge: Implicit and explicit

Implicit knowledge is knowledge which cannot necessarily be clearly articulated and which can only be passed on by close personal contact. Although companies do possess knowledge stored in an explicit form, they also have a good deal of unconscious knowledge, which is tied into routine behaviors. Because routines are constantly repeated, they are a kind of "memory" for knowledge which cannot be made explicit (Nelson and Winter, 1982).

Implicit knowledge is part of the special relationships between people and is linked to groups, processes and routine procedures within an organization. Strategically relevant resources can often only be acquired through learning processes, because they are closely tied to the company and cannot be sold on the market as uniform standard solutions. Acquiring implicit knowledge presupposes strategic visions and involves long development times and continuous collaboration at the personal level. For these reasons, it can be useful to encourage the development of strategically relevant knowledge within one's own company in order to be independent of competitors.

Explicit knowledge is a different matter. It exists in codifiable form, for example in documents, patents or products, or it is capable of being put into such a form. Explicit knowledge can be acquired on the open market and bought according to need. However, cost is often an obstacle to acquiring knowledge from outside.

On the subject of cost, it is often more favorable to concentrate on producing a few strategically important products in one's own company and to bring in other products and services from outside. A reason for not producing everything internally is that it is extremely time-consuming. It can be more reasonable to buy up-to-date products as needed.

## Joint ventures as a way of learning and acquiring knowledge

One way around the difficulties of developing knowledge internally and acquiring implicit knowledge is to found a joint venture with another company. This is particularly useful when a company needs to update its own knowledge quickly. An advantage of a joint venture is that the partners can work on special problems in a separate unit, which is outside the sphere of the partner's everyday business. Close collaboration with another company can also reduce the risk or uncertainty of acquiring knowledge on the open market. Figure 10.1 provides an overview of the three alternative ways of acquiring knowledge, that is on the market, through internal development or through a joint venture.

The idea that joint ventures can be used as an instrument for learning or for acquiring knowledge is relatively new. According to accustomed views, their purpose is primarily economic or strategic. In this chapter, we shall consider the theoretical and practical implications of a learning perspective on joint ventures. We shall start by examining the particular characteristics of a learning view as an additional way of looking at

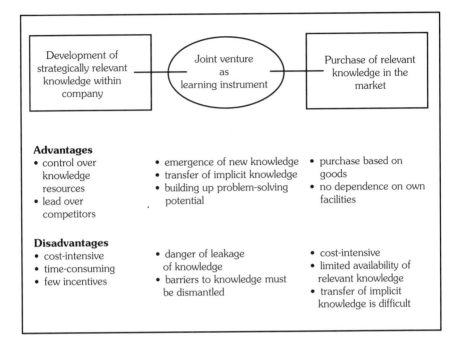

**Figure 10.1**  Advantages and disadvantages of different ways of acquiring knowledge

cooperative relationships. In reality, learning alone is not sufficient to ensure the survival of the joint venture; economic success is needed as well. However, a learning perspective offers an additional approach and helps companies to build up problem-solving potential for later use. A learning approach to joint ventures has four essential implications: a changed view of the cooperation, a changed view of its duration, a different approach to problems and an effort to achieve a win–win situation for all the companies in the joint venture system.

The different concept of the joint venture which a learning orientation entails is evident primarily in the way the results of the venture are judged. It is no longer simply a question of achieving directly quantifiable results, for example increasing market share by a given percentage or making a particular profit. Part of the objective is to build up potential for taking action, solving problems and acquiring knowledge; this potential will only bring concrete results at some time in the future. It is not visible today which makes it much more difficult to define and to measure the fulfillment of any learning objective.

The success of the learning process for the joint venture partners only becomes apparent when the knowledge gained in the joint venture is transferred back to the parent company and applied there. A learning orientation therefore affects the time-scale of the joint venture, which should be set with a view to the time companies need to learn from each other. On the one hand, it is useful to limit the duration of any particular joint venture so as to gain experience with different partners. On the other hand, a joint venture which is set up for a longer period permits the development of trust, which is needed for the transfer of sensitive knowledge. If a company wishes to acquire from its partner's skills which are relatively easy to transfer, then it makes sense to limit the duration of the joint venture. If, however, it desires to acquire "implicit" knowledge which depends on the experience of individuals, it will usually take some time for the employees to collaborate sufficiently for the transfer to take place. It is only when employees have become familiar with each other that they discuss problems, develop joint solutions and exchange experiences through working together.

As trust develops, both within the joint venture and in its relationship with the partners, a different view of problems appears. Problems are no longer regarded as obstacles which have to be cleared out of the way. From a learning viewpoint, joint ventures are consciously recognized as a field for experimentation. They can be used for trying out different solutions, developing alternatives and trying out unusual methods of problem solving.

The final distinguishing feature of a learning perspective is the emphasis which it places on mutual benefit and sharing. A learning-oriented joint venture will only be successful in the long term if all the companies learn from each other, not work against each other. The whole joint venture system must be seen as a win–win situation in which the partners can only increase their knowledge if they do it together. The benefit which one partner can gain from the learning opportunity will always bring benefit to the other partner.

Table 10.1 contains a summary of the main features of a learning approach to joint ventures.

| Characteristic | Manifestation |
|---|---|
| Concept of cooperation | Success judged in terms of potential |
| Duration of cooperative relationship | Deliberate decision is made regarding duration |
| Attitude to problems | Problems seen as learning opportunities |
| Attitude to benefits | Long-term benefit can only be achieved if there is a win–win situation for all parties |

**Table 10.1**   Main characteristics of learning-oriented joint ventures

## LEARNING AT DIFFERENT LEVELS IN THE JOINT VENTURE SYSTEM

In this section, we shall look more closely at the bases of learning processes in the joint venture system. First, we need to answer the question, "What does learning in the joint venture system mean?" Several examples may come to mind intuitively: Toyota learned something about the US supply and transport system when they entered a joint venture with General Motors; Siemens learned to produce the one-megabit memory chip through its cooperation with Toshiba; International Digital Communication Corporation, an agreement between Cable & Wireless and several smaller Japanese partners, wanted to transfer knowledge from the partners to the corporate headquarters in London, but failed.

These cases offer different answers to our question. Learning in the joint venture system means transferring knowledge from the joint venture back into the partner company and integrating it into the knowledge base so that the company can use it later for its own purposes. In the following sections, we shall use the following points as a basis for discussing learning in the joint venture system:

- Agents: "Who learns in the joint venture system?"
- Content: "What is learned?"
- Process: "How is it learned?"

# Agents of learning in the joint venture system

It seems obvious that the agents of learning in a company are the individual employees. The same is true, of course, of a joint venture. However, when we come to consider how a manager's knowledge is preserved when he or she leaves the company, the question becomes more difficult. Individual managers learn and store knowledge in their memories, but there must also be other ways of ensuring that their knowledge is not lost if they leave. The following distinctions between individual learning and organizational learning may help to clarify the problem.

## *Individual learning and organizational learning*

Organizational learning can be less than the sum of the learning of individuals, for example if the results of individual learning are not passed on and considered by others, and therefore do not become part of the shared body of thought in the organization.

Organizational learning can be more than the sum of learning of individuals, for example if individual employees store the available knowledge in an "organizational memory" (Walsh and Ungson, 1991). This may take the form of data bases and archives, or routines and specific behaviors.

These distinctions show that there is a quantitative and qualitative difference between individual and organizational learning. The concept of organizational learning focuses on a two-way relationship between the individual employee and the organization. First, organizational learning should not be equated with the sum of individual learning processes, even though these are necessary for organizational learning to take place. Second, the interactive component between the organization and the individual is the more important factor for understanding the concept of organizational learning. The emphasis is on the sharing of individual knowledge and the need for communication. Our discussion will therefore be based on the following definition of organizational learning, which takes into account the two-way relationship between the individual and the organization, and stresses the qualitative difference between individual and organizational learning.

## *Organizational learning*

Organizational learning is the process by which the organization's knowledge base changes, leading to improved problem solving ability and capacity for action (Probst and Büchel, 1997, p. 15). Organizational learning is based on individual learning, but the results of individual learning
must be communicated to others within the company in order to trigger
a collective learning process.

The essential point in this definition is the fact that employees share
their knowledge. If individual members possess or acquire knowledge but
do not pass it on, then it is useless to others (Nonaka, 1994). It need not
necessarily be transmitted by means of verbal communication: in view of
our distinction between explicit and implicit knowledge, we must also
consider ways in which implicit knowledge can be acquired from others,
for example by simply watching or working with them.

## Ways of transferring different kinds of knowledge

The following model shows different ways in which individual knowledge
can be made collective; it embraces both implicit and explicit knowledge
(Nonaka and Takeuchi, 1995).

The first stage is to transfer knowledge from one person to another.
Knowledge which is possessed by individuals must be made accessible to
others and this happens most readily through the process of socialization.
In the course of socialization, knowledge and skills which are subjective
or difficult to articulate can be transferred without being made explicit,
that is through "learning-by-doing". In this first phase, we are still
concerned with learning by individuals; individual learning has not yet
been transferred to a larger group or generally communicated within
the company.

The second phase in the transfer process is to communicate the experiences of the individual to a larger circle of people. Nonaka (1991) calls
this "articulation". It constitutes a qualitative "leap"; knowledge is no longer
traceable to particular individuals, but has gained an independent quality
through the process of articulation and collective discussion. This also
makes the knowledge easier to store and transfer.

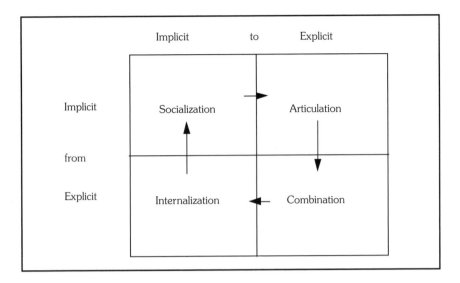

**Figure 10.2**  Ways in which knowledge can be transferred
Source: Based on Nonaka, I. and Takeuchi, H. (1995) *The Knowledge-Creating Company*, New York: Oxford University Press, p. 62

In the third phase, previously articulated knowledge is standardized and combined with other knowledge to produce new solutions ("combination"). This happens, for instance, if routines are developed, and perhaps partly formulated in writing. The knowledge then becomes available to many people. If in the course of further development new strategies are formed, the knowledge can be used as a basis for planning ("internalization"). It thus represents a potential which can be used in strategy formulation and implementation (Figure 10.2).

The internalization phase completes the cycle of knowledge transfer. In the optimal case, these four phases (socialization, articulation, combination and internalization) form a circular knowledge process in which implicit knowledge is communicated to a wider group and externalized, thus making it possible for individual knowledge to become organizational knowledge (Nonaka, 1991).

We shall return to this idea of a knowledge cycle in the following sections, and show that different phases in the cycle take place at different levels in the joint venture system.

## Learning processes and knowledge management

Before we move on to consider the specific problems which affect the development or acquisition of knowledge at different levels in the joint venture system, it will be helpful to make a distinction between learning processes and knowledge management. Learning processes cannot be prescribed or controlled; at best, companies can provide conditions and incentives which encourage learning. Knowledge management, however, involves structuring and organizing, and the targeted use of "instruments of knowledge management" (Figure 10.3).

Knowledge management consists of making targeted interventions in the organization's knowledge base. Concepts and methods are available for this purpose. The individual elements in the knowledge process, which

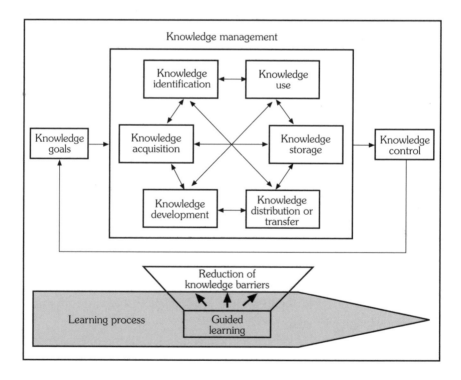

**Figure 10.3**  Knowledge and learning processes in the joint venture system
Source: Based on Probst, G., Raub, S. and Romhardt, K. (1997) *Wissen managen*, Wiesbaden: Gabler, p. 56

we try to influence by the use of "knowledge management instruments", will be discussed in more detail in relation to the different levels in the joint venture system. At this point, we shall simply offer an overview of what we mean by the elements in the knowledge management process.

## Knowledge goals

By knowledge goals we mean the conscious development of goal categories which emphasize the acquisition of specific knowledge in the joint venture. The deliberate formulation of knowledge goals is in itself a way of influencing the knowledge base of the organization. A description of the knowledge goals answers the question: "What goals are being pursued through this joint venture with regard to knowledge?"

### GOALS FOR LEARNING AND KNOWLEDGE

In an internal Ericsson document, the following statement was made:

When the Japanese form cooperative ventures with overseas companies, they always have learning in mind. For Japanese companies, one of the most frequent reasons for forming an alliance is a lack of strategically relevant knowledge. Western companies have quite different reasons, though for them too it is important to learn from the partner. Learning is an extra benefit of cooperation, and it brings the employees of two companies closer together. There is nothing bad about learning from other companies. On the contrary, it is something which should be specifically planned. It should be made clear from the beginning what the companies expect from each other. We ought to make a list of the knowledge which is to be transferred between the companies. In all cases, it is important that the transfer of knowledge should be a two-way process, and that there should be an open dialogue. It is very important to put all one's cards on the table.

## Knowledge identification

Identification of knowledge is the process of creating transparency in the internal and external knowledge environments. Knowledge identification provides answers to the question: "What kinds of knowledge exist inside and outside the organization?"

In order to identify knowledge in the joint venture partner organizations, knowledge transparence needs to be given. This applies to both transparence of the internal and the external environment of the joint venture. Identification may be based on traditional portfolio-models, judging knowledge components according to their strategic importance and immediate or long-term availability. Also, data banks or knowledge charts may be used to achieve transparence about the current state of knowledge and future knowledge needs. Identification should not only be based on the analysis of explicit and visible knowledge, it should also account for invisible or tacit knowledge components that are more difficult to identify. Suitable identification methods may be in-depth interviews that account for the unconscious knowledge components managers may not be immediately willing to articulate.

## ACQUIRING MANUFACTURING KNOWLEDGE

As Xerox in the US realized that its position in the copier industry was declining in the 1980s, the importance of the Fuji Xerox joint venture began to increase. The CEO of Xerox started to take a closer look at the internal management activities of Xerox Fuji since the manufacturing costs and the reject rates were substantially lower than in the American operations. Soon, Xerox executives visited the Fuji Xerox operations and started to employ similar management practices like the benchmarking and qualify program implemented within the joint venture. In the late 1980s and early 1990s, these efforts started to bear fruits and Xerox increased its competitiveness in the American market.

## Knowledge distribution or transfer

By knowledge distribution we mean the process by which knowledge is transferred between the members of an organization or between organizational units (e.g. the joint venture and the joint venture partners). The question is: "How is knowledge shared?"

Knowledge transfer relates to sharing processes between both partner organizations and the joint venture. When knowledge is to be transferred within the joint venture entity, internal barriers have to be torn down. These may result from differences in learning style or different goals formulated by each joint venture partner. Once knowledge is transferred within the joint venture entity, it encounters a second barrier that is between the joint venture entity and the partner organization. Boundaries both internally and externally should be actively managed in order to facilitate knowledge transfer.

## Knowledge development

The process of knowledge development focuses on the emergence of new knowledge within the organization. The question is: "By what means is new knowledge generated?"

When we talk about knowledge development in joint ventures, we refer to the development of new knowledge. But even though this is the major focus, the development of new knowledge needs to be based on knowledge that is already given. Certain structures, processes, and tools need to be shared in order to build on them as a joint basis for further development. Joint venture partners also need to consider the time necessary to build up this joint basis and whether this time is compatible to the knowledge objectives it has formulated for the joint venture. Thus, the management of knowledge development is related to duration management of the joint venture.

## Knowledge acquisition

The process of knowledge acquisition is that of gathering information from different sources, mainly external. The question is: "Where does knowledge come from?"

In contrast to knowledge transfer, we talk about knowledge acquisition when the joint venture enlarges or changes its knowledge base while receiving environmental input from outside the joint venture system. For instance, when a joint venture system is developing in quantum leaps, the required technology may not be available from any of its partners. When knowledge development is the explicit goal, minimal technological standards may be required that can be jointly purchased from an external industry leader. Once acquired, this knowledge serves as a minimal standard for joint knowledge development.

## Knowledge storage

Processes and media for storing knowledge are needed so that the knowledge which is acquired will remain available for a longer period. The question is, "What media are available for storing knowledge and is it in fact possible to store knowledge permanently?"

In order to be of long-term use, knowledge needs to be stored in some sort of memory. In the first instance, suitable storage bins need to be identified. These can either be of a formal or informal nature. What matters most is that people are willing to document their knowledge in some form of collective memory that is then accessible to a wider public.

## Knowledge use

Acquiring knowledge does not guarantee that good use will be made of it. The procedures for making use of knowledge should therefore be examined. The question is: "How can knowledge be used internally and marketed externally, for example in the form of competencies?".

Knowledge need not only be acquired or developed, but also applied. Application is the relevant process which decides on the success of given knowledge. If it is not used either in the present or in the future, economic benefits will not arrive. Even when knowledge application is considered from a long-term perspective it is the market value or knowledge that will finally determine the joint venture success.

## Knowledge control

Knowledge control is the general evaluation of knowledge. In the context of joint ventures, we use the term in the narrower sense of avoiding an undesired leakage of knowledge from one partner to the other. The question is: "How can we control our own strategically relevant knowledge and avoid uncontrolled leakage?"

By knowledge control, we not only understand the overall notion of evaluating knowledge, but also the supervision of the joint venture's internal flows of knowledge. This applies to voluntary knowledge transfer and involuntary knowledge loss. Thus, knowledge control is a question of boundary and barrier management that requires active involvement of all participating joint venture managers. Barriers to successful learning may be structural, strategic, cultural, individual, or political. In the joint venture itself, they are most likely to be individual or cultural in nature. Between the joint venture and the partners there may be structural, strategic and cultural barriers. At the level of the joint venture system, political barriers are the most probable.

## LEARNING WITHIN THE JOINT VENTURE

In this section, we shall be concerned with learning processes in the joint venture itself. This is no different in principle from organizational learning in any company. In practice, the special feature is that employees entering a joint venture have widely differing skills and knowledge to exchange. It is useful to ask the following questions:

- What are the important knowledge processes which take place in the joint venture?
- How can different kinds of knowledge be transferred in the joint venture?
- How does new knowledge arise?
- What are the barriers to knowledge which must be overcome in the joint venture?

The most significant knowledge processes in the joint venture are the development of knowledge, the transfer of knowledge between employees from different partner companies, and the control of knowledge. The aims are to create new knowledge within the joint venture, to exchange existing knowledge amongst the employees and to control unwanted leakage.

The most important factor in knowledge development within the joint venture is the process of socialization between employees from two different partner companies. For knowledge to develop, the employees from the two companies must work closely together, and learn simply through watching, or acquire new skills under specialist guidance. This is only possible if there is a close and trusting relationship, in which people can allow others to gain insight into their own capabilities.

The ability to absorb new knowledge can be reduced in the joint venture by differences in cultural background or training and by differing views on the objectives of the joint venture. It is only when previously accepted values are reconsidered or even renounced completely that there will be space for something new. This means that people may have to question or let go, or in other words "unlearn". The need to "unlearn" particularly affects established companies whose accumulated knowledge often bears no relation to the strategically relevant knowledge which they currently require. People are often not prepared to learn until the pressure increases, and the discrepancy between the existing knowledge resources and those which the company needs becomes obvious.

It is also important to support the transfer of knowledge. The readiness to pass on knowledge which was previously present in implicit form, and to develop new knowledge through creative collaboration within the joint venture, can be facilitated by careful molding of contextual factors. The basic factors are commitment, trust and sensemaking. Others include the creation of open structures, versatile communication systems, learning incentives and a learning-oriented team structure.

The main reason for supporting communication within the joint venture is to create cohesion. Communication spreads a feeling of belonging which increases readiness to learn. If cohesion exists, substantial amounts of information and knowledge can be exchanged, and it is useful to have a new and open communication system for this purpose. The cooperation between the Dresdner Bank and the Banque Nationale de Paris provides an example of the importance of shared communication systems.

## STRUCTURING COMMUNICATION IN A COOPERATIVE RELATIONSHIP

The production of a combined telephone book absorbed the most effort. For more than a year, high-level managers in the Dresdner Bank and the Banque Nationale de Paris worked on an index through which every employee of the German bank could find his or her partner on the French side and vice versa. For how could a cross-border cooperation between two institutions be expected to work if nobody knew who to talk to?

Another important way of encouraging knowledge transfer is to create material and non-material incentives. A joint venture pay system based on short-term assessments and purely material incentives offers little stimulus to learning. We have already seen that when joint ventures are being evaluated, non-financial aspects of performance must be measured in order to encourage learning. The same applies to assessments of individuals. The readiness to share knowledge should be included in employee evaluations and a "knowledge-based remuneration system" instituted. For a number of years, the American company Salomon Brothers Inc. has been using a pay system of this kind, which it calls "performance-related pay", "qualification-oriented remuneration" or "knowledge-related compensation". This pay system differs from others in that employees are paid for professional qualifications, social openness and ability to learn. All employees are paid according to a pay scale, like students who are given marks for their efforts. Pay raises are given for projects, which are completed by teams. The following measures might be taken to introduce a system of this kind into a joint venture, so as to recognize and reward learning:

- get rid of everything that could have demotivating effects;
- avoid guidelines and practices which reward preservation of the status quo;
- clarify learning expectations by describing accurately the scope of a particular position, or the level of competence needed for it;
- assign different tasks and projects;

- offer opportunities to present that which has been learned; and
- recognize and reward learning progress.

A final important factor in knowledge transfer is the team structure of the working group. By increasing autonomy within small groups in the joint venture, the traditional form of work division, according to which people performed narrowly defined and simple activities, can be broadened considerably. This increases the learning potential of the employees. However, as things are at present, their potential is far from being fully exploited. Joint venture managers tend to favor teamwork, but they often continue to think in terms of narrow job descriptions. Outmoded ideas of this kind must be dismantled if successful learning is to take place within the joint venture. Attitudes should be rethought according to the following principles:

- accept that all employees are capable of personal development and of learning together; and
- depart from compartmentalized thinking and narrowly defined areas of activity; concentrate instead on the nature of the work that has to be done.

Up to this point, we have considered how to achieve maximum transfer of knowledge amongst employees. However, this can be taken too far if "secret knowledge" is revealed, that is when the outflow of knowledge is not controlled. Knowledge control serves to prevent the unconscious leaking of knowledge. The simplest solution is to designate certain areas taboo and to exclude them from transfer right from the beginning.

Table 10.2 contains an overview of knowledge processes within the joint venture and ways in which they can be supported:

| Knowledge processes | How to support them |
|---|---|
| Knowledge development | • Encouragement of socialization processes<br>• Daily collaboration |
| Knowledge transfer | • Open communication<br>• Learning incentives<br>• Team structures which support learning |
| Knowledge control | • Designate taboo areas |

**Table 10.2**   Important knowledge processes in the joint venture

For the efficient structuring of knowledge processes in the joint venture, it is not enough to set the conditions. Barriers to the development and transfer of knowledge must also be dismantled. Within the joint venture, the barriers usually result from cultural and individual factors.

Cultural barriers arise in joint ventures because employees from two companies with different cultures come together in the new company. There may also be barriers arising from the national culture, or a culture specific to a branch of industry. Cultural barriers are amongst the most serious for learning, because they cannot be avoided simply by changing the system. They often exist at an unconscious level in the minds of the employees and cannot be explained rationally. The following steps may help to reduce cultural barriers:

• Make people aware that the barriers exist.
• Institute continuous interchange between hierarchical levels.
• Encourage the exchange of information.
• Manage conflicts in such a way as to support shared opinions.

Individual barriers are mainly a matter of the difference between "I can" and "I will". It is often the case that employees lack particular skills, but could learn them with suitable training. However, their ability to learn usually has less to do with the outcome than with their psychological resistance. It is more difficult to overcome the "not-invented-here" attitude than it is to make up a training deficit; the worst obstacles lie within us. When attempts are made to transfer knowledge between the joint venture partners and the new company, the problem of psychological resistance may arise in acute form unless the learning intentions have been rigorously discussed and clarified at the start. If the learning intentions could be not only formulated on paper, but also absorbed and "lived" by every employee, individual barriers might not arise in the first place. The importance of the "individual element" is apparent in the following description of German–French joint ventures:

> In every cooperation, there must be people on both sides who push the partnership forward and give it life. The boss of a German subsidiary in France has to be ready to attempt the impossible. He must be an

ambassador in both directions: on the one hand, he must uphold the parent company's business interests in the foreign country; on the other, he must make clear to the parent company the justified interests of the foreign employees and the different conditions in the foreign market. And he must do all that without each side thinking that he is an undercover agent for the other.
(*Manager Magazin*, **9**, 1993, p. 154)

The following steps may help in dismantling individual barriers to learning:

- develop suitable pay and incentive systems;
- target the motivation of the employees;
- encourage creativity and tolerance;
- allow people to think differently; and
- tolerate mistakes.


## LEARNING OF THE PARTNER COMPANIES

Once successful learning has taken place in the joint venture, the question for the partners is how to transfer the resulting knowledge back into their own companies, and how to store and use it. The key issues are as follows:

- What are the necessary conditions for transferring knowledge from the joint venture to the partners?
- What are the difficulties in transferring knowledge from the joint venture to the partners?
- What are the barriers which have to be overcome?
- How can the learning outcomes, which initially consist of undirected potential, be transformed into real competitive advantages?
- How can knowledge be stored?

The processes of combination and internalization are particularly important for the transfer of knowledge between the joint venture and the joint venture partners. Communication must be increased between the employees of the joint venture and those of the partners, so that the partner companies are enabled to make new combinations. Storage of knowledge is mainly a question of internalization; it makes the information part of the partners' knowledge base.

For transfer of knowledge to take place, one of the first essentials is to create conditions which give people access to the knowledge acquired in the joint venture. The process of knowledge transfer between the joint venture and the partners then becomes one of the key processes in the whole system.

One of the most important preconditions for transfer of knowledge from the joint venture to the partners is the existence of a learning intention. At the beginning of this chapter, we drew attention to the fact that a learning perspective involves adopting a different approach to problems. This new approach should be explicitly formulated as a learning intention. If the learning intention is drawn up when the joint venture is founded, there can be an open exchange of information from the beginning; companies can then explore each other's learning needs and agree on joint learning targets. However, cooperation of this kind will only be possible if the partners try to create a win–win situation for all the companies in the joint venture system. In the case of EHPT, the learning intentions of Ericsson and HP were formulated at the outset.

## LEARNING INTENTIONS OF ERICSSON AND HP

When EHPT was created, the partners were already planning to acquire knowledge through the joint venture. The following are observations made by Ericsson and HP employees regarding each others' learning intentions.

- "By joining with HP, Ericsson can get access to computer knowledge."
- "HP expects to get more telecom knowledge and software by working together with Ericsson."
- "Ericsson wanted to know how the computing technology will influence their marketplace and how to use that to strengthen the position."
- "From Ericsson we said that we needed a partner that is very

> knowledgeable in computer equipment, data application, things that are broader than telecom."
>
> These remarks show that in addition to economic success, the partners hoped that the joint venture would bring them access to knowledge.
>
> After the joint venture had been operating for a year, the partners were satisfied with its economic performance, but their learning objectives had not been met. Ericsson gained very little by way of HP skills through the joint venture, and HP increased its knowledge of the telecommunications market only to a very small extent though both companies had expected to gain access to the core skills of the partner.
>
> Although the partners shared these learning objectives, neither did much to realize them. The interfaces which were needed to increase the exchange of information between the organizations were not created and there was no transfer of personnel, which would have permitted employees to transfer skills between the companies. The partners therefore had to rely on their own employees returning from the joint venture to bring them knowledge.

An important instrument for knowledge transfer, but one which has been little used as yet, is rotation of staff between the joint venture and the partners. Inkpen (1995) reports a study in which he found that only six percent of knowledge transfer takes place via staff rotation. This is not surprising, because frequent changes of staff require a great deal of planning and employees resist too many moves. Other and easier ways of transferring knowledge are therefore more common. These include:

- regular visits to the joint venture by the CEOs of the partner companies;
- intensive exchange of information between the joint venture and the partners;
- involvement of senior management in the activities of the joint venture; and
- building up closer links between the partners and the joint venture.

Even if knowledge is successfully transferred, it has not yet met the partners' final criterion of success. The knowledge acquired through the joint venture need not be immediately visible in economic results, but this is undoubtedly the objective in the long run. It is important to consider how the newly acquired knowledge can be integrated into the internal knowledge base of the partners, thus raising their problem solving skills and their business potential. The knowledge must also be capable of transformation into competencies which can be sold on the market. The answers to the following three questions will show whether a company is capable of using its knowledge and transforming it into competencies (Prahalad and Hamel, 1990; Barney, 1991):

- Can the company use the knowledge to gain access to a wide range of markets?
- Can the knowledge be used and embodied in a product which customers will prefer to the alternatives?
- Is it difficult for competitors to imitate the knowledge or the end product?

In addition to making use of the knowledge, the partners must be able to preserve and store it. The knowledge acquired in the joint venture is often tied to individual persons and does not exist in the form of documents, computer records, etc. It must therefore be put into some form of "memory" which others can use (Walsh and Ungson, 1991). Making the knowledge widely accessible to members of the partner company is more important than trying to store it permanently. Storage media, which might include the company culture, its structures or routines, should normally satisfy three criteria: knowledge should be accessible, explicable and not dependent on individuals (Gomez and Probst, 1995).

Table 10.3 contains a summary of the main knowledge processes which take place between the joint venture and the partners, and ways in which they can be influenced.

There are barriers to knowledge processes between the partner companies just as there are within the joint venture itself. At partner level, the barriers are mainly structural and cultural. Structural barriers to knowledge often take the form of interrupted or inadequate flows of information and communication. The technical infrastructures of the companies, from the computer systems they use to the number of levels in their hierarchies, are often not compatible. The following methods may be used for breaking down structural barriers:

| Knowledge processes | How to support them |
|---|---|
| Knowledge transfer | • Increase exchange of information<br>• Communicate learning intentions |
| Knowledge storage | • Choose storage media<br>• Check criteria, e.g. accessible, explicable, not dependent on individuals |
| Knowledge use | • Check compatibility with existing knowledge<br>• Check opportunities for market access<br>• Make imitation difficult |

**Table 10.3**  Important knowledge processes to the joint venture partners

- Encourage informal exchanges.
- Create structures which permit a flow of information across separate functions and market areas.
- Increase spatial proximity.

There are also cultural barriers to be overcome at this level. The appropriate measures have already been suggested, so we will not discuss them again.

## LEARNING IN THE JOINT VENTURE SYSTEM AS A WHOLE

This brings us back to an important point which we discussed earlier, namely, that learning is a joint process; one company cannot learn at another's expense. For learning to take place, all parties must feel that they are in a win–win situation.

This idea has far-reaching implications for understanding and managing joint ventures, because in a cooperative situation, the competitive mentality must give way to jointly attainable goals. The point is not to optimize the learning outcomes for individual companies, but to optimize them for the whole system. The concept of optimizing the system suggests that it has "development potential".

If the idea of "togetherness" is well established, whether in written form or in the structure of daily activities, no one need fear losing knowledge or suffering some other disadvantage within the joint venture system. The basic factors mentioned in Chapter 8 are particularly important here. Learning is not possible without trust, because it always involves admitting that one's own company knows less than others in a particular area and this increases its vulnerability. Second, learning will only take place where there is commitment and once again, this must be mutual. We have argued that learning cannot be prescribed. No one can compel a manager to learn in a joint venture; there must be fundamental commitment and recognition of a shared meaning or sense. This completes the cycle: trust, commitment and sense are preconditions of learning processes, and they also result from them.

These three basic factors are particularly effective weapons against barriers to learning at the level of the whole joint venture system. The barriers at this level are primarily political. They usually affect the information available to particular groups in the company and they reflect power interests. If the joint venture system is based on the understanding that it is development-orientated, then there will be, de facto, no political barriers. However, this is an ideal situation towards which the participants must work, so we shall make some suggestions as to how it might be achieved, and how to recognize and dismantle any political barriers:

- Expose the power structures.
- Deliberately bring the "political" opponents together.
- Clarify promotion prospects and decision criteria.

If the companies in the system are to achieve a joint increase in knowledge, this should be established as an explicit common objective when the venture is founded. We shall end our discussion of learning in joint ventures with a remark made by an HP manager: "We are both learning from one another...and we are making the joint venture a success..."

## Questions to address

- What are the learning objectives to be achieved through the joint venture?

- Have the learning objectives been clearly stated in the form of a learning intention?
- Is the planned duration of the cooperation consistent with achieving the learning objectives?
- Are problems in the joint venture system perceived as learning opportunities?
- Is there an awareness of possible barriers to learning at all levels in the joint venture system?
- What knowledge is to be acquired in the joint venture?
- What methods are being used to encourage the development of knowledge?
- What instruments are being applied to support transfer of knowledge?
- Is there fear of possible loss of knowledge?
- What ways of storing knowledge are available and how are they used?
- How is the knowledge acquired in the joint venture to be used?

# CHAPTER ELEVEN

# CONCLUSION: LEARNING THROUGH COOPERATION

The idea of learning through cooperative ventures featured throughout this book. In the course of our discussion, we have addressed a number of aspects of learning. The first issue which we considered was how to master the art of cooperating within the framework of a challenging form of business enterprise, that is the joint venture.

Trying to understand the many different forms which joint ventures can take is in itself a daunting task. We must then confront the variety of problems which arise at different levels and in different stages in the development of joint ventures. These problems correspond to four major areas of management: strategy development, structural design, culturally sensitive management and human resource management. We also discussed three basic factors on which the cohesion of the joint venture system depends, namely trust, commitment and sensemaking. These basic factors cannot be managed within a particular functional area or by a particular person; they must lie at the heart of management thought and action at all levels and in all areas of the joint venture system.

Successful management of joint ventures involves a great deal more than managing economic, financial and strategic issues. This becomes especially clear when it is necessary to evaluate the success of a joint venture. Joint ventures are often assessed by a number of people who have different viewpoints and use different criteria, and their conclusions can differ to an astonishing degree. For this reason, a joint venture should be judged not only according to how far it meets the goals set by the partners, but also from a strategic point of view as a "stand-alone". The cooperative and communicative processes in the joint venture system as a whole should also be assessed.

We have supplemented the traditional ways of evaluating joint ventures by adding a learning perspective. This approach focuses on knowledge, learning and the ability to solve problems in the joint venture system, rather than on immediate economic success. From this viewpoint, joint ventures are seen as a way for companies to acquire external knowledge, combine complementary skills and gain a lead in the development of knowledge. The learning perspective emphasizes the joint accumulation of potential for success in the medium to long term.

The factors which influence success in joint venture management must be sought in a number of different areas. If a joint venture is to be successful, it is not enough to optimize performance in relation to a narrow range of preselected variables. In several joint ventures which we have studied in recent years, we have found that factors which are vital to success often lie in areas which traditional approaches overlook. One of the most important aims of this book is to show that in all the stages of their development, joint ventures must be structured so as to encourage learning. Only when this is achieved can we say that the joint venture is being successfully managed in the broad sense. Companies will therefore benefit from learning to cooperate and cooperating to learn.

Managing a joint venture is a demanding leadership task in which the main day-to-day challenge is to resolve the difficult conflicts which repeatedly threaten the existence of the cooperation. The scope of management thus extends far beyond organizing the operational side of the company and assigning tasks to different people. It is a complex process which takes place at different levels in the joint venture system and which cannot be reduced to a matter of formal rules, contracts, business procedures or sequential planning.

When we come to consider the management as a system function, the attempt to analyze and make structural recommendations reaches the limits of its usefulness. When future-oriented companies use cooperative relationships as a way of shaping their strategies, they need qualities such as creativity and innovation, not checklists and patent remedies. From this viewpoint, the main success factor is the ability of companies to learn together within the joint venture system and its environment.

One of the greatest challenges in managing joint ventures is learning to cope with paradoxes and dilemmas at all levels. The autonomy of individual companies pulls against the integration of the joint venture system as a whole and competition between the partner companies conflicts with the notion of interorganizational learning. Individual power and influence must be balanced against the need to share knowledge and skills, and the unavoidable differences between the partners must be reconciled with the unity of the whole system. In all these dimensions, there is tension between two opposing principles, that is trust and competition. It is the task of joint venture managers to make use of both principles and to bring them into a state of equilibrium.

In the past, joint ventures were often founded with a single objective such as making greater use of production capacity or gaining access to new markets through shared use of sales channels. Today, however, we see increasing numbers of cooperative ventures being created because both the founder companies hope to acquire new competencies by combining their resources in a process of interorganizational learning. Knowledge can be used jointly and combined across different functions, though this can only succeed when both partners see the cooperation as offering a win–win situation. If one partner hopes to learn at the expense of the other, the cooperative venture cannot be learning-oriented in the full sense of the term.

As we have shown in our case studies, the road to creating a learning-oriented cooperative venture is long and difficult, and often winding and stony. If this book has provided some guidelines along the way, it has more than fulfilled its purpose.

# APPENDIX

## AN ILLUSTRATION OF A JOINT VENTURE AGREEMENT

Prepared by a group of participants in the EMBA program of the School of Management, Asian Institute of Technology, Bangkok, Thailand. This agreement has been prepared as a response to a simulation exercise involving the launch of a joint venture between a Japanese and a Thai company. The joint venture will undertake manufacturing and marketing of boilers in Thailand.

THIS AGREEMENT is made on 14 March 1998.

**BETWEEN**

1. **ASAHI STEAM COMPANY LIMITED**, a company incorporated in Japan whose office is located at No. 349 Kawaminami, Wakayanagi Machi, Kurihara-Gun, Miyagi 989-58, Japan, hereinafter will be referred to as Asahi on the one part; and

2. **VICHAK BOILER COMPANY LIMITED**, a company incorporated in Thailand whose registered office is situated at 99/69 Moo 11 Thanya-Lamlookka Road, Thanya-Ongkarak, Pathumthani 12111, Thailand, hereinafter will be referred to as Vichak on the other part.

## WHEREAS

The parties desire to enter into a joint venture partnership in order to establish a boiler manufacturing and marketing joint venture to be based in Thailand, in which Vichak wishes to undertake through its Manufacturing Division the assembly manufacture and distribution of the range of boilers designed and manufactured by Asahi. The parties agree to the terms and conditions stated herein as follows:

This agreement shall remain in force for seven years from the date hereof and unless terminated by either party through unilateral pullout.

## Article 1:   Formation of Partnership for Joint Venture

The parties hereby enter into partnership under the laws of Thailand solely for the purpose of establishing a boiler manufacturing plant in Pathumthani province, Thailand.

It is clearly understood that the parties are not in partnership in respect to any other business, and that no party shall represent itself to others as being in partnership with the other, except in respect to each other.

## Article 2:   Partnership Share

Each party shall have an equal 50-50 share in the loss, profit and liability of the partnership.

## Article 3:   Joint Responsibilities

The parties shall be jointly and severally responsible for the obligations of the partnership. Subject to the power granted to the Managing Director, where Vichak will name the person, that all operations under the joint venture legal documents, invoices, decisions affecting the partnership generally shall be approved by all the parties. For greater certainty, but without restricting the generality of the foregoing, no agreements shall be made without the consent of both parties involved.

## Article 4:    Organization and Board of Directors

Asahi shall name an individual who will be the Chairman, where Vichak shall name an individual who will be the President (or Managing Director) to run the newly established joint venture. Inclusively, each party shall name an individual who has the authority to bind legal matters for the purpose of this agreement and these individuals shall be the members of the Board of Directors ("the Board") of the partnership.

The affairs of the partnership shall be managed by the Board, in this case it has been agreed that the Board will be a 50-50 consensus from both parties. No decision of the Board shall be made except by unanimous agreement of the four members of the Board. No decisions of the Board shall be made except by unanimous agreement of ALL the four members of the Board.

Asahi
- Manufacturing Director
- R&D Controller
- Product Development
- Quality Control Director
- Engineering Director

Vichak
- Managing Director
- Marketing & Sales Director
- Finance & Accounting Director
- HR & Administrative Director

## Article 5:    Joint Venture Proceeds

Both parties agree in the first two years that Asahi will supply Vichak with semi-knocked down boilers for sale, in which after the second year, the joint venture will begin producing these boilers themselves in Thailand, using Asahi technology and key components. From year one to seven, both parties agree that distribution of completed boilers will be sold under Vichak's brand name.

## Article 6:    Manufacturing Team

The Board shall name the Manufacturing Director from Asahi, who shall be responsible for heading a team of individuals ("the Manufacturing Team") to undergo construction of the boiler manufacturing plant. The Manufacturing Director shall select for the team such individuals from the personnel of the parties or from personnel of the partnership's subcontractors and suppliers, as would be most advantageous to the construction of the boiler manufacturing plant.

## Article 7:   Power and Duty of Manufacturing Director

Immediately after the signing of this agreement, the Board shall pass a resolution defining the power and authority of the construction of the boiler manufacturing plant.

## Article 8:   By-Laws & Territory

Immediately after the signing of this agreement, the Board shall prepare and approve by-laws of the partnership consistent with the provisions of this agreement. In addition, the Territory agreed will mean Thailand and other ASEAN countries.

## Article 9:   Equal Contributions

a. Capital
   Each party shall contribute equally to the capital considered by the Board to be necessary for the purposes of the partnership with total investment of US$40 million.
b. Resources
   Each party shall contribute as equally as possible the personnel and other resources necessary for the purposes of the partnership.

## Article 10:   Subcontractors and Suppliers

The parties understand and agree that portions or phases of the construction of the manufacturing plant may be awarded to such subcontractors and suppliers (including a party to this agreement) considered by the Board to be advantageous to the joint venture, provided that in respect to an award to a party to this agreement:

a. the award shall be made only with the prior approval of the Board, and

b. the duties of the awarded party qua subcontractor or supplier shall be in addition to its duties qua partner under this agreement.

## Article 11: Liability

Each party shall indemnify and save harmless the other party to this agreement against losses, damages and liabilities of any nature or kind whatsoever arising out of that party's failure to perform its responsibilities in accordance with the terms of this agreement.

## Article 12: Termination

Under this agreement, both parties have the right to a termination of the joint venture under unilateral pullout, meaning either party could enter the Thai/ASEAN market directly at any time or tie up with other firms.

From the date of expiry of this agreement or the date of its termination for any reason whatsoever, both parties will take into consideration of the option to continue to joint venture after the seventh year.

## Article 13: Standards of Competence

The parties shall maintain good engineering practices in relation to the joint venture and all work shall meet standards of competence normally attained by the parties hereto.

## Article 14: Boiler Models and Quantities

The parties agree to assemble two models of imported boiler kits for the first two years of the joint venture and accept the terms and conditions of the pricing strategy set by Vichak, where the minimum guaranteed quantity is the average of the first two years.

| Year | Boiler model | FOB pricing US$ | No. of units |
|:---:|:---:|:---:|:---:|
| 1 | Scout | 95,000 | 100 |
| 2 | Inferno | 130,000 | 100 |

The boiler model "Bagheera" will further be revised for production after the review of the first two years' performance of the above mentioned boiler models and to further study the marketing trend according to the turn of economic status in Thailand. During the first two years, "Bagheera" model will be imported by the joint venture from Asahi on a need to order basis.

## Article 15:   Royalty

The royalty shall be paid as follows:

a. The royalties after pro-rating in the third year shall be paid on the 1st day of January in each year during the continuation in force of this agreement the first payment to be made on 1 January 2000.
b. On the 30th day of June and December in each year during the continuation in force of this agreement, Vichak shall remit Asahi the royalty on net sales calculated in accordance with the rate of 3% in respect of the immediately preceding six month periods ending 31 June and December respectively.

   In determining the amount of these semi-annual royalty payments, Asahi shall give and Vichak shall receive credit for the fixed royalty paid on the 1st January 2000. The computation of royalties shall be made in US dollar payments and will be remitted in US dollars to the account of Asahi at a bank to be designated by it at the rate of exchange ruling on the date of remittance.
c. Coincident with the remittance of semi-annual royalty payments, Vichak shall provide Asahi statements setting forth a list of all Units or components of the Units sold and if so requested by Asahi the names of the customers therefore during the relevant semi-annual period. Interest shall be charged on all overdue royalty

payments at the rate of 3% per annum above the Bank base rate at the time being calculated and payable monthly.

d. Vichak agrees to maintain books records and accounts in accordance with generally accepted accounting principles covering its operations and containing all information necessary for the accurate calculation of the net sales of boilers or components of the boilers and will deliver Asahi with each remittance referred to in Article 15 subclause (b).

## Article 16:   Procurement by Asahi

a. Asahi hereby agrees to provide the supply to Vichak of the boilers and components of the boilers at the prices shown in Article 14 standard price list. Asahi shall inform Vichak on each occasion that there is a requirement for an adjustment to Asahi's standard price lists and agrees to accept orders for shipment within 90 days following the notification of such adjustments at pre-adjustment prices for quantities of the same boilers or components of the boilers up to the number ordered during the three months immediately preceding such notification but after the expiry of the said period of 90 days such revised prices shall forthwith be applicable to all boilers supplied to Vichak and shall be accepted without demur.

b. Asahi agrees to facilitate shipment of purchases by Vichak through the forwarding agents and to the destination in the Territory and in such manner as Vichak may from time to time request.

c. Asahi agrees to assist Vichak in promoting sales of the boilers in the Territory by making available on loan existing artwork and the like for the preparation by Vichak of promotional materials.

d. Asahi agrees to provide complete on the site training to selected personnel from Vichak for the first two years with continuous support of technological update and training throughout the joint venture along with bearing the responsibility and expense incurred for training.

e. Asahi agrees to permit Vichak to use Vichak's brand name in association with sales by Vichak of the boilers and components of the boilers within the Territory for the life of the joint venture of the agreement where Vichak maintains the standard quality prescribed by Asahi.

f.  Asahi agrees to procure the supply to Vichak of information assistance and expertise available at Asahi in connection with the assembly manufacture and sale of boilers and components of the boilers. For this purpose, Asahi shall procure that Asahi shall make available personnel to visit the factories of Vichak or distributors or customers in the Territory up to a commitment of not more than four man days per week per year as may be mutually agreed.

Additionally, Asahi shall procure that Asahi shall accept visits by Vichak personnel to Asahi's factory if required up to a total commitment of not more four man days per week per year or as may be mutually agreed.

g.  Asahi agrees to procure that Asahi shall inform Vichak of evolutionary improvements which Asahi may make in connection with the design of the boilers or their components or for the materials or techniques used in their manufacture and provided that the same are not subject of patents or patent applications permit Vichak to adopt and use the same without payment of any royalty additional to that herein before set out. In the case of improvements the subject of patents or patent applications Asahi agrees not to grant to any party other than Vichak in the Territory the right to use the same without having first offered such right to Vichak nor subsequently to grant such rights to any third party on terms more favourable to such third party than those finally refused by Vichak.

## Article 17:  Procurement by Vichak

a.  Vichak agrees to procure use of its best endeavour to promote sales of the boilers in the Territory on a scale consistent with early achievement of maximum market penetration.

b.  Vichak agrees to pay for goods purchased from Asahi within 90 days from dispatch of each shipment from Asahi's factory in such a manner as Asahi may from time to time stipulate it being clearly understood that notwithstanding Asahi's Conditions of

Sale property in such goods shall not pass to Vichak until payment in full therefore shall have been received by Asahi.

c. Vichak agrees to pay the royalties reserved under Article 15 hereof in accordance with the provisions contained therein.

d. Vichak agrees to maintain accurate accounts books and records of all transactions and activities relating to the sale and manufacture of boilers and components of boilers and make the same available for inspection by a member of Asahi's auditors or accountants for the purpose of verification.

1) Prominently display Vichak's trademark on each boiler sold by Vichak and indicate that the trademark is a registered trademark provided that registration in the Territory shall have taken place.

2) Use Vichak's trademark in all promotional and packaging material associated with the boilers and where practical the components of the boilers and acknowledge in the case of each such use that Vichak's trademark is the property of Vichak of Thailand.

3) Maintain the standard of quality prescribed by Asahi in respect of units or components of boilers assembled or manufactured by Vichak and make such products available for inspection by Asahi.

4) Take complete responsibility with regard to boilers or components of boilers sold by Vichak which have neither been manufactured by Vichak nor upon which Vichak has carried out any assembly operation for any warranty which Vichak may give to Vichak's customers which is more favourable to such customer than any warranty given by Asahi to Vichak.

## Article 18: Liability Insurance

Vichak hereby certifies that it carries liability insurance covering Vichak against suits claiming product or public liability and Vichak agrees to furnish to Asahi a certificate of insurance showing that such coverage is adequate in amount and in full force and effect and further agrees to keep such insurance in force at all times during the term of this agreement.

## Article 19: Priority Supplier

Vichak agrees that during the existence of this agreement and for seven years, upon the selection of supplier, Asahi will be given special priority in providing Vichak price quotation as priority supplier in which the requirement includes that the pricing must be competitive as to other supplier also.

## Article 20: General Provisions

Vichak and Asahi agree that:

a. each party will bear its own expenses in connection with visits made by its representatives or personnel to the other's country provided that in the case of the visits made by Vichak's representatives/personnel for the purpose of on site training, the expenses will be borne by Asahi under the negotiation terms.
b. each party will maintain and will procure that its respective employees (including employees of Asahi and Vichak) will maintain in the strictest confidence all and any technical and commercial information which it receives from the other and at no time disclose the same to any third party except in so far as such disclosures may be necessary to enable the party properly to fulfill its obligations under this agreement.
c. neither party shall be entitled to assign the benefit of this agreement other than for the purpose of amalgamation or reconstruction without the prior written consent of the other which consent shall not unreasonably be withheld.
d. this agreement shall be construed in accordance with and governed in all respects by the laws of Thailand.

## Article 21: Governing Law

The parties hereto agree that this agreement shall conclusively be deemed to be contract made under, and for all purposes be governed and construed in accordance with the laws of Thailand.

## Article 22:   Arbitration

Any dispute arising out of or in connection with this agreement which the parties are unable to settle between themselves within one month of the appearance of the dispute shall be submitted to arbitration on the application of either party.

Final settlement shall be made by a single arbitrator appointed in accordance with and operating under the rules of conciliation and arbitration of the International Chamber of Commerce of Thailand. Any such arbitration shall take place in Bangkok, Thailand. The parties accept that any arbitral awards shall be binding upon them and executed against them. All charges relating to arbitration to be borne by the losing party.

This agreement is written in both English and Japanese (02 copies each) with the equal validity. Asahi keeps 2 copies (English and Japanese), and Vichak keeps 2 copies (English and Japanese).

This contract takes effect from the signing date until the expiration of warranty time.

For & on behalf of                    For & on behalf of
ASAHI STEAM                           VICHAK BOILER
COMPANY LIMITED                       COMPANY LIMITED

# REFERENCES

Ahlert, D. (1982) Vertikale Kooperationsstrategien im Vertrieb, In: *Zeitschrift für Betriebswirtschaft*, **1**, 62–79.

Anderson, E. (1990) Two Firms, One Frontier: On Assessing Joint Venture Performance, In: *Sloan Management Review*, **Winter**, 19–30.

Anderson, E. and Weitz, B. (1992) The Use of Pledges to Build and Sustain Commitment in Distribution Channels, In: *Journal of Marketing Research*, **24**, 18–34.

Anderson, J. and Narus, J. (1990) A Model of Distributor Firm and Manufacturer Firm Working Partnerships, In: *Journal of Marketing*, **54**, 42–58.

Argyris, C. and Schön, D.A. (1978) *Organizational Learning. A Theory of Action Perspective*, Reading, MA: Addison-Wesley.

Arrow, K. (1980) *Wo Organisation endet*, Wiesbaden: Gabler.

Badaracco, J.L. (1991) *The Knowledge Link*, Boston: MA: Harvard Business School Press.

Baird, I.S., Lyles, M.A. and Reger, R.K. (1993) Evaluation of Cooperative Alliances: Integration and Future Directions, Working Paper, Academy of Management, Atlanta, Georgia.

Barney, J. (1991) Firm Resources and Sustained Competitive Advantage, In: *Journal of Management Studies*, **17(1)**, 99–120.

Bierhoff, H.W. (1987) Vertrauen in Führungs- und Kooperationsbeziehungen, In: Kieser, A., Reber, G. and Wunderer, R. (Hrsg.) *Handwörterbuch der Führung*, Stuttgart: Poeschel, 2028–2038.

Bleeke, J. and Ernst, D. (1993) *Collaborating to Compete: Using Strategic Alliances and Acquisitions in the Global Marketplace*, New York: Wiley.

Bleicher, K. (1992) Der Strategie-. Struktur- und Kulturfit strategischer Allianzen als Erfolgsfaktor. In: Bronder, C. and Pritzel, R. (ed) *Wegweiser fir strategische Allianzen.* Gabler. Frankfurt, 265–292.

Bromiley, P. and Cummings, L.L. (1993) Organizations with Trust: Theory and Measurement, Working Paper, Academy of Management, Atlanta, GA, August.

Bronder, C. (1992) (Hrsg.) *Wegweiser für strategische Allianzen: Meilen- und Stolpersteíne bei Kooperationen,* Wiesbaden: Gabler.

Bronder, C. and Pritzel, R. (1992) Ein konzeptioneller Ansatz zur Gestaltung und Entwicklung strategischer Allianzen. In: Bronder, C. and Pritzel, R. (ed) *Wegweiser fir strategische Allianzen.* Gabler. Frankfurt, 15–44.

Browning, L.D., Beyer, J.M. and Shetler, J.C. (1995) Building Cooperation in a Competitive Industry: SEMATECH and the Semiconductor Industry, In: *Academy of Management Journal,* **38(1)**, 113–151.

Büchel, B. (1997) *Development of Joint Ventures: Conditions, Influences, Relationships,* Wiesbaden: Gabler.

Butler, J.K. (1991) Toward Understanding and Measuring Conditions of Trust: Evolution of a Condition of Trust Inventory, In: *Journal of Management,* **17(3)**, 643–663

Cauley de la Sierra, M. (1995) *Managing Global Alliances: Key Steps for Successful Collaboration,* Wokingham: Economist Intelligence Unit, Addison-Wesley.

Chakravarthy, B.S. and Lorange, P. (1991) *Managing the Strategy Process: A Framework for a Multibusiness Firm,* Englewood Cliffs, NJ: Prentice-Hall.

Connolly, T., Conlon, E.T. and Deutsch, S.J. (1980) Organizational Effectiveness: A Multi-Constituency Approach, In: *Academy of Management Review,* **5**, 211–217.

Contractor, F.J. and Lorange, P. (1988) *Cooperative Strategies in International Business: Joint Ventures and Technology Partnerships between Firms,* Lexington, MA: Lexington Books.

Cullen, J.B. and Johnson, J.L. (1995) Japanese and Local Partner Commitment to International Joint Ventures: Psychological Consequences of Outcomes and Investments in the IJV Relationship, In: *Journal of International Business Studies,* **1**, 91–115.

Daft, R.L. (1992) *Organization Theory and Design,* St. Paul, MN: West Publishing.

Drucker, P.F. (1993) *Post-Capitalist Society*, New York: Harper Business.

Dwyer, F.R., Schurr, P.H. and Oh, S. (1987) Developing Buyer-Seller Relationships, In: *Journal of Marketing*, **51**, 11–27.

Feldman, D.C. and Arnold, H.J. (1983) *Managing Individual and Group Behavior in Organizations*, New York: McGraw-Hill.

Fishman, M. and Levinthal, D.A. (1991) Honeymoons and the Liability of Adolescence: A New Perspective on Duration Dependence in Social and Organizational Relationships, In: *Academy of Management Review*, **16 (2)**, 442–468.

Galbraith, J. (1973) *Designing Complex Organizations*, Reading, MA: Addison-Wesley.

Geringer, J.M. and Hebert, L. (1989) Control and Performance of International Joint Ventures, In: *Journal of International Business Studies*, **20(2)**, 235–254.

Golembiewski, R.T. and McConkie, M. (1975) The Centrality of Interpersonal Trust in Group Processes, In: Cooper, C.L. (ed.) *Theories of Group Processes*. New York: Wiley, 131–185.

Gomez, P. and Probst, G.J.B.(1995) *Die Praxis des ganzheitlichen Problemlösens*, Bern: Haupt.

Gundlach, G.T., Achrol, R.S. and Mentzer, J.T. (1995) The Structure of Commitment in Exchange, In: *Journal of Marketing*, **59**, 78–92.

Hamel, G., Doz, Y.L. and Prahalad, C.K. (1989) Collaborate with Your Competitors—and Win, In: *Harvard Business Review*, **67(1)**, 133–139.

Harrigan, K.R. (1986) *Managing for Joint Venture Success*, New York: Lexington Books.

Helleloid, D. and Simonin, B. (1993) Collaborative Know-How: Can Firms Become More Competent International Collaborators? Working Paper, Academy of Management Meetings, Atlanta, GA.

Hergert, M. and Morris, D. (1988) Trends in International Collaborative Arrangements, In: Contractor, F. and Lorange, P. (eds) *Cooperative Strategies in International Business*, Lexington, MA: Lexington Books, 99–110.

Hermann, R. (1988) *Joint Venture-Management*: Strategien, Strukturen, Systeme und Kulturen, Dissertation. St.Gallen.

Hirschman, A. (1970) *Exit, Voice, and Loyalty*, Cambridge, MA: Harvard University Press.

Hofstede, G. (1980) *Culture's Consequences: International Differences in Work-Related Values*, Beverly Hills, CA: Sage.

Inkpen, A. (1995) *The Management of International Joint Ventures: An Organizational Learning Perspective*, London: Routledge.

Kanter, R.M. (1994) Collaborative Advantage: The Art of Alliances, In: *Harvard Business Review*, **72**, 96–108.

Killing, J.P. (1983) *Strategies for Joint Venture Success*, Westport, CT: Praeger.

Klimecki, R.G. and Probst, G.J.B. (1992) Interkulturelles Lernen, In: Haller, M., Brauchlin, E. and Wunderer, R. (Hrsg.) *Globalisierung der Wirtschaft—Einwirkungen auf die Betriebswirtschaftslehre*, Bern/ Stuttgart: Haupt.

Kogut, B. (1988) A Study of the Life Cycle of Joint Ventures, In: *Management International Review*, **28**, 39–52.

Kolb, D.A. (1984) *Experimental Learning*, Englewood Cliffs, NJ: Prentice-Hall.

Korsgaard, M.A., Schweiger, D.M. and Sapienza, H.J. (1995) Building Commitment, Attachment, and Trust in Strategic Decision-Making Teams: The Role of Procedural Justice, In: *Academy of Management Journal*, **38(1)**, 60–84.

Krubasik, E. and Lautenschlager, H. (1993) Forming Successful Strategic Alliances in High-Tech Businesses, In: Bleeke, J. and Ernst, D. (eds) *Collaborating to Compete: Using Strategic Alliances and Acquisitions in the Global Marketplace*, New York: Wiley, 55–66.

Kumar, S. and Seth, A. (1994) The Design of Coordination and Control Mechanisms for Managing Joint Venture-Parent Relationships, Working Paper, University of Houston.

Lalit, J.M. "A Framework for Designing Pre-negotiation Strategy", Working Paper, Asian Institute of Technology.

Larson, A. (1991) Partner Networks: Leveraging External Ties to Improve Entrepreneurial Performance, In: *Journal of Business Venturing*, **6(3)**, 173–188.

Lewis, J.D. (1990) *Partnerships for Profit: Structuring and Managing Strategic Alliances*, New York: Free Press.

Linn, N. (1989) *Die Implementierung vertikaler Kooperation: Theoretische Konzepte und erste empirische Ergebnisse zum Prozess der Angleichung logistischer Teilaufgaben*, Darmstadt: Lang.

Lorange, P. and Roos, J. (1990) Formation of Cooperative Ventures: Competence Mix of the Management Teams, In: *Management International Review*, **30**, 69–86.

Lorange, P. and Roos, J. (1991) Analytical Steps in the Formation of Strategic Alliances, In: *Journal of Organizational Change*, **4**, 60–72.

Lorange, P. and Roos, J. (1992) *Strategic Alliances: Formation, Implementation and Evolution*, Cambridge, MA: Blackwell Business.

Luhmann, N. (1989) *Vertrauen*, Stuttgart: Enke.

Lützig, W.-P. (1982) *Die vieldimensionale Kalkulation der Kooperation*, Dissertation, Berlin.

Lyles, M.A. (1987) Common Mistakes of Joint Venture Experienced Firms, In: *Columbia Journal of World Business*, **22**, 79–85.

Madhok, A. (1995) Opportunism and Trust in Joint Venture Relationships: An Exploratory Study and a Model, In: *Scandinavian Journal of Management*, **11(1)**, 57–74.

Milkovich, G.T. and Boudreau, J.W. (1991) *Human Resource Management*, Homewood: Irwin.

Mohr, J. and Spekman, R. (1994) Characteristics of Partnership Success: Partnership Attributes, Communication Behavior, and Conflict Resolution Techniques, In: *Strategic Management Journal*, **15**, 135–152.

Moran, R. (1993) Making Globalization Work, In: *World Executive Digest*, **14(1)**, 16–19.

Naujoks, H. (1994) *Autonomie in Organisationen: Perspektive und Handlungsleitlinie des Managements*, Dissertation, St. Gallen.

Nelson, R.R. and Winter, S.G. (1982) *An Evolutionary Theory of Economic Change*, Boston, MA: Belknap Press.

Newman, W.H. (1992) Launching a Viable Joint Venture, In: *California Management Review*, **35**, Fall, 68–80.

Nonaka, I. (1991) The Knowledge-Creating Company, In: *Harvard Business Review*, **69(6)**, 96–104.

Nonaka, I. (1994) A Dynamic Theory of Organizational Knowledge Creation, In: *Organization Science*, **5(1)**, 14–37.

Nonaka, I. and Takeuchi, H. (1995) *The Knowledge-Creating Company*, New York: Oxford University Press.

Peng, M.W. (1992) The China Strategy: A Tale of Two Firms, In: Hill and Jones (eds), *Strategic Management an Integrated Approach*, Boston: Houghton-Mifflin Company, C519–C532.

Petermann, F. (1985) *Psychologie des Vertrauens*, Salzburg: Müller

Peters, T. (1992) *Liberation Management*, London: Macmillan.

Pfeffer, J. and Nowak, P. (1976) Joint Ventures and Interorganizational Dependence, In: *Administrative Science Quarterly*, **21**, 398–418.

Prahalad, C.K. and Hamel, G. (1990) The Core Competence of the Corporation, In: *Harvard Business Review*, **68(3)**, 79–91.

Prange, C., Probst, G. and Rüling, C. (1996) Lernen zu kooperieren-Kooperieren, um zu lernen, In: *Zeitschrift für Führung und Organisation*, **1**, 10–16.

Probst, G.J.B. (1987) *Selbst-Organisation: Ordnungsprozesse in sozialen Systemen aus ganzheitlicher Sicht*, Berlin/Hamburg: Parey.

Probst, G. and Büchel, B. (1994) *Towards a New Framework of Cooperative Endeavors—The Organizational Learning Perspective*, Cahier de Recherche no. 1994.18, HEC, Université de Genève.

Probst, G.J.B. and Büchel, B.S.T. (1997) *Organizational Learning: The Competitive Advantage of the Future*, London: Prentice-Hall.

Pucik, V. (1988) Strategic Alliances, Organizational Learning, and Competitive Advantage: The HRM Agenda, In: *Human Resource Management*, **27**, 77–93.

Quinn, R.E. and Rohrbaugh, J. (1983) A Spatial Model of Effectiveness Criteria: Towards a Competing Values Approach to Organizational Analysis, In: *Management Science*, **3**, 363–377.

Raffée, H. and Eisele, J. (1994) Joint Ventures—nur die Hälfte floriert, In: *Harvard Business Manager*, **3**, 17–22.

Reich, R.B. and Mankin, E.D. (1986) Joint Ventures with Japan Give Away Our Future, In: *Harvard Business Review*, **March-April**, 78–86.

Ring, P.S. and Van de Ven, A.H. (1992) Structuring Cooperative Relationships Between Organizations, In: *Strategic Management Journal*, **13(7)**, 483–498.

Ring, P.S. and Van de Ven, A.H. (1994) Developmental Processes of Cooperative Interorganizational Relationships, In: *Academy of Management Review*, **19**, 90–118.

Rössl, D. (1994) *Gestaltung komplexer Austauschbeziehungen: Analyse zwischenbetrieblicher Kooperation*, Wiesbaden: Gabler.

Schaan, J. (1988) How to Control a Joint Venture Even as a Minority Partner, In: *Journal of General Management*, **14**, 4–16.

Schein, E. (1985) *Organizational Culture and Leadership: A Dynamic View*, San Francisco: Jossey-Bass.

Serapio, M.G. and Cascio, W.F. (1996) End-Games in International Alliances, In: *Academy of Management Executive*, **10(1)**, 62–73.

Swierczek, F. and Hirsch, G. (1994) Joint Ventures in Asia and Multicultural Management, In: *European Management Journal*, **12(2)**, 197–209.

Teagarden, M.B. and Glinow, M.A. (1994) Beijing Jeep Corporation—American Motor's Experience in China, In: Moran, Bratten and Walsh, *International Business Case Studies—for the Multicultural Marketplace,* Houston: Gulf Publ. Co, 97–116.

Tsui, A.S. (1990) A Multiple-Constituency Model of Effectiveness: An Empirical Examination at the Human Resource Subunit Level, In: *Administrative Science Quarterly*, **35**, 458–483.

Ulrich, P. (1984) Systemsteuerung und Kulturentwicklung. Auf der Suche nach einem ganzheitlichen Paradigma der Managementlehre, In: *Die Unternehmung*, **38(4)**, 303–325.

Ulrich, H. and Probst, G.J.B. (1988) *Anleitung zum ganzheitlichen Denken und Handeln: Ein Brevier für Führungskräfte*, Bern/ Stuttgart: Haupt.

Van de Ven, A.H. and Walker, G. (1984) The Dynamics of Interorganizational Coordination, In: *Administrative Science Quarterly*, **29**, 598–621.

Walsh, J. and Ungson, G. (1991) Organizational Memory, In: *Academy of Management Review*, **16(1)**, 57–91.

Weick, K.E. (1995) *Sensemaking in Organizations*, London: Sage.

Williamson, O.E. (1985) *The Economic Institutions of Capitalism: Firms, Markets, Relational Contracting*, New York: Free Press.

Williamson, O.E. (1991) Comparative Economic Organization: The Analysis of Discrete Structural Alternatives, In: *Administrative Science Quarterly*, **36(2)**, 269–296.

Williamson, O.E. (1992) Markets, Hierarchies, and the Modern Corporation. An Unfolding Perspective, In: *Journal of Economic Behavior and Organization*, **17**, 335–352.

Wolfe, D. and Kolb, D. (1979) Career Development, Personal Growth and Experimental Learning, In: Kolb, D., Rudin, J. and McIntyre, J. (eds) *Organisational Psychology*, Englewood Cliffs, NJ: Prentice-Hall, 535–563.

Wörner, H. (1992) Bosch-Siemens Hausgeräte GmbH—Vom Management einer strategischen Allianz, In: Bronder, C. (Hrsg.) *Wegweiser für strategische Allianzen-Meilen- und Stolpersteine für Kooperationen*, Wiesbaden: Frankfurter Allgemeine Zeitung, 356–376.

Yoshino, M.Y. and Rangan, U.S. (1995) *Strategic Alliances: An Entrepreneurial Approach to Globalization*, Boston, MA: Harvard Business School Press.

Zahra, S. and Elhagrasey, G. (1994) Strategic Management of International Joint Ventures, In: *European Management Journal*, **12(1)**, 83–93.

Zajac, E.J. and Olsen, C.P. (1993) From Transaction Cost to Transactional Value Analysis: Implications for the Study of Interorganizational Strategies, In: *Journal of Management Studies*, **30**, 131–145.

Zeira, Y. and Shenkar, O. (1990) Interactive and Specific Parent Characteristics: Implications for Management and Human Resources in International Joint Ventures, In: *Management International Review*, Special Issue, 7–22.

# INDEX